DESTINATION
MOSCOW

DESTINATION MOSCOW

⚽ An Alternative look at Manchester United's triumphant 2007–08 season ⚽

JUSTIN BLUNDELL

First published in Great Britain in 2008 by

The Breedon Books Publishing Company Limited

Breedon House, 3 The Parker Centre, Derby, DE21 4SZ.

ISBN 978-1-85983-673-6

Printed and bound in Page Bros (Norwich) Ltd.

Contents

To my brilliant Mum and Dad
&
Kiana, Kristian, Matilda, Samuel and Thomas

About *Destination Moscow*

Most books on football seem to think that football fans stop being interested in their team once the final whistle blows. Of course that's not true. And that's why *Destination Moscow* is different from every other season review. It doesn't just cover every United match. It also gives a round-up of all the news, trivia, humour, gossip and rumours affecting United – and our fiercest rivals – between games.

How *Destination Moscow* works

Here's what you'll find in *Destination Moscow*. For every single match there's a punchy round-up of the game, a rundown of all the moments that matter, the best quotes and headlines plus a selection of views from the press box. And after each game there is a review of all the following week's news and gossip. In addition, for the major games you'll find an entertaining, savagely Red-eyed, minute-by-minute guide to the action.

Thanks and acknowledgements

Destination Moscow quotes from a wide range of sources, including all the major national newspapers, *Red Issue* and *United We Stand*. Every effort has been made to acknowledge each source when it has been used. If I have failed to acknowledge it, I apologise and if you contact me I will make sure this is rectified in any future editions.

I would especially like to acknowledge the excellent *Red News* news service (please visit *www.rednews.co.uk*) as well as the Mediawatch column in *football365.com*.

Comments

This is the first time I've written a season review like this. And as always there is plenty of room for improvement and new ideas. If you have any suggestions or comments about *Destination Moscow* please contact me at blundelljustin@hotmail.com.

League tables

The figures in the League tables 7 (3) are number of points from (number of games).

Abbreviations used

YCNMIU = You couldn't make it up
ABU = Anyone but United
NWAF = No women at football

Introduction

As the credits rolled on the 2006–07 season, it felt great to be a Red. Sure, Chelsea had just taken the double from us. But we had won the trophy we wanted the most. And Milan had just done us a favour by turning Liverpool over in Athens.

The summer was an enjoyable one too. Four impressive new players came in from Bavaria, Portugal and the East End. There was no Ronaldo drama for a change. And the club broke their duck at the new Wembley by beating Chelsea on penalties in the Community Shield.

But it wasn't all good news. The Glazers' hated ACS (Automatic cup scheme) priced United out of the reach of thousands more lifelong Reds. Giuseppe Rossi, the best 'home-grown' centre-forward since Mark Hughes, was flogged to Villarreal. Thaksin Shinawatra 'rescued' City from their latest financial crisis. Fergie's rumoured top target Dimitar Berbatov remained at Spurs. And former crowd favourite Gabriel Heinze developed a bizarre desire to play for Liverpool.

And as the Red Army piled down Sir Matt Busby Way for the season's opener against Reading, another nasty surprise lay just around the corner…

United 0 Reading 0   12/08/2007

The first day back at Old Trafford should be about swapping Wembley stories with your neighbours, groaning that no one's been found who can do a better job with the mic than Alan Keegan, counting how many regulars have fallen victim to the Glazers' latest ticket atrocities…and watching United stroll to victory against half-baked opponents whose main ambition is to avoid starting the season with a battering.

It shouldn't be like this. First Rooney falls victim, once again, to the curse of the metatarsal. Then United, with O'Shea bizarrely pushed into action as an emergency centre-forward, bang their heads fruitlessly against a 10-man Reading brick wall. The man from *The Guardian* gets it spot on, musing 'Seldom has an opening-day fixture been more painful for so many people.'

The moments that mattered
BROKEN! (39): I could talk about Giggsy's volley against the post in the first half. I could talk about the series of saves Marcus Hahnemann made in the second. But there was only one moment that really mattered here: Rooney tries to get in front of Duberry at the near post, the big defender accidentally treads on the top of his left foot and, as Rooney limps back to the halfway line, it's obvious that something is seriously wrong. Hospital scans later confirm the news that he has broken a metatarsal for the third time in as many years.

What was good?
☺ Not a lot. United were tidy in possession but really struggled without a focal point up front. They even made Michael Duberry look good, and that hasn't happened since he used to hang around with Bowyer, Woodgate and the rest of the 'Majestyk' crew.

What was bad?
Where do you start…?
☺ The new Premiership anthem and handshake. What the devil?
☺ Reading's support – or, to be precise, the lack of it. Have there ever been more red seats visible in the away end for the first match of the season?
☺ Reading's tactics – I don't want to come over all Arsene Wenger, but has an away team ever come to Old Trafford with less intention of scoring a goal? It's a bit depressing when a team's attacking plan is to send aimless balls down the channels.

☺ The lines on the back of United's new kit – they look alright on the players, but if you don't buy a number and name for the back of your replica they look a bit weird. A sneaky way to milk more money out of the fans perchance?

What was ugly?

☺ The studs-up lunge by Dave Kitson on Evra that earned him a red card just 37 seconds after coming on. It was the fifth quickest sending off in Premiership history. It was also the second time that a Reading sub had seen red at Old Trafford in successive seasons. Last year Sodje managed to get booked twice in the space of 10 minutes.

View from the broadsheets

☺ 'Manchester United have spent in excess of £40 million to reinforce their attacking armoury since securing a ninth Premiership title last May, so it was unexpected, to say the least, to see John O'Shea occupying the centre-forward role as the champions tried in vain to begin the defence of their Championship with victory against Reading at Old Trafford.' – *The Telegraph* picks up on the weirdest sight of the day.

Forum post of the day

'60 million quid to end up with that t*t up front, f***ing disgrace.'…and so does Karlos on the RED NEWS Forum.

Worst headline of the day

'Foot And Out' – *The Star* tries to make a pun out of Wayne's fractured metatarsal. And fails.

Reading – the verbals

☺ 'If Wayne had stayed on, we would have gone on to win the match. That lack of a central striker cost us.' – Fergie states the obvious.

☺ 'After watching the guys on TV, I almost feel like I have to apologise. It does bother me because I want people to think we are more than just a defensive side. But your season-long dreams can be shattered very quickly here. I would have loved to have gone 4–4–2 and seen what happened, but we would have got hammered.' – Stevie Coppell torments himself.

☺ 'I think visiting goalkeepers must be Man of the Match at our ground more than at any other.' – Fergie sulks after Reading 'keeper Hahnemann plays like he's got buckets for hands.

Match facts

United: Van der Sar, Brown, Ferdinand, Vidic, Silvestre, Ronaldo, Carrick, Scholes, Evra, Giggs, Rooney (Nani half-time)

Reading: Hahnemann, De la Cruz, Ingimarsson, Duberry, Shorey, Murty, Ki-Hyeon* (Oster 57*), Harper, Gunnarsson, Hunt (Bikey 87), Doyle (Kitson 72†) [Coppell] FAPL 16.00 (Sky). Att: 75,655. Ref: R. Styles. Half-time: 0–0
*Yellow card † Red card

Other scores
Chelsea 3 (Pizarro, Malouda, Essien) Birmingham 2 (Forsell, Kapo); Aston Villa 1 (Barry pen), Liverpool 2 (og, Gerrard); West Ham 0 City 2 (Bianchi, Geovanni); Arsenal 2 (Van Persie pen, Hleb) Fulham 1 (Healy)

Reading to Portsmouth
'Even the smell of the hot dogs is great'

Just deny it
'He himself is personally absolutely confident, as we are, that the boot had nothing to do with his injury.' – Nike's Charlie Brooks gets all defensive after accusations that Nike's new boots contributed to Rooney's latest foot injury. But if the new, lighter football boots aren't contributing to the recent spate in fractured metatarsals, what is?

Quotes of the week
- 'It was a good contract and a fine opportunity, but money is not the only thing in life. I could not sign for Newcastle out of respect for Ousmane Dabo.' – Mickey Silvestre reveals why he turned down a £6 million summer move to Newcastle. His name is Joey Barton.
- 'I was excited, and it takes a lot to get me excited...ask my wife.' – Keano reveals too much after Sunderland score in injury time to win their Premiership opener against Spurs.
- 'It's great to be back in the Premiership – even the smell of the hot dogs is great.' – Brucie's back in the big time too. How do the hot dogs smell in the Championship?
- 'There are moves to give the World Cup to England. I must fight that. Nobody in Europe likes England. England invented the sport but has never made any impact on world football.' – Good to see FIFA vice-president Jack Warner remaining objective.

Minor spat of the week
From *The Sun*:
    'Red-faced Dave Kitson was involved in a four-letter tunnel row with Sky pundit Ruud Gullit after the game at Manchester United. The Reading striker's appearance as a sub

lasted just 37 seconds before he was sent off for a crude tackle on Patrice Evra. Gullit asked him when he was going to learn to play football properly. Kitson told the former Chelsea boss to mind his own business and the pair went eyeball to eyeball for a few seconds.'

Spot the difference

✪ 'Every time I saw him playing for West Ham last year, I thought to myself, I just wish we had done it last year. But there were too many complications at the time.' – Fergie looks back wistfully as Carlos Tévez is officially unveiled as a United player, August 2007.

✪ 'Tévez was never on the shopping list.' – Gill denies all interest in Tévez, August 2006.

Why didn't they think of that earlier?

'Not only have they taken my arms and legs off, now they've cut my balls off as well' – Dennis Wise provides inadvertent justification for Leeds's 15-point deduction.

Money for nothing

Totesport reveal their leading contenders for the 2007–08 golden boot. Hope you didn't get sucked in by the favourites:

7/1 Drogba, 9/1 Van Persie, 10/1 Berbatov, 11/1 Shevchenko, 14/1 Tévez, 16/1 Ronaldo, 18/1 Owen, Martins, McCarthy, D. Bent, Torres, 20/1 Anelka, Pizarro, Rooney, 22/1 others.

Portsmouth 1 United 1 15/08/2007

Scholes 15, Benjani 53

Football, bloody hell, as Fergie would say. First Reading come to Old Trafford, park their buses in front of goal and break Rooney's foot. Then United travel to Portsmouth, give them a football lesson for 45 minutes and still allow them to scramble a point. Oh, and Ronaldo gets sent off for the year's least-threatening headbutt. And one more thing, Chelsea escape from a first-half battering at Reading to open up a four-point lead. Any chance of the season starting again?

Match action
1–0 (15): First the fun bit…Nani drives down the left, cuts inside and plays in debut-boy Tévez on the edge of the box. Tévez kills the ball instantly, holds off two markers and passes back to Scholes who thumps the ball low past James's right hand.

1–1 (53): Then this happens…Taylor makes headway on the left and smashes a cross into the United area, which Benjani, steaming late into the area, heads powerfully into the bottom-left corner. Annoyingly, it's the only decent effort Portsmouth have all night.

10 (83) versus 10 (85): And this…First, Muntari trips Carrick and receives a second yellow. So far, fair enough. Then a minor tussle in the area finishes with Ronaldo nuzzling heads with Pompey no-mark Richard Hughes. Steve Bennett, who's got history with Ronaldo after sending him off for next to nothing at City, can't get his red card out quickly enough. Depressingly, that was the last we'd see of either of the two 'R's until 22 September.

Rant of the night
Headbutts are bad and should result in red cards. But nuzzling foreheads like dogs? Surely no one has to walk for that. And what is it about United players that makes them nuzzle rather than butt? Coley at Liverpool, Coley at Sunderland, Gary Neville against City, Silvestre at Arsenal and now this. If you're going to get sent off for going head to head with someone like McManaman, then you might as well make it count.

View from the broadsheets
⚽ 'At times United threatened to tear Portsmouth's defence apart, but even with Tévez at the point of their attack, they did not have the natural finisher to put the game out

of sight. With Ryan Giggs playing just behind Tévez, and Nani and Ronaldo occasionally brilliant on the wings, it is a team of attacking talent just lacking the goalscorer to complete the ensemble.'

☺ *The Independent* expresses the fear of every Red. Is this the year we turn into the Arsenal of old – lots of pretty play but no finish? Where is the guy who scores the scruffy goals, the ones from a yard off his testicles? In short, is this the year we'll really suffer for Fergie falling out with Ruud?

Fratton Park – the verbals

☺ 'It was a disappointing result but a good performance. We played some fantastic football but were wasteful with some of our chances certainly. We were unfortunate not to get the three points.' – Fergie can't believe we didn't kill the game off.

☺ 'I have tried to look at the replay, and there was nothing conclusive there. In fact you cannot really see anything. But my take is he was provoked and he has fallen for it. But that referee Steve Bennett sent him off at City, and he will have loved that opportunity to send him off.' – Fergie bemoans the Ronaldo red.

☺ 'I was pushed in the area. He came straight to me, put his hand on my neck and I opened my arms in a "that's enough" way. We pushed each other but nothing serious. We leaned heads against each other, but that was all. Absolutely nothing else happened. When I saw the red card, I couldn't believe it, the situation was so surreal. And it's absurd, because I'm aware that now I'll sit out a ban for something I didn't do. I feel dejected and very sad.' – So does Ronaldo himself.

Match facts

Portsmouth: James, Cranie (Traoré 45), Pamarot (Hughes 64), Distin, Hreidarsson, Mwaruwari, Mendes (Taylor 45), Muntari** 83, Utaka, Davis*, Nugent [Redknapp]
United: Van der Sar, Brown (Eagles 88), Ferdinand, Vidic*, Evra, Ronaldo† 85, Carrick, Scholes, Nani, Giggs (O'Shea 81), Tévez
FAPL 19.45 Fratton Park. Att: 20,510. Ref: S. Bennett. Half-time: 1–0
*Yellow card **Two yellow cards. † Red card

Other scores

Reading 1 (Bikey) Chelsea 2 (Lampard, Drogba); City 1 (Johnson) Derby 0; Brucie 2 Keano 2

Champions League qualifiers:

Toulouse 0 Liverpool 1 (Voronin); Sparta Prague 0 Arsenal 2 (Fabregas, Hleb)

Portsmouth to City
'Chelsea are a pure and naïve team'

No hard feelings

'It wasn't a Glasgow kiss, I've received harder headbutts than that!' – Portsmouth's Richard Hughes doesn't seem to rate Ronaldo's butting technique. It didn't stop him reeling away and holding his face, mind, did it?

Huh?!

'I think I have a naïve team. They are naïve because they are pure and they are clean. We don't have divers, we don't have violent people, we don't have people with nasty tackles or people diving into the swimming pool. Chelsea are a pure and naïve team.' – Jose Mourinho.

Four sides to every story

⚽ 'Manchester United is linked to many players in every transfer window. The club have categorically not made any offer for Dimitar Berbatov.' – United try to distance themselves from the Berbatov rumours.

⚽ 'They (Spurs) informed us that there's a query from Manchester United about the possibility of Berbatov joining them.' – Berbatov's agent Emil Danchev has a different take on things.

⚽ 'I had one approach, and I said I'd rather die than sell him.' – Martin Jol restarts the rumour mill.

⚽ 'We made an inquiry about a striker not so long ago. The club concerned would not sell and it remains that way.' – Who was Fergie talking about?

News

Not a lot happened this week: United reserve-teamer Ritchie Jones joins Yeovil on loan. Keano tries to take the spirit of '99 to Sunderland by bringing in Coley to play alongside Dwight Yorke (what next? Maysie May gatecrashing the team photo?). Fletcher is named as Scotland's skipper for the next round of internationals. Eriksson buys a £415 bottle of Cabernet Sauvignon to give to Fergie after the weekend's derby.

This is how it feels to be City

⚽ 'The only danger now is people getting carried away and expectation going through the roof. So we have to keep a lid on it.' – Richard Dunne tries to switch off the giddyometer after, er, City win their first home game of 2007.

⚽ 'City and United's rivalry is omnipresent. Contrary to what we could think, people from the city are clearly Manchester City fans.' – New Blue Gelson Fernandes goes through the brainwashing process early.

⚽ 'It is a pity, as fans want to see the best players performing.' – Eriksson reckons it's a pity that City won't be facing Rooney and Ronaldo in the derby. We believe you Sven. Yes, we do.

Bitter-sweet memories

'Last year was amazing. They spent a fortune on those blue-and-white scarves for all the fans, and they never had a shot at goal or tried to beat us. We were trying to win the League, and they were quite happy.' – Fergie has a nice dig at City before the derby.

Best of enemies

'If Sven gives it [a bottle of wine] as a present, I'll accept it. But I'm not going to be sharing it with him. I'll be taking it home.' – Fergie reacts like a spoilt toddler to the news of Eriksson's gift. He really can't stand him can he?

City 1 United 0   18/08/2007

Geovanni 31

Only six League games separated United's latest visit to Eastlands from the one before. But it could have been six years for all the changes that had taken place. Back in May, when Ferdinand and Van der Sar were battling with jobsworth stewards to celebrate the 1–0 win with travelling Reds, United had one hand and four fingers on the Premiership trophy and a Wembley Final on the way. City, meanwhile, had no money, a comedy team that hadn't scored at home for 212 days and a young Irish midfielder with the same hairstyle as Peter Swales.

Now City had a mountain of tainted bahts, a collection of exotic names and a 100 per cent record. Stephen Ireland had more hair than the four Beatles, plus Dick Best, combined, and after just eight days of the season Fergie was saying that it would be an uphill struggle to retain the League. Unbelievable!

The game was pretty unbelievable as well. Richards and Dunne were immense. Without ever looking in control, Schmeichel junior got himself in the way of everything he had to stop. But everywhere else on the pitch City players were outpassed and outplayed to an almost embarrassing degree. They didn't manage to win a corner all game, they hardly had the ball in United's half, but they still managed to end up with the points. Has there ever been a better performance by a losing derby team?

Goal!

0–1 (31): Johnson nudges the ball into Geovanni's path in the final third. He strides forward and hits a speculative shot that takes an enormous deflection off Vidic's backside and reverse swings past Van der Sar.

Headline of the day

'Swede 1 Beetroot 0' – *The Times* man guarantees himself a look down the barrel of Fergie's hairdryer.

Pub quiz question of the week

Peter and Kasper Schmeichel have now both beaten United in derby games. Which other father and son team has tasted victory against United?

*Answer: The Lampards.

17

View from the broadsheets

◉ 'Ferguson looked like a man locked into a nightmare of shocking proportions. In a way it was because, short of a touch more precision in front of goal, Ferguson could not have asked a lot more from a team apparently determined to wipe away the uncertainties that came with draws against Reading and Portsmouth and the injury to Rooney and suspension of Ronaldo.'

◉ 'Paul Scholes put in his usual 90-minute stint of superior grafting, albeit without one moment of truly devastating insight, Ryan Giggs ran elusively and with much skill, and new signing Owen Hargreaves at times suggested he might bring more than mere energy and hard professionalism to the United midfield. The more United dominated, and the more their opportunities drifted away, the more Hargreaves attempted to make sense of the imbalance between effort and result. He will play a lot less convincingly than this, you have to believe, and be part of a crushing victory rather than a defeat that when this game is played back, reel by reel, will never cease to be amazing.' – *The Independent* can't believe we didn't win it either.

City – the verbals

◉ 'We could have beaten them by six.' – Wes is in shock.

◉ 'It's a fantastic game, a difficult game and we were lucky and if their chances had hit the target we would have lost. It was a battle but we defended very well. I would have liked to have kept the ball better. Three wins, it's very, very good. Absolutely no to winning the League.' – Is Sven the luckiest man alive?

Match facts

City: Schmeichel, Garrido, Richards, Dunne, Corluka*, Geovanni (Ball 74), Hamann*, Johnson, Petrov, Bojinov (Mpenza 8), Elano (Bianchi 63) [Eriksson]
United: Van der Sar, Brown* (O'Shea 73), Ferdinand*, Vidic, Evra, Hargreaves, Scholes, Carrick (Campbell 73), Giggs, Nani (Eagles 60), Tévez
FAPL 12.45 (Sky) Eastlands. Att: 44,955. Ref: M. Clattenburg. Half-time: 0–1
*Yellow card

Other scores

Liverpool 1 (Torres) Chelsea 1 (Lampard pen); Blackburn 1 (Dunn) Arsenal 1 (Van Persie)

League table

1. City 9 (3) 2. Chelsea 7 (3) 3. Wigan 6 (3) 4. Everton 6 (3)…16. United 2 (3)

City to Spurs
'I still think they will recover and come back. Three games played is not a lot.'

News I

Gabriel Heinze loses his legal battle to force through his move to Liverpool, as virtually everyone outside the Anfield boot room knew he would. Unsurprisingly, the arbitration panel found that the famous letter from United only envisaged an international transfer. And, in any case, it only constituted an 'agreement to agree', rather than a binding agreement to sell to any club who coughed up £6.9 million. Still, it didn't stop Benitez from launching a tirade almost as amusing as his new goatee beard...

You cannot be serious

'I would like to ask the Premier League a number of questions. How can a player with a signed agreement be treated like this?'

Because United made it clear he wasn't going to Liverpool, and it wasn't a legally enforceable document, Rafa...

'He has a document, which is clear, but the Premier League prefers to believe the word of someone else who made a mistake. How can this be allowed?'

Because United made it clear he wasn't going to Liverpool, and it wasn't a legally enforceable document, Rafa...

'Then I would like to ask the Premier League why is it that Liverpool always plays the most fixtures away from home in an early kick-off, following an international break?'

Because United made it...What? You're lashing out at anything now man. For the record, United have had more lunchtime kick-offs than anyone else over the last five years.

'Then I want to ask the Premier League why it was so difficult for Liverpool to sign Javier Mascherano, when we had to wait a long time for the paperwork, but it was so easy for Carlos Tévez to join Manchester United?'

You've got to admit, he's got a point here. Liverpool had to wait all summer to sign Mascherano and saw the whole affair turn into a soap opera involving West Ham, the Premier League and the courts. United, meanwhile, bent the rules and snapped up Tévez inside a month. Oh no, hang on a minute, it was the other way round!

The dive and the drive

Amusing conspiracy theory of the week, courtesy of *The Sun*:

'THE referee who sparked a storm by awarding Chelsea a dodgy penalty on Sunday [Styles was the only man in Anfield to see a foul when Malouda barged into Finnan] also paved Blues owner Roman Abramovich's drive.

Rob Styles, whose decision let Chelsea sneak a 1–1 draw with Liverpool, is on the board of builders Oakwood Groundworks Ltd. The company was paid a five-figure sum for work at billionaire Abramovich's 440-acre country estate last summer.

Styles, 43, has been dropped as a ref for this weekend's Premier League matches following his apparent howler that drew furious protests from Liverpool.'

I like the use of the word 'apparent'. A bit naughty that, Rupert.

International Friendly Reds

Ferdinand, Brown and Carrick all feature as Germany claim their fifth straight Wembley win, beating England 2–1. Van der Sar misses out on Holland's defeat in Switzerland after being nobbled by Scouser Kuyt in training. Evra's France win 1–0 in Slovakia. O'Shea's Republic of Ireland thrash Denmark 4–0 away, with Darron Gibson coming on as sub. Fletcher plays a captain's role for Scotland, setting up the only goal of their home game against South Africa. Meanwhile, in the Euro qualifiers, Ronaldo salvages a 1–1 draw for Portugal in Armenia, while Vidic's Serbia lose 3–2 in Belgium.

News II

Platini's plans for a Champions League place to go to FA Cup winners get a widespread kicking. Fergie rightly points out that beating Millwall, as United did in 2004, should not earn you a free ticket into football's top competition. United win the inaugural Champions Youth Cup in Kuala Lumpur, seeing off Porto, Boca Juniors, Inter Milan, Barcelona and Flamengo before beating Juve 1–0 in the Final. Fabien Brandy scores the winner. Lee Daley leaves his role as United commercial director after just four months. Surprise, surprise, the Glazers offer no official explanation.

Deluded moi?

Micah Richards after City win their third game on the row:

'Some of the football we played against Newcastle was amazing. Look at our performance against Manchester United too. We didn't just beat them 1–0 – at stages we were passing the ball around them. I have not seen a City team do that!' – Neither did anyone else Micah.

Prediction of the week

'I still think they will recover and come back. Three games played is not a lot.' – Wenger can't see a pizza thrown from five yards, but it appears he can see the future.

News III

After losing out on the chance to be the new Phil Chisnall, Heinze signs for Real for £8 million. It's a good deal all round. Real have a decent replacement for Roberto Carlos.

Heinze gets to live in Madrid rather than Liverpool. And United get rid of a player who turned up late in his first season, wrecked his cruciate and asked for a transfer in his second, messed up his rehab by rushing back for the World Cup and came back demanding double wages. Oh, and they bag £1.1 million more than they were prepared to accept at the start of the summer for a player whose legs look shot (by the Milan semi Heinze made John O'Shea look lightning).

Blessed is the man

- ❂ 'We're disappointed because he was a great warrior for us. But the role of agents these days – there are different types and some are completely in control of their clients. They do their banking, their investing, their holidays, so they become controlled by them and dependent on them. I don't think Gabby was getting the right information from his agents.' – Fergie is remarkably cool about Heinze's betrayal.
- ❂ 'I don't think I left Manchester United under a cloud, I left as a League champion.' – Heinze is officially mad.
- ❂ 'I deserved better treatment after my efforts for the club.' – What?
- ❂ 'Manchester United fans are not stupid. They will not forget everything I did for the club and everything we won together, so I am not worried about their reaction. The fans know how I feel and what I am like.' – You've just agitated for a move to Liverpool, Judas boy. I'm not sure you'll be getting hugs and kisses if you come back.

Bleeding hearts

'It's going to be very difficult for us to win the Premier League because the other teams are so strong, but I want our supporters to know that despite the disadvantages we have, we will fight all the way. We will fight to cope with our more difficult kick-off times and all the other decisions which are going against us.' – Yes, Benitez is still whining. Perhaps he wouldn't feel so hard done by if he reflected on managers who actively unsettle players when they're under contract at other clubs.

Lower than a snake's bottom

Heinze's agents really are a class act from *The Mail*:

'Crystal Palace were offered an astonishing "commission", thought to be around £1 million, to act as a go-between in an elaborately conceived transfer plot to get Gabriel Heinze from Manchester United to Liverpool.

'The plan, allegedly thought up by Heinze's representatives, called for Palace to buy the player from United then sell him on to Liverpool. It foundered when the London club refused to cooperate and, instead, made both Manchester United and the Premier League aware of the approach.'

United 1 Spurs 0   26/08/2007

Nani 68

It's one of the great unsung goals of the Fergie era. United were playing at The Dell in one of those horrible blue numbers they wore in the early 1990s. The game was on the verge of ending in a dire 0–0 when the Southampton 'keeper half saved, half fumbled Darren Ferguson's low centre at the feet of Dion Dublin. He made no mistake from close range and, in an instant, the hangover that had gripped the club since Leeds had snatched the title, was cured. United, with just one point from their first three games, went on to win six games on the spin before losing their way again. But Big Dion's goal, and the last 18-point haul of the BC (Before Cantona) era, made all the difference when the title jinx was finally broken the following May.

And the reason I've brought this up now? Simple. For the first time since that first Premiership campaign United had failed to win any of their opening three games. They desperately needed to turn Spurs over, but the tension was getting the better of them. If anything, the visitors – who had endured an even worse start to the campaign than United – looked the likelier winners. And then Nani jinked inside from the left and thumped in a 30-yarder that nicked off Tévez's neck and flew high into Robinson's goal. It was ridiculously early in the season. But just like the Dell in 1992, it felt like a major corner had just been turned.

The (five) minutes that mattered
0–0 (64): One-time United target Gareth Bale threads a ball through the middle towards Berbatov. Berbatov survives a tangle with Vidic and prods the ball past Van der Sar. If he'd got a slightly better contact he would certainly have scored. As it is, Ferdinand's pace allows him to clear off the line.

0–0 (66): Berbatov hurdles Van der Sar and flicks the ball goalwards. Brown dives in and clears the ball with what looks – to Spurs – like a combination of chest and arm. TV replays prove without question that Wes saves it with his left nipple. Not that that stopped the press pack banging on about phantom penalties the next day.

1–0 (68): Nani's moment. When was the last time a United player scored a better first goal? Neil Webb against Arsenal on Michael Knighton day?

What was good?
- Berbatov. Looked every inch a United player – the closest thing to Cantona I've seen. And with his vampire complexion he'd look much better in red than white.
- Bale. Superb left foot. And stronger and quicker than I imagined. A missed opportunity?

What was bad?
- United's passing. So good in the first three games, so bad here. But we won. Go figure.

View from the broadsheet
- *The Times's* Martin Samuel goes leftfield with his description of Nani's goal. Funky who?

    'Timing is all. At the moment when, stung by what was wrongly perceived to be a harsh penalty call, the travelling Tottenham Hotspur contingent chose to voice their displeasure with a taunt of "that's why you're champions", Nani unleashed a shot that defied all obstacles, including terrace sarcasm. No, that's why we're champions, it seemed to say.

    'From a distance of 30 yards, the ball dipped and clipped the top of Carlos Tévez's head, eluding Paul Robinson, the goalkeeper who, Steve McClaren, the England head coach, will ruefully note, is having one of those weeks. Beaten last Wednesday by a Germany striker whose alter ego is a rapper called Funky Pee, his tormentor on this occasion celebrated his goal with a series of somersaults and back-flips. It is as if the circus has come to town, and is camped on his lawn, mocking him through the windows.'

Tottenham – the verbals
- 'He used everything that a 'keeper uses except that he is not a 'keeper, he is a defender.' – Martin Jol won't let himself believe the replays.
- 'He must have been a wizard to keep the ball out of the goal.' – Nice quote though.
- 'The first time all season we have had a little break.' – Fergie's just glad the nightmare's over.

Match facts
United: Van der Sar, Brown*, Ferdinand, Vidic, Evra, Nani, Hargreaves, Carrick (Eagles 57), Scholes, Giggs*, Tévez (Fletcher 77)
Spurs: Robinson, Chimbonda, Rocha (Zokora 83), Gardner*, Lee (Taarabt 75), Malbranque, Jenas, Huddlestone*, Bale, Berbatov*, Keane (Defoe 75) [Jol]
FAPL 16.00 (Sky). Att: 75,696. Ref: H. Webb. Half-time: 0–0
*Yellow card

Other scores

Arsenal 1 (Fabregas) City 0; Sunderland 0 Liverpool 2 (Sissoko, Voronin); Chelsea 1 (Lampard) Portsmouth 0

League table

1. Chelsea 10 (4) 2. City 9 (4) 3. Wigan 7 (4) 4. Liverpool 7 (3)…10. United 5 (4)…17. Spurs 3 (4)

Spurs to Sunderland
'Don't you take my Solskjaer away'

Farewell legend

'After much deliberation and with deep sadness, Ole Gunnar Solskjaer today announces his retirement from his playing career. The decision was reached after continuing problems with his knee injury. Ole will remain at the Club in a coaching capacity and will represent Manchester United as an official Ambassador.' – The official website brings the news we all knew would come, but hoped would be delayed till Moscow in May…Ole's knee finally forces his retirement at the age of 34.

Ole – the quotes

- ⚽ 'I've told the boss and David Gill that I won't be able to play this year. I was training last week and the knee blew up and I'd reached the end of the line, it was an easy decision to make. It's been a fantastic 11 years, and I'm privileged to play for this club, in front of the Stretford End, and serve the Gaffer and proud to play for Manchester United…'
- ⚽ 'There are quite a few stand-out moments. My debut, scoring, turning around and seeing Eric Cantona. Obviously the goals against Bayern Munich and Liverpool. Last year leaving the pitch scoring and seeing my son proud that his dad had scored for Manchester United. The goal against Celtic in the Champions League; to be able to thank them, the Stretford End, for all the support they'd given me was a big motivation. Re-paying the Gaffer because he's been so loyal to me…'
- ⚽ '1999 was a great night for everyone concerned for the club. I think everyone in Manchester has shook my hand and said "I was there" – I think there must have been two million there!'

Ole – the tributes

- ⚽ 'Ole is a fantastic professional. A wonderful human being, a dedicated footballer. Everything that everyone knows about Ole is true, there's no myth about him. A credit to this football club and himself and his family.' – Fergie.

- 'Ole is a man who is respected and loved by everyone at Old Trafford and, as far as I'm concerned, he's up there with the likes of Law, Best and Charlton as one of the legendary figures in United's history. Ole has done things for Manchester United that people only dream about.' – Paddy Crerand.

- 'He's the nicest bloke I ever met in football. He ranks up there with Eric Cantona, and the fans certainly think so. Even when he was out, they never stopped singing his name, the same as they do with Eric. That's what he means to them. The banner above the Stretford End that says "Legend" sums up his place up in United's history. He was blessed with something money can't buy. He is one of the greats in every way.' – David May.

- 'It's a shame. He's a fantastic lad and probably the best all-round finisher I ever played with. Now people will look at that and say, "What? Better than Shearer? Better than Klinsmann?" But in terms of right foot, left foot and heading, he knew exactly where the goal was. He would put the ball through people's legs and in the corners. Brilliant.' – Teddy Sheringham.

- 'The understanding between supporters and players is sadly missing these days. But Solskjaer's approachable, he's a gentlemen, he is almost without fault. As much as for what he did on the pitch, fans have always loved Solskjaer's genuine connection with them.' – IMUSA's Andy Walsh.

Ole – the numbers

216 (starts); 150 (subs appearances); 126 (goals); 67 (Norway caps); 25 (most goals scored in a season, 2001–02); 23 (Norway goals); 9 (trophies won); 2 (4-goal hauls); 1 (red card)

News

In a tragic week for football, three players suffer heart attacks in a matter of days. Leicester's Clive Clark survives, but Sevilla left-back Antonio Puerta and Walsall teenager Anton Reid sadly both die. United are paired with Sporting Lisbon, Dinamo Kiev and, as sod's law would have it, Roma in the group stages of the Champions League. To the chagrin of every ACS victim, United get a home draw – against Coventry – in the Carling Cup. Ex-United disaster zone David Bellion wins the French Player of the Month award for August after scoring four goals in as many games.

Que sera sera...

City win their first Carling Cup tie for three years, beating Bristol City 2–1.

Lucky sevens

William Hill announce their Champions League odds:

Barcelona 5/1, Chelsea 13/2, Man Utd 7/1, AC Milan 8/1, Inter Milan 8/1, Real Madrid 9/1, Liverpool 10/1, Arsenal 16/1, Roma 33/1, Sporting Lisbon 100/1, Dynamo Kiev 150/1, an all-British Final 9/2

United 1 Sunderland 0 01/09/2007

Saha 72

This was the first time that all four of United's summer signings played in the same game. But it was the one player that Fergie didn't sign that dominated pub talk before and after the game. When Ole retired, it seemed certain he'd bring in a new striker – maybe Berbatov or, more likely, the apparently uber-keen Anelka. Instead the window slammed shut, with United boasting just three established strikers, including only one out-and-out front man, the glass-kneed Louis Saha.

The effect the 'fourth striker' factor could have on United's game was immediately obvious here. In the first half, United, with Tévez and Anderson looking confused up front, had absolutely no cutting edge. When Saha, all power and aggression, came on at half-time, they looked far more like their normal selves. It sounds ridiculous looking back, but as the final whistle blew on the week's second tepid 1–0, it really did seem that United's season would stand and fall by how successful Rob Swire was in keeping Saha's knees – and Rooney's feet – on the pitch.

Moments to savour
- Winner: Old Trafford rises to welcome back one legend (Keano) and say farewell to another (Ole). Thank god they didn't play Barcelona. There wouldn't have been a dry eye in the house.
- Runner-up: The winner. Nani curls in a near-post corner from in front of the tunnel, the otherwise immaculate Craig Gordon comes but doesn't collect and Saha heads the ball into the empty net.

Question of the day
Who will go down as the greater United hero? Keane, the great captain and the heartbeat of the club for a decade, or Solskjaer, the permanent reserve who won every Red's heart.

Worry of the month
In terms of raw ability United boasted the finest collection of strikers in the League. In terms of strength in depth they lagged behind just about everyone apart from City. Even Derby started the season with a better fourth option than Dong Fangzhou (though it's unlikely that lumbering Geordie Steve Howard sells as many shirts).

Views from the broadsheets

⊛ 'Sunderland could not manage a miracle on Roy Keane's return to Old Trafford, though Louis Saha did provide a lesson: Manchester United cannot function without a centre-forward. Before his goal, United were in danger of surrendering another two points to determined but ordinary opponents. Things should improve when Cristiano Ronaldo returns from suspension and Wayne Rooney from injury, and they need to. On this evidence the idea that Carlos Tévez can lead the United attack appears wildly misplaced.' – *The Observer* frets about the lack of a target man too.

⊛ 'Mark Hughes, Steve Bruce and Steve Coppell have all returned to Old Trafford in charge of Premier League teams and will do so again this season, but it is fair to say that none received as rapturous a welcome as Keane's. Never one to bask in adoration, let alone milk it, he walked along the touchline with nothing more than an occasional nod of acknowledgment. He looked more comfortable offering his own applause to a former teammate Ole Gunnar Solskjaer, who took a bow to say sad farewells to the crowd after being forced to retire last week.' – *The Independent on Sunday* on Keano's return. I reckon Robbo's was just as loud in 1995.

Quote of the day

⊛ 'Our first-half passing was far too slow. We lacked weight up front and weren't making many chances. It was a long day.' – Fergie.

⊛ 'They'll be fine. They'll be safe.' – Keano's grinning reply when pressed for his views on United's prospects.

⊛ 'One lapse and you lose the game, that's why the Premiership is so tough. I don't want to be over-critical, though, it was a very good delivery and Louis is a bloody good player. He changed the game when he came on, gave them something different, a bit of physical presence.' – Keano again.

I know they have tight deadlines but...

The Sunday tabloids battle it out for the corniest headline award:

'Keano sunk by sub' – *The Sunday Mirror*
'Keane at a Lou's End' – *People*
'Roy's on a Lou-ser' – *The Daily Star Sunday*

Match facts

United: Van der Sar, Brown, Ferdinand, Vidic*, Evra, Eagles (Fletcher), Hargreaves, Scholes, Nani (O'Shea), Anderson (Saha half-time), Tévez

Sunderland: Gordon, Nosworthy, McShane, Higginbotham, Collins, Leadbitter*, Yorke, Etuhu (Miller 82), Wallace (Stokes 82), Chopra*, Jones (Murphy 69) [Keane]
FAPL 17.15 (Set). Att: 75,648. Ref: M. Atkinson. Half-time: 0–0
*Yellow card

Other scores
Liverpool 6 (Alonso 2, Torres 2, Babel, Voronin) Derby 0; Aston Villa 2 (Knight, Agbonlahor) Chelsea 0; Arsenal 3 (Adebayor pen, Fabregas, Rosicky) Portsmouth 1 (Kanu); Blackburn 1 (McCarthy) City 0

League table
1. Liverpool 10 (4) 2. Arsenal 10 (4) 3. Everton 10 (5) 4. Chelsea 10 (5)...8. United 8 (5) ...17. Sunderland 4 (5)

Sunderland to Everton
'Fergie, Fergie, shut your mouth'

News
Fergie gets hit in the groin by drunk Scotsman, Kevin Nicholls, outside Euston station. It later emerges that Nicholls, who head-butted and racially abused the policeman who tried to restrain him, had no fewer than 105 previous convictions. Scholesy is named *MEN* Player of the Year. Giggsy marries his long-time girlfriend Stacey Cooke. Most of the Sunday papers report that Chinese and Arab consortiums are set to make £1 billion bids for United. Ronaldo and his flatmates make headlines in *The News of the World* – the naughty scamps.

Euston, we have a problem
- ☺ 'I'm sorry Fergie. I did not know it was you' – 'Fighting drunk' Kevin Reynolds convinces nobody after punching Sir in the nads.
- ☺ 'Fergie, Fergie, shut your mouth' – Especially after chanting this at him.

Oh the irony
After reports suggested that several parties were considering making a £1 billion bid for ManYoo, the Glazer family issued a firm denial that they were looking to make a quick buck on the club. The statement opened with: 'Manchester United is not for sale'.

The Three Amigos

The News of the World reveals that Ronaldo, Nani and Anderson celebrated the win against Spurs with a cosy night at home – featuring vodka, red bull, a fat limo driver and five prostitutes from Leeds. Blimey. What will they get up to if we actually win something?

That's not what we've heard

Sir Fergie seemed blissfully unaware of what his charges had been up to if his post-match quotes are anything to go by. After the Sunderland game:
'We do lack penetration…You have to look at the front four. They have never played with each other.' – From *football365.com*

Fergie's quotes of the week

☺ 'What the hell are you doing?' – What Sir Alex reportedly said to ABUs' favourite drunk.

☺ 'I think the BBC is the kind of company that never apologises and they will never apologise. They are arrogant beyond belief. They did a story about my son that was a whole lot of nonsense. It was all made-up stuff with "brown paper bags" and all that kind of carry-on. It was a horrible attack on my son's honour and he should never have been accused of that' – Fergie sticks it to Auntie. Looks like Charlie Q will be stuck with *Match of the Day* duties for the foreseeable future then.

☺ 'At the time he had just come back from an Achilles injury and we thought he had just lost a little bit. We got the offer from Lazio – £16.5 million for a centre-back that was 29. It was an offer I couldn't refuse. But in playing terms it was a mistake.' – Five years on, Fergie finally admits he got it wrong trading Laurent Blanc for Jaap Stam.

Euro 2008 Reds

England cruise to successive 3–0 home wins against Estonia and Russia. Ferdinand plays in both matches, scoring the third against the Russians. Fletcher plays the full game as Scotland beat Lithuania 3–1 but fractures his leg as the Scots shock France 1–0 in Paris. Jonny Evans's Northern Ireland lose to second-half own-goals in both Iceland (1–2) and Latvia (0–1). Van der Sar keeps a brace of clean sheets as Holland beat Albania 1–0 and Bulgaria 2–0. O'Shea's Republic of Ireland (when did people stop calling them Eire?) are held 2–2 in Slovakia and lose 1–0 at home to the Czechs. Ronaldo scores the second as Portugal draw 2–2 in Poland. Vidic's Serbia are held 0–0 at home by Finland, then Ronaldo versus Vidic ends in a 1–1 draw and a 30-man melee.

Pub question of the week

Rio scored against Russia. But when was the last time a United defender scored for England?

International story of the week

City's Stephen Ireland lies about the death of BOTH his grannies to secure his withdrawal from the Republic of Ireland squad after the Slovakia game. It later emerges that the real reason he wanted to leave was that his girlfriend had just had a miscarriage. Though even that explanation would start to smell fishy a few weeks later (see p58)...

International quotes of the week

- ✪ 'There's more chance of me flying Concorde to the moon blindfolded than there is of you taking Wales to the World Cup.' – Robbie Savage sticks it to Wales manager John Toshack.
- ✪ 'It's nearly time to book your tickets for Austria.' – The tannoy announcer at Wembley gets ahead of himself. Steady on chaps.
- ✪ 'Ray Clemence has got more chance of starting a game than me at the moment.' – Scott Carson doesn't fancy his chances of getting a start for England. If only things had stayed like that.

Quotes of the week

- ✪ 'The Chinese people literally have billions behind them and the Dubai group are not far behind. It could turn into a bidding war and that will push up the price. That will leave the Glazers facing huge pressure to sell. They have an enormous debt which was raised when they bought United and the temptation to cash in and make a profit of over £295 million will be hard to resist.' – United 'source' to the *News of The World*.
- ✪ 'I think they [the Glazers] are as big a supporter as anybody really.' – Did Bobby Charlton really say that?

Careless

'McKenzies model escorts also make ideal companions for dinner dates, afternoons sampling the delights of Manchester's many art galleries and exhibition spaces, or evenings at an award-winning production in one of Manchester's many impressive theatres.' – The advert for the escort agency used by Ronaldo & co. forgets to mention the full sex.

Everton 0 United 1   15/09/2008

Vidic 83

In a first month full of surprises, none bigger than United's transformation from the great entertainers to Chelsea in red, this was a welcome return to normality. United almost always beat Everton at Goodison. The only real unknown is how they're going to do it – easily, dramatically, luckily, professionally or with a wonder volley from Lee Sharpe.

As it turned out, this latest win was a mix of everything bar a Sharpie shuffle. First Ferdinand and Vidic subdued the threat of the Everton forwards. Then, just when it was becoming clear that no one else had goals in their boots, Vidic marched up the other end and powered in Nani's corner. United in crisis? For 45 minutes, Vida's header put us top of the League.

Moment of the match

The Sunday Times sets the scene nicely as Hibbert concedes a corner with seven minutes to go...

'At this point everyone, except Vidic, had settled for a draw. Fairness demanded it. Both teams had played for almost an hour and a half, competing fiercely, and yet neither goalkeeper had been asked to make a worthwhile save. United were neat in everything they did, they played with a lot of energy too but it was artistry without substance.

'Everton were less pretty but efficient. They knew how to counter United and it was quite an achievement to introduce a new goalkeeper, Stefan Wessels, and then ensure he had an almost idle afternoon. Alas for Everton, their industry and organisation didn't create much at the other end of the pitch. Yakubu and Andy Johnson started as if they meant business but, by half-time, Vidic and Rio Ferdinand, had lowered their expectations.

'So that's where it was as Nani delivered that late corner. Standing centre of goal, Vidic surged towards the near post, Yobo went with them but as the ball arrived, Vidic jumped early, hung momentarily in the air and then powered a header into the roof of the net. It was the game's outstanding moment and coming from Vidic, about as predictable as these things can be.'

Line of the day

'Hampered by injuries, suspensions, a dearth of strikers and makeshift XIs featuring young newcomers, Manchester United sit inside the top four, within a win of the top, after three consecutive 1–0 victories. A stutter? This is how thoroughbreds stutter.' – *The Independent*

Runner-up

'This was not the most inspiring of games, nor the most convincing of performances from either side, but at least Manchester United have achieved their first objective of the season. They are now higher in the table than Manchester City.' – *The Observer*

What was good?

☺ We keep on getting away with it. And we're one game closer to getting Rooney and Ronaldo back.

What was bad?

☺ Mickey Silvestre was carried off with a damaged cruciate ligament and won't be back till spring.

Goodison – the verbals

☺ 'We knew we could get a goal like we did. We came for that and we got it' – Vidic makes a revealing admission.

☺ 'That's the kind of defending you need to win titles. Once you do that, and when we get the other top players back and the consistency of performance, we will be OK.' – Fergie sounds confident…in public at least.

Match facts

Everton: Wessels, Hibbert, Yobo, Lescott, Baines, Arteta, Jagielka, Neville* (McFadden 85), Osman (Pienaar* 73), Johnson, Yakubu (Anichebe 74) [Moyes]
United: Van der Sar, Brown, Ferdinand, Vidic, Silvestre (Nani 41), Ronaldo*, Carrick, Scholes*, Evra, Giggs (Saha 63), Tévez, Nani (Pique 85)
FAPL 12.00 Goodison Park. Att: 39,364. Ref: A. Wiley. Half-time: 0–0
*Yellow card

Other scores

Chelsea 0 Blackburn 0; Portsmouth 0 Liverpool 0; Spurs 1 (Bale) Arsenal 3 (Adebayor 2, Fabregas)

League table

1. Arsenal 13 (5) 2. City 12 (6) 3. Liverpool 11 (5) 4. United 11 (6)…7. Everton 10 (6)

Everton to Sporting
'I realise now it was a mistake to say that my grandmother had died'

Gossip

United are linked with Sevilla's Russian forward Alexander Kerzhakov, South Korean starlet Ki Sung-yong and, mischievously, with Benitez's former assistant, Pako Ayesteran. The agent of Brazilian seal-boy Kerlon claims he was close to signing for United until he injured his knee in the summer. Plans are announced for a British musical based on the life of Roman Abramovich. *The Mail* says that Tévez and Mascherano could face up to five years in jail for alleged tax evasion in Brazil – as if they haven't been caught up in enough controversy already.

Cracking up

'The style of how we play is very important. But it is omelettes and eggs. No eggs – no omelettes! It depends on the quality of the eggs. In the supermarket you have class one, two or class three eggs and some are more expensive than others and some give you better omelettes. So when the class one eggs are in Waitrose and you cannot go there, you have a problem' – Mourinho flips his lid after his two main goalscorers, Drogba and Lampard, both pick up injuries. Maybe he shouldn't have put all his eggs in two baskets.

You were saying?

August 29:

'I would have expected United to have started a bit better, but a lot of clubs have bought really well over the summer. Five points is a hell of a gap to have this early on. It's going to be difficult for United.' – John Terry.

September 8:

United go top of the League.

Stereotypical

Everton fan Carl Lloyd calls in the police after accusing Ronaldo of assaulting him at Goodison. The 34-year-old, who said Ronaldo stamped on his arm when he reached for the ball near the hoardings, told *The Daily Post*: 'I've been in excruciating pain. I don't know if I'll work again any time soon.' You don't say la', you don't say!

Quotes of the week I

☉ 'I realise now it was a mistake to say that my grandmother had died' – Everyone's favourite grandson, Stephen Ireland, finally puts his hands up.

⚽ 'As long as he keeps getting away with it, I am happy. His father was the same because he got away with a lot too. Maybe it runs in the family' – Sven Goran Eriksson explains why he keeps picking Kasper Schmeichel, despite the mounting proof he's not actually any good.

⚽ 'Rafa would be very lucky to be in a job if he hadn't got to two Champions League Finals, because they have had some very, very poor finishes in the Premier League.' – Sam Allardyce (trophies won, 0) earns himself a whole lot of grief by asking what Benitez has ever done for Liverpool. Mind you, he's got a point…

No Mr Bond, I expect you to die

Peter Kenyon comes over all Dr Evil again, predicting world domination for London's third-biggest club:

'Over a 10-year period, you need two European Cups to be a world club. You have to dominate your domestic League. We have to have an infrastructure to deal with that and people to deal with it. We will win the Champions League. It's just "when?" is the question. We've got a squad, a structure, a belief and we've got quality. And I do believe the Champions League is not that far away.'

Amusingly, on the same day Kenyon's comments become public, Chelsea have to slash their prices for their Champions League opener against Rosenborg…and still only pull in a crowd of 24,973.

Using double barrels

'It's bulls**t' – Arsenal chairman Peter Hill-Wood blasts Chelsea's world domination plans.

Quotes of the week II

⚽ 'Money is irrelevant to history and how big your club is. I don't want to run Chelsea down, but one has to concede Manchester United and Liverpool are probably the biggest names in UK football and probably throughout the world. For Chelsea to think they are suddenly going to dominate Manchester United and Liverpool is fantasy.' – Peter Hill-Wood continues to stick it to Chelski.

⚽ 'Over a 10-year period, you need two European Cups to be a world club.' – Kenyon's mission statement is news to the likes of United and Barcelona, who have only won two European Cups each in 50 years but still manage to be revered across the globe.

⚽ 'It is amazing to put pressure on the lad to win two European Cups.' – Fergie, who knows more than most how hard it is to win the big one, sticks up for Jose. Have any other managers had more stabs at it than Fergie? Answer: No.

Sporting Lisbon 0 United 1   19/09/2007

Ronaldo 62

In many ways this game was an exact replica of the 1–0 win at Benfica at the same stage last year. United began stodgily, passed the ball sloppily and spent most of the first half on the back foot, while the opposition 'keeper barely got a sweat on. Just as they had against Benfica. Then half-time came and seemed to drain Sporting of their extra spark and energy. Just as it had to Benfica. And, finally, just after the hour-mark, United scored a classy breakaway goal that was totally out of keeping with everything that had gone on before it. Just as they had against Benfica.

There was, however, one vital difference between the two Portuguese 1–0s. At the Stadium of Light, the locals had treated Ronaldo (a national hero when wearing the maroon of Portugal) like he'd been wearing 666 on his back. This time he was treated like Figo, Eusebio and Vasco da Gama all rolled into one. It didn't even matter that he scored the goal that condemned his old team to an undeserved defeat. In fact, his respectful, bowing reaction to his diving header provoked one of the images of the season: a standing ovation that swept round the stadium like a high-speed Mexican wave.

'Ronaldo – adored in Manchester', as the banner in the United end said. But he's also adored in Lisbon – the green-and-white half anyway.

Goal!

1–0 (62): United take the first step on the road to Moscow. Scholes and Rooney build the move, Carrick finds Brown on the overlap, and his exquisite cross is headed in by a diving Ronaldo. For an instant he looks like he is going to celebrate, but then he remembers where he is, makes a prayer sign and applauds the home support. Within seconds a wave of applause rings around the stadium. A remarkable moment.

View from the broadsheets

⚽ 'For once the script went to plan, and there was barely a dry eye in the house. There will certainly be none in the Madeira home in which Cristiano Ronaldo grew up after this. On his return to Sporting Lisbon, the club which took his raw talent and moulded him into a starlet, Ronaldo scored the goal which brought up Manchester United's century of victories in this competition. Yet despite this devastating blow to Sporting's hopes of progressing in the Champions League, Ronaldo was still accorded an ovation when he left the field. Such is the love his rare talent inspires, and the humility with which he displayed it last night.' – *The Independent*

Ronaldo – the verbals

- ✪ 'Red is my colour and I want to win for United. I said before the game that Sporting Lisbon is my second home, and I feel a little bit sad [they lost], but the most important thing is United. They are my team, and I'm very happy with the victory.'
- ✪ 'It was a perfect night – I score, I win, it was great for Manchester United.'
- ✪ 'The reaction of the Sporting fans towards me was very special. It made me feel very proud, maybe the proudest moment of my career so far.'

Match facts

Sporting: Stojkovic, Abel, Tonel, Anderson Polga, Ronny (Pereirinha 74), Izmailov (Vukcevic 55), Veloso, Moutinho, Romagnoli* (Purovic 67), Djalo, Liedson [Bento]
United: Van der Sar*, Brown, Ferdinand, Vidic, Evra, Carrick, Scholes, Nani*, Giggs (Anderson 76), Ronaldo (Tévez 86), Rooney (Saha 72)
CLF 19.45 (Sky). Att: 39,514. Ref: H.Fandel (Ger). Half-time: 0–0
*Yellow card

Other scores

Roma 2 Kiev 0; Porto 1 Liverpool 1; Chelsea 1 Rosenborg 1; Arsenal 3 Sevilla 0

Sporting to Chelsea

'I will miss the Manchester United fans, even though they shout things at me that I don't like.'

News

Not much to report…except that Chelsea boot out their most succesful manager of all time – a man who never lost a match at Stamford Bridge – and replace him with Israeli poodle Avram Grant.

Right behind you (holding a knife)

- ✪ Agent Kenyon, January 2007: 'Mourinho has a contract until 2010. He is happy here. His family are here. He knows he has a job to do. The board and Jose want to follow up on two fantastic seasons.'
- ✪ Agent Kenyon, April 2007: 'Jose has contract to 2010 and he wants to stay. We are not going to sack him, he has the club's support. That's the situation and we are agreed on it.'

- Agent Kenyon, 18 September 2007: 'There's loads of speculation that if we don't win (against Rosenborg) Jose gets fired, but that's not the way we think.'
- Chelsea, 20 September 2007: 'Chelsea Football Club and Jose Mourinho have agreed to part company today by mutual consent.'

Rumour of the week
'CHELSEA'S stars are revolting over Avram Grant being named boss. A furious row broke out at the team meeting after training yesterday. Angry words were exchanged between big-name players as they argued about Grant taking over from Jose Mourinho. Among those most upset over Mourinho's departure were striker Didier Drogba, winger Florent Malouda and defender Ashley Cole.' – *The Sun*

What a performance
'Jose leaving Chelsea is a disappointment for the game. He was terrific for football and terrific for Chelsea. He brought something fresh and new to our game and I enjoyed the competition with him. I wish him well, but I just don't know what I am going to do with my wine now' – How did Fergie manage to keep a straight face?

Rumour of the week II
Abramovich reckons he can do the job himself. In fact, he'd already started before Mourinho left. From *The Observer's* report on the Rosenborg game:
'In front of the entire Chelsea team, but while Mourinho was occupied with press conference duties, the Russian billionaire decided to hand out an impromptu tactics lesson to Michael Essien. Employing striker Andriy Shevchenko as translator, he instructed midfielder Essien, Player of the Year last season, to hit passes wide rather than through central areas where the Norwegians had compressed play.
'Abramovich is expected to take an increasingly hands-on role in the team following the appointment of Grant to replace Mourinho and, according to several sources, will effectively select the side.'

Not so special
'We haven't played so well this season. We played one game against Birmingham, which was fantastic, we played well for 20 minutes against Reading. We haven't scored enough goals, and there are many things to improve' – Avram Grant lays into his predecessor.

Outburst of the week
'He will be always remembered as the man who pushed away Jose Mourinho. To be honest, if there are people who hate Israelis now they hate us more because of Avram.

I think the way that Grant got his job was disgusting. As a human being I would be ashamed to walk on the streets after the things Avram has done...I have the feeling Grant will be successful but there is one problem, though. He became hated in the United Kingdom.' – Eyal Berkovic lays into Grant.

Quote of the week

'I love English football, the fans, the match, even the supporters of other teams! I will miss the Liverpool and Manchester United fans, even though they shout things at me that I don't like. It is part of the culture. I know that I have a place in the history of Chelsea, and for me I will always love the fans and they will always love me.' – We'll miss you too Jose, but probably not as much as you think...

United 2 Chelsea 0

23/09/2007

Tévez 48, Saha 90 (pen)

The really surprising part about the Special One's departure wasn't that he had been given the boot. Everyone knew that a rift the size of Mourinho's ego had opened up between him and Abramovich. The really shocking part was the timing. Peter Kenyon had had all summer to sharpen his dagger, so why wait until mid-September to use it? And strangest of all, why time it so that Avram Grant's first-ever match in charge of a half-decent team would be at Old Trafford (was it because Mourinho would have been unsackable if he'd beaten United)? Whatever the reasons – and it reeked of another Kenyon cock-up to many – the events of the week played straight into United's hands. Chelsea were anything but special ones in the opening exchanges. When Mikel was harshly sent off for lunging into Evra, they went extra-negative. And when Tévez flicked in his first United goal, they effectively settled for a low-key defeat. Amusingly, it was the only goal they managed to hit all afternoon.

As for United? They certainly didn't play well. Ronaldo was quiet, Rooney and Tévez didn't look a good fit again, and they couldn't quite decide whether to try and sweep Chelsea aside in the second half or just close the game out. But they were the better side when it was 11 versus 11. And they were hugely comfortable when it went 11 versus 10. It wasn't exciting, it wasn't impressive, but it was easily enough.

How the match unfolded

ROONEY. SAVE! (1): Rooney charges down the inside-left channel, cuts inside Ben Haim and curls in a right-footer that Cech just manages to fingertip behind. It's a decent effort and a cracking save. Or as Andy Gray growls in classic Gray style: 'Top football all round. The closing down of Scholes. The run of Rooney. The attempt from Rooney. And finally, what a save!'

PENALTY! NO! (17): Tévez holds off Ferreira on halfway and passes back to Carrick who instantly lofts a left-footer into the space where the Chelsea right-back should have been. Evra beats Joe Cole in a foot race, charges into the area and is taken down by Cole's desperate last-ditch lunge. It's a clear penalty, a definite yellow card, and a borderline red one. Mike Dean awards a goal-kick.

GIGGS. MISS! (29): Essien, under no pressure in his own area, sends a panicky toe-pecker straight at Rooney. Rooney chests it down and floats a lovely ball to the back post which practically begs Giggs to dive and head in. Instead Giggs opts to let the ball come across him and try a sidefoot volley from a far more difficult angle. Three times out of 10 he might well have made it. Unfortunately, this is one of the other seven and the ball balloons over Cech's bar.

OFF! (32): Mikel shows too much of the ball to Evra and steams into a tackle, catching Evra on the top of the foot and sending him flying. Scholes, Rooney and half the Chelsea team surround the referee as he calmly reaches for his cards. When Terry sees what colour Dean picks out he makes a desperate, and extraordinary, attempt to grab it out of his hand (such exemplary behaviour from the England captain). It makes no difference. The red card is held aloft and Mikel is off. It looks a harsh decision – he didn't go over the top of the ball, and he didn't go in two-footed. But Mikel did launch himself with one set of studs at Evra, so it certainly wasn't the total miscarriage of justice it was portrayed later.

TÉVEZ! GOAL! (47.30): Ronaldo forces a corner on the right. As Giggs steps up to take it, Martin Tyler muses, 'Having seen a big refereeing decision go against them, imagine if Chelsea conceded a goal here, right on half-time.' Then, as Chelsea clear the corner and Brown recycles the ball to Giggs, he adds, 'There's still a chance that might happen because it's Giggs…'
    Tyler couldn't have set up what happened next any better. Giggs bends in a near-post cross with the outside of his left foot. Cech makes the decision to come for the ball and Tévez dives in front of him to flick the ball into the net for his first United goal. Or as Tyler puts it, 'TÉVEZZZZZZZZZZ! They have!'

GIGGS. OVER! (59): United have clearly sussed out that the right side of Chelsea's defence looks vulnerable against the long ball. This time Carrick drops a pass over Ferreira and Giggs smashes a 'one in 20' volley into the wheelchair section.

OFF! NO! (72): Joe Cole launches a terrible, almost cowardly, lunge at Ronaldo, raking his Achilles with his studs. Fergie goes berserk, marching into the technical area and screaming 'It's a f***ing red card' straight into the Sky mics. Dean would surely have got out his red card if he hadn't used it already. As it was, Cole – who should have been at least booked in the first half, remember – gets away with a yellow.

PENALTY! SAHA! GOAL! (88): That long ball over Ferreira catches out Chelsea once again. Saha pulls down Ferdinand's raking pass brilliantly with his left foot and then flicks the ball away with his right. As he does, Ben Haim catches him slightly on the shin. Which is enough contact for Saha to do an arched-back, Drogba-style collapse. And for Dean to point to the spot. Saha, not Ronaldo, steps up to take the penalty, and he scores with a low side-foot down the middle.

Chelsea – the verbals

- 'I thought the referee was excellent' – Avram Grant tries out sarcasm. Though, let's face it, Mike Dean was just as bad for both teams.

- 'I've seen the sending-off incident and it was maybe a bit harsh, but there was intent there. It could have hurt the boy [Evra], but a lot of referees would have let it go. Then, when you see Joe Cole's tackle in the second half on Cristiano Ronaldo, that should have been a straight red card. It was right down the Achilles, which is happening repeatedly to Cristiano. I think the referee was perhaps balancing it out. The foul on Louis Saha for our penalty was a bit harsh, but I think that cancels out the one we should have got in the first half. We should have had a penalty-kick [for Joe Cole's foul on Evra] in the first half, I think the cameras clearly show that.' – Fergie gets it spot on.

Views from the broadsheets

- 'Mike Dean had some big calls to make at Old Trafford yesterday. It really would have spoilt it had he got one right. He gave a penalty that was not; missed a penalty that was; sent off a player that did not deserve it; merely cautioned one that did. When Sir Alex Ferguson describes a red card to an opposition player as harsh, it would suggest an extreme miscarriage of justice. If the jury is out on the new Chelsea manager, Avram Grant, it is because the performance of the referee ruled this match a mistrial.' – *The Times*

- 'On the day that "Avram Who?" became "Avram Why?", Chelsea lost a player, two goals and three points to compound the disaster of losing the inspirational Jose Mourinho. If they are to rebuild for the future, Chelsea must appoint a more substantial successor to Mourinho than Avram Grant, who possesses neither the leadership skills nor the coaching licence.' – *The Telegraph*

- 'No points but at least Grant had plenty of excuses when Abramovich pushed open the door. Specifically, they will have focused upon the referee Mike Dean who made two erratic decisions, the first when he failed to award a penalty to Manchester United for Joe Cole's crude challenge on Patrice Evra on 17 minutes. Then, more crucially from Grant's point of view, there was the poorly-judged dismissal of John Obi Mikel on 32 minutes for a challenge on Evra that was worth of a booking yet ended up tipping the balance of the match.' – *The Independent*

- 'Once United had scored, with Carlos Tévez notching his first goal for the club, Chelsea enjoyed no more than a meaningless rally. Sir Alex Ferguson's side remembered to keep ample numbers behind the ball and spirited breaks by the visitors petered out, with no genuine saves required of Edwin van der Sar. Those seeking to have their emotions stirred were best advised to keep their eyes on the referee.' – *The Guardian*

- 'As Chelsea owner Roman Abramovich sat alone with his thoughts in a deserted directors' box at the break, serenaded by United chants of "You've Lost Your Special One", even the Russian oligarch must have acknowledged that success comes to those who employ high-class managers and then leave them alone. Arsene Wenger's vibrant Arsenal lead the Premier League followed by Sir Alex Ferguson's Manchester United, who are beginning to find their elegant stride.' – *The Telegraph*

Quote of the day

'Chelsea pushed the violence to the absolute limit, and there could have been other red cards during the match. But justice prevailed in the end and we deserved to win. Our game is totally superior to Chelsea's this season, and the scoreline was actually short of what we deserved. I have seen the problems at Chelsea with the change of coach, but this season they have just not developed the rhythm of the other years. Chelsea were very nervous, and it was impossible that we were going to lose the match.' – Carlos Tévez after becoming the third Argentine to score for United.

Match facts

United: Van der Sar, Brown*, Ferdinand, Vidic, Evra, Ronaldo, Scholes, Carrick, Giggs, Tévez (Saha 79), Rooney*
Chelsea: Cech, Ferreira, Ben-Haim, Terry*, A.Cole, Makelele, Essien, Mikel† 32, J.Cole* (Pizarro 76), Shevchenko (Kalou 59), Malouda (Wright-Phillips 69) [Grant]
FAPL 16.00 (Sky). Att: 75,663. Ref: M. Dean. Half-time: 1–0
*Yellow card † Red card

Other scores

Arsenal 5 (Adebayor 3 [1 pen], Diaby, Fabregas) Derby 0; Liverpool 0 Birmingham 0; Fulham 3 (Davies, Bouazza, Murphy) City 3 (Petrov 2, Mpenza)

League table

1. Arsenal 16 (6) 2. United 14 (7) 3. City 13 (7) 4. Liverpool 12 (6)…6. Chelsea 11 (7)

Chelsea to Coventry
'No wonder any player who comes to Manchester United never wants to leave.'

Be careful what you wish for

According to *The Daily Star*, Mariah Carey has 'discovered she is related to footballer Ashley Cole'.

'The R&B diva, 37, traced her family tree because she was convinced the late Nat King Cole was from the same stock. Instead, her search revealed she does have a Cole in the family – Chelsea left-back Ashley, 26.'

Says the singer: 'I'm such a huge fan of his. That would be wonderful and would explain so much.' (I'm guessing she's talking about Nat there, not Ashley.)

You were saying

A good spot from *football365.com*:

Here's an extract from an interview with John Terry in *The Observer* in May 2006:

'And when I feel that a decision should have gone our way, then it's down to the players to make a point to the ref. But we do have to stop running up to him, in his face, if there's 10 of you. Certainly the captain should be allowed to go up and have a decent conversation.'

So Terry must think a 'decent conversation' involves swarming all over the ref, showering spittle in his face and then trying to wrestle the red card out of his hand.

You're nicked

Another good 'un lifted from *football365.com*:

Reported *The Guardian* the Friday before the Chelsea game:

'Avram Grant, the former Israel manager, yesterday led his first training session since taking charge of the first team. He will face Manchester United on Sunday and has been told it is his job to lose.' So far so good then.

Oh, this one could prove very useful later on...

Said Avram Grant after the FA rejected Obi Mikel's appeal against his red card on Sunday:

'One of the things I always teach my players and even my children is that when you make a mistake, you can admit it. I promise that if I make a mistake, I will say I did one because it happens to all of us and no-one is perfect.'

Spot the difference

- ⚽ 'Arsenal said on Monday annual pretax profit dropped 65 per cent to 5.6 million pounds from 15.9 million last year as the club refinanced the debt it borrowed to build its Emirates stadium...The result would have been worse but for the sale of talismanic striker Thierry Henry' – Reuters
- ⚽ 'Arsenal announce record profits – Arsenal have announced record operating profits of £51.2 million for the year ending May 2007 – a 274 per cent increase on the previous year...Match-day revenues from the club's first season at their new home rose to £90.6 million, which amounts to £3.1 million per game and is more than double the £44.1 million accrued from the team's final season at Highbury' – Setanta

Yellow peril

'Chelsea's new manager, Avram Grant may be happy describing himself as "normal" – as opposed to "special" like his predecessor Jose Mourinho – yet the same can hardly be said of his wife, Tzofit…She has drunk her own urine for breakfast and has bathed in chocolate. The 43-year-old actress-cum-exhibitionist has been called the Ruby Wax of Israeli television…On one memorable occasion she knocked back a whisky tumbler of her own urine live on air to explore whether or not it had any health benefits.' – *The Daily Mail* with the celebrity scoop of the week.

United quotes of the week

- 'I can't even begin to estimate how many tickets I have been offered at knock-down prices by season ticket holders who don't want to go to this game.' – IMUSA's Mark Longden predicts swathes of red seats for the midweek Coventry game.
- 'I've never seen such a good atmosphere as I have here, even with the players who can't speak English. Anderson and Nani can barely speak any English and they are in on every joke. I don't know how they do it. There's always music playing before games. In Germany that is unheard of. It's very relaxed here. The atmosphere is great and the staff contribute to that. No wonder any player who comes to Manchester United never wants to leave. The attention to detail here is fantastic. It's bigger than Bayern, better organised.' – Ever get the feeling Owen Hargreaves is happy to be here?

Chelsea daggers

'When Mourinho went to say goodbye for the last time in the dressing room it only lasted five minutes, but it was an immensely strong moment and very moving. To watch him empty his locker so quickly and with such little fuss was terrible. Some around me were crying. It's a shame if you are sensitive. He kissed us, one by one – except a few! Then he said "I wish you good luck to you and to your families and I thank you all. Even those who betrayed me."' – Drogba spills the beans on Mourinho's farewell. Breaks your heart doesn't it?

Unshocking quote of the week

'It's a long while since I've had sex.' – Coventry boss Iain Dowie.

United 0 Coventry 2　　　　　26/09/2007

Mifsud 27, 70

Oh dear. This was all a bit embarrassing wasn't it? Somehow, though, watching the United team slope off the pitch at the end was all very reassuring. After all, United haven't been this consistently bad in the League Cup since they were really good in everything else.

Goal action

0–1 (27): Coventry tear United's young defence apart down the left, their captain Michael Doyle crosses low to the far post and Malta international Michael Mifsud arrives late to slide in.

0–2 (70): Mifsud rounds off another quick break on the left to complete Coventry's best night for years – and his country's biggest sporting night since Tony Drago, the 'Maltese whippet', reached the quarters at the Crucible in 1988.

View from the broadsheets

- 'This time last week everyone was struggling to contain their amusement at Chelsea shooting themselves in the foot. Now, just as suddenly, it is Manchester United's turn to look very silly indeed.
  'Going out of the Carling Cup at home to Coventry City was one thing, but doing so in front of a record crowd of 74,055, many of whom did not want to be there in the first place and had reluctantly shelled out money to find themselves watching an unrecognisable team, was a public-relations fiasco that will take some living down.' – *The Observer*

Quote of the night

'It's a big shock to us all and we just hope the young players look at it and improve themselves. These are players whose talents we have been trumpeting for a while but I was flabbergasted with the performance.' – Fergie's in shock.

What was bad?

- Where do you start?

What was good?

☺ United's early knockout meant we wouldn't be forced to shell out another £25-plus to watch the reserves again. It also meant we'd be spared another 90 minutes of Dong Fangzhou – surely the worst centre-forward ever to pull on a United shirt?

Question of the day

The official attendance was 74,055. But how many people were really in the ground?

Headline of the day

'Sud It' – Full marks to both *The Mirror* and *The Sun*.

Match facts

United: Kuszczak, Bardsley (Brown 45), Evans (Carrick 56), Pique, Simpson, Nani, Martin (Campbell 45), O'Shea, Eagles, Dong, Anderson
Coventry: Marshall, Osbourne (McNamee 8), Ward, Turner, Borrowdale, Simpson, Hughes, Doyle, Tabb, Mifsud, Best (Adebola 90) [Dowie]
CCC3 20.00. Att: 74,055. Ref: M.Halsey. Half-time: 0–1

Selected Carling Cup third-round results:

Hull 0 Chelsea 4; Arsenal 2 Newcastle 0; Reading 2 Liverpool 4; City 1 Norwich 0

Coventry to Birmingham
'The boys I put out are good enough to win the Carling Cup'

If it wasn't for those pesky kids

'For some reason, the technique and ability we know these young players have just wasn't there, which was a big disappointment.' – John O'Shea gives a masterclass in passing the buck. He was only captain against Coventry after all.

Building them up

From Fergie's programme notes for the Coventry game:

'Tonight's team will be built round the talented young players who are now back with us after spending most of last season out on loan. We have an exceptionally gifted group of young men who are in critical need of a higher grade of football.'

'The boys I put out are good enough to win the Carling Cup. I would have no qualms playing any of them in our first team.'

It's a scandal

'Manchester United serves up the WORST footie food in Europe, says a survey. In the grub stakes, Glasgow clubs Rangers and Celtic had the next most disliked meals, followed by Tottenham and Chelsea. Arsenal's Emirates Stadium was the top culinary experience, along with Barcelona while Delia Smith's Norwich was third.' – *The Sun*

But who cares about that when you've got all those chip, pie and gravy emporiums (the Ming Dynasty is my favourite at the moment) outside?

More famous last words

'I think we've got a terrific bunch with Dong, Campbell, Martin, Gibson, Eagles – who has come on unbelievably well – Pique, Evans, Simpson...they're all excellent.' – Fergie again.

Seriously though...

The superb results Arsenal's kids keep on getting in the Carling Cup, the unbelievable talent that's emerged out of Barcelona and even the number of decent players City have been bringing through the ranks only serve to highlight how few success stories there have been from United's academy. Amazingly, since the class of 1992, United haven't produced a single player who has ended up as a first-team star.

The Magnificent Seven?

Home-grown United first-teamers since the class of '92: Pip Neville, Brown, Fletcher, O'Shea, Chadwick, Wallwork, Richardson (Pique and Rossi don't count – they were nicked).

Reeking of menace

'These boys will take some lessons from this, but they will have to learn them fast.' – Fergie lays down the law.

Non-football rumour of the week

'Tom Cruise is on a secret *Mission Impossible* to recruit Posh and Becks to Scientology, says a new book. Author Andrew Morton, 54, claims the movie star wants to convert pals David and Victoria Beckham to the controversial church. He makes a string of allegations about the 45-year-old actor and the religion in a new unauthorised biography.' – *The Daily Star*

Birmingham 0 United 1   29/09/2007

Ronaldo 51

Birmingham were much better than United in the first half. United weren't much better in the second half, but they defended OK and nicked the win when Ronaldo scored. Well, if United can get away with doing just enough, so can I...

Goal!

1–0 (51): As Fergie admitted afterwards, United were lucky to be level at half-time, with Van der Sar saving well from Queudrue and Jerome and Ferdinand clearing McSheffrey's header off the line. But underdogs often pay for failing to take their chances, and that's what happened here. Queudrue makes a terrible hash of dealing with Ferdinand's straightforward heave up the pitch, Ronaldo beats him to the bounce, skilfully evades Ridgewell and Taylor and passes the ball into the net.

Views from the broadsheets

- 'Birmingham have not beaten United since November 1978, the month when the bakers' union went on strike. Steve Bruce's side used their loaves well enough in the first half on Saturday to put this record straight but were thwarted by a combination of Edwin van der Sar's saves and the support he enjoyed from his centre-backs, Rio Ferdinand and Nemanja Vidić.' – The game was so dull at times that *The Guardian's* legendary sportswriter David Lacey ends up obsessing about a 30-year-old bread strike.

- 'Up front Carlos Tévez resumed his partnership with Wayne Rooney, but the best double acts thrive on contrasts of style and method and this pair are too alike to surprise defences with something unexpected; two Ernie Wises looking for the same punchline.' – Lacey's words sound silly now. But we were all thinking this at the time.

- 'It is more 1980s Liverpool – or, in terms of results, Arsenal under George Graham – and it probably would not measure up for Roman Abramovich in terms of winning with style. But, having taken eight matches and seven weeks to manage what Portsmouth achieved in 90 mad minutes at Fratton Park on Saturday, Manchester United are bearing a certain ominous look early in their title defence. Unfamiliar as the "1–0 to the United" chant is, momentum is steadily growing in a manner that must make their rivals wonder what will happen when the shackles do come off.' – *The Independent*

St Andrews – the verbals

- ☻ 'We made a horrible mistake and got punished. To lose like that is cruel.' – Brucie's gutted.
- ☻ 'They are the best side we have played this season. They were very athletic, very aggressive and very quick about the pitch, and even at 1–0 I was still praying we would get through the match.' – Fergie's just pleased to have got this one out of the way.

Match facts

Birmingham: Taylor, Kelly, Djourou (Schmitz 75), Ridgewell, Queudrue*, Larsson*, Muamba (Palacios 70), Nafti* (O'Connor 84), McSheffrey, Jerome, Kapo [Brucie]
United: Van der Sar (Kuszczak half-time), Brown, Ferdinand, Vidic, Evra*, Ronaldo, Scholes, Carrick, Giggs (Saha 63), Rooney, Tévez (O'Shea 88)
FAPL 15.00 St Andrews. Att: 26,526. Ref: S. Bennett, Half-time: 0–0
*Yellow card

Other scores

Wigan 0 Liverpool 1 (Benayoun); Chelsea 0 Fulham 0; West Ham 0 Arsenal 1 (Van Persie); City 3 (Petrov, Mpenza, Elano) Newcastle 1 (Martins)

League table

1. Arsenal 19 (7) 2. United 17 (8) 3. City 16 (8) 4. Liverpool 15 (7)…13. Birmingham 8 (8)

Birmingham to Roma
'I'm fed up with the f**king thing. Shove it up wherever.'

How to pick up Page Three girls at 41

'2 Time Out bars, 5 tins of Foster's lager, 1 Caramel bar, 4 tins of Red Bull, 1 jar of Tesco's strawberry jam, 5 bottled beers, 1 jar of Colman's horseradish sauce, 2 bottles of Dom Perignon, 1 tub of Flora, 2 bottles of white wine, 1 jar of Colman's mustard, 1 carton of milk, 6 (slightly rotten) tomatoes.'

The Sunday Times goes rooting in Teddy Sheringham's fridge for the secret of permanent youth. And finds this. Chocolate, champagne and Colmans. What a boy…

Who'd have thought it?

'Despite the long-suffering Nancy sporting an engagement ring, Sven has allegedly been seeing single mum Saima Ansari since returning to Britain as City manager this summer.' – *News Of The World*

Quotes of the week

- ⊛ 'I'm fed up with the f**king thing. Shove it up wherever. I've had 17 million questions about second-season syndrome.' – Stevie Coppell feels the strain after struggling Reading score four goals at Portsmouth and still get hammered.
- ⊛ 'The first match generated so much controversy. United then profited from these circumstances by doing all they could to create a totally unjust atmosphere against us. United deserved to win, but some of their players abused this superiority. We see this as an opportunity to exact revenge. I have never suffered on the field like I did that day last season.' – Roma greaseball Christian Panucci thirsts for revenge on the eve of their return to Old Trafford.
- ⊛ 'The only way for us to forget about what happened last season is to beat United by 7–0. I want my revenge, and if I was asked to choose between beating Inter Milan or Manchester United, I would prefer to win in England. Any Serie A game is important; however, we all want a great and beautiful revenge against United.' – Francesco Totti comes over all emotional too.

Pot...kettle...taxi

- ⊛ 'At the end of the game the referee told me to f*** off.' – After Leeds draw at Gillingham, Dennis Wise reveals why Danny McDermid is an early contender for referee of the year.
- ⊛ 'I think it is totally unacceptable and we as a club will be reporting him,' whines Wise, the same Wise who was sacked from Leicester after breaking Callum Davidson's nose and jaw, who was convicted of assaulting a London cabbie, who could start a fight in an empty room, who...

A double-edged sword

Roma's Francesco Totti and teammate Damiano Tommasi send a message of apology to Carly Lyes, 23, one of the victims of the police violence in Rome in March:

'We would like to apologise for the treatment you received in Rome last season and hope it has not damaged the opinion that you and your fellow supporters have of Rome.'

It's a nice touch from the two of them, no question about it. It's just a shame they had to spoil it by saying this:

'We would also like to invite you to the Olympic Stadium for the game later this year and treat you as our guest.'

The b***ards!

Quote of the week

'When we were 6–0 up [against Roma], one of their players said "don't do any more dribbles", almost begging. Other players ask me to go to play on the opposite side and others don't show any humour when they make threats to my physical integrity.' – Diplomacy, Ronaldo style.

United 1 Roma 0   02/10/2007

Rooney 70

So what do you think? Was Roma 'keeper Doni really ill, like he said he was when he pulled out of this game minutes before kick-off? Or did he bottle it? Remember, the last time he played at Old Trafford he had the mother of nightmares, the football equivalent of soiling yourself during a crucial interview. But if Doni really did pull a sickie, he chose the wrong night to do it. United were still stuck in Chelsea mode. Old Trafford, which had been a crackling bear pit during April's 7–1, barely cleared its throat. And Roma, as Fergie said, were more pumped up for this match than any other. But they still weren't good enough to get the revenge they so obviously craved, which, in a sense, must have made this latest visit to M16 just as painful as the one before.

Goal action

70 (1–0): This game didn't have the thrills or the atmosphere of Roma's last visit. Nothing like, in fact, but it was an intriguing watch none the less – a footballing chess match full of thoughtful passing and canny defence. Roma had the chances late on to get a draw, but United just about deserved their checkmate, if only because of the quality of the decisive goal. Carrick one-touches the ball to Nani, he feeds Rooney and he makes a hugely difficult task (finding the corner with a low, angled shot on the run) look easy.

What was bad?
- The accidental (?) elbow from Vucinic that left Ronaldo needing four stitches in his eyebrow.
- The accidental penalty-box collision that left Carrick with a fractured arm (amazingly, he finished the game).
- Roma's finishing at the end.

What was good?
- Roma's finishing at the end!
- Rooney's goal ends a drought stretching back to the Goodison 4–2 on 28 April.
- Ferdinand. The best defender on the planet?

Views from the broadsheets
- 'Revenge – or, more precisely, vendetta – has been the dirty word doing the rounds in Italy this week, but, for one of AS Roma's crestfallen players, it was to take the most

cowardly form. A stray elbow from Mirko Vucinic in the final moments of the game last night left Cristiano Ronaldo with a bloodied face and a quivering lip. Fortunately for Manchester United, it was the only time all evening that a Roma player managed to hit his target.' – *The Times* doesn't believe Roma's claim that Vucinic didn't mean it.

Roma – the verbals

- ☻ 'It's a disease, I'm trying to get a vaccine for it! It's not a concern. The goals will come.' – Fergie after United's sixth 1–0 in eight games.
- ☻ 'I'm pleased because they're a good team, it was a good game and a good European night. A bit tactical at times but a good result for us.' – Fergie again.
- ☻ 'If anyone deserved to score more goals today it was us rather than Manchester.' – Spalletti is sick of coming to Old Trafford.

Worst headline of the day

'Wayne Netter' – *The Daily Mirror* thinks it's 1991. From *football365.com*

Match facts

United: Kuszczak, O'Shea, Vidic, Ferdinand, Evra, Ronaldo, Carrick, Scholes, Nani (Giggs 79), Saha (Tévez 66), Rooney (Anderson 84)
Roma: Curci, Cicinho, Mexes*, Juan, Tonetto, De Rossi, Aquilani (Pizarro 61), Giuly (Esposito 79), Perrotta, Mancini (Vucinic 74), Totti [Spalletti]
CLF 19.45 (ITV). Att: 73,652. Ref: M.E.M. Gonzalez (Sp). Half-time 0–0
*Yellow card

Other scores

Kiev 1 Sporting 2; Steaua Bucharest 0 Arsenal 1; Liverpool 0 Marseille 1; Valencia 1 Chelsea 2

League table

1. United 6 (2) 2. Roma 3 (2) 3. Sporting 3 (2) 4. Kiev 0 (2)

Roma to Wigan
'It's not a problem. In four or five days I will be beautiful once again'

News

Ronaldo and Paddy Crerand bring out new books, *Moments* and *Never Turn The Other Cheek*. No prizes for guessing which is the better read. Carrick's fractured elbow takes the number of injured first-teamers to a painful nine. Milan 'keeper Dida embarrasses himself at Parkhead by collapsing to the turf in fake agony after a pitch invader brushes against his face. Proving he has absolutely no shame, he then allows himself to be stretchered off.

The new Matthew Simmons

'It was just the emotions of the night and the booze. I tried to pat Dida on the shoulder and said, "Unlucky Dida."' – Celtic pitch invader Robert McHendry convinces nobody with his version of events at Parkhead. Have you ever met a drunk Glaswegian who doesn't swear?

Harsh

According to *The Sun*, 'a conman described as a "ginger Wayne Rooney" has been fleecing victims out of cash for fake goods' in Brighton. They don't give a full description, but they do describe the villain as 'fat' and 'balding'.

One victim said: 'I couldn't believe the likeness to Rooney – it was uncanny.'

Momentous

According to Ronaldo, the title of his book, *Moments*, sums up 'the essence of his work'. Here are a few more pearls of wisdom. How many do you reckon he came up with himself?

- ✪ 'My passion for football is obvious. I also have a boyish side I don't want to lose ever.' *Maybe.*
- ✪ 'I like to improvise, as ball-dribbling, posing, speaking a sentence or whatever one has to do flows more naturally when improvised.' *Not a chance.*
- ✪ 'Football is my absolute priority, but I do recognise that I am very fond of advertising.' *I really hope not.*

A life less ordinary

'I have come a long way. I have 24 brothers and sisters, including eight from the same two parents as me – my father was married three times. My progress through life has been like nobody else's. I left home to play in Italy aged 17, having never gone through a training academy. I played in Serie C for Marsala, in Sicily, a little town where there was just one bar, and I would often find myself in tears. I was paid just £100 a month. Even my mum wondered what was going to become of me. On my first day in Italy I got lost on their rail network. I ended up being taken in by a Senegalese family who I did not know, and the next morning they put me on the right train.' – Paddy Evra gives us a glimpse of his life story. Now that is a book that's crying out to be written.

He'll be some player when he gets some confidence

- 'Chelsea without Mourinho, that's a completely different team. You can never write Chelsea off, but I have a feeling that this will not be a good season for them.' Ronaldo writes off Chelsea by not writing them off.
- 'Milan are inferior to Manchester United: I think we are the real favourites to win the Champions League, with the Milan teams and the Spanish teams immediately behind us.' Ronaldo forgets last May's 3–0.
- 'It's not a problem. In four or five days I will be beautiful once again.' Ronaldo brushes off the gashed head he received against Roma. The whole of Canal Street celebrates.

The curse of Carrington

First reserve-teamers Mads Timm and Callum Flanagan drive themselves into jail, then Fletch messes up his Range Rover, now this. From *The People*:

'Man United stars Wayne Rooney and Rio Ferdinand had an amazing escape when Rio's Range Rover swerved into a 10ft ditch and rolled over. Rooney, a passenger in the £70,000 motor, had to kick out a window to get free. Starlet Chris Eagles was also in the vehicle driven by £29 million-rated Rio.' – Perhaps he forgot to look where he was going.

Quote of the week

- 'I met 10 of them in the middle of the night in Derry. They were working-class lads, and I told them that they needed to renounce violence. I said the only way of solving problems is by dialogue, not by shooting each other, but all they wanted to talk about was United and Celtic' – Paddy Crerand recalls his encounter with the IRA in 1975.

United 4 Wigan 0   06/10/2007

Tévez 54, Ronaldo 59, 76, Rooney 82

Remember the famous anecdote about Bestie? The one where the waiter goes into his hotel room, sees Bestie in bed with Miss World and a mountain of fivers, and asks him where it all went wrong. Well, this season, as United had churned out one uninspiring 1–0 after another, the Old Trafford press pack had started to sound just like that waiter. 'So, Sir Alex,' you could imagine them saying, 'you're second in the League, you've only let in two goals all season and you're already well on the way to qualifying for the next round of the Champions League…Where did it all go wrong?'

It was ridiculous really, the amount of stick United had been getting for achieving results that keep-it-tight merchants like Benitez and Mourinho would have been delighted with. Even so, it was a relief for everyone when Wigan showed up at Old Trafford. United always put a few past the pie-eaters, and when the excellent Anderson set up the equally excellent Tévez to break the deadlock there was only one way this match was going. It had taken 55 days, and 1,044 minutes of football, but as Tévez & co. hugged and grinned in front of the Stretford End it finally felt like normal service had been resumed.

Goal action

1–0 (54): What a difference a goal can make. For 54 minutes Old Trafford sweated as United struggled to come to terms with dogged Wigan defending and another wave of injuries. Then Anderson, who was only on because of Vidic's concussion, sends Tévez charging through the Wigan defence. Tévez beats Kilbane and Bramble for speed, then he beats them for skill and balance before walking the ball past Kirkland and finding the net left-footed.

2–0 (59): Now comes the deluge that Fergie had promised – Noah-style – in his programme notes. First Ronaldo nods in to an empty net after Kirkland dives full-length to paw away Giggs's deflected shot…

3–0 (76): Then Rooney sets up Ronaldo for a simple sidefoot…

4–0 (82): And finally, Rooney heads in from Simpson's excellent cross from the right.

What was good?

- Tévez. Energy, pace, power, commitment, touch, class…as Alan Hansen might say.
- Anderson. I knew he'd be quick and excellent technically (thank you *youtube*), but I never thought a teenage Brazilian with a fondness for bling would be this strong and have such an English-style appetite for getting stuck in. When we signed him I presumed he'd be a highlights player. Now I can see why Fergie has earmarked him as the successor to the Ginger King (Scholesy's surely not a prince any more).

What was bad?

- The injuries to O'Shea, Vidic and Saha (who managed to injure himself – not for the first or last time – in the pre-match warm-up), which left United in the midst of a genuine injury crisis. Not that the press would remember it when they were bemoaning Chelsea and Arsenal's problems later in the season.

Views from the broadsheets

- 'The romantic notion that any Premier League team can beat any other took another pounding here as an initially disjointed Manchester United side, missing 11 players and losing another three on the day, settled down to dismiss Wigan's feeble challenge with four second-half goals. After the champions' recent drought – only Derby had scored fewer goals – this sudden flood carried them to the top of the table, at least until Arsenal attempt to roast Sunderland for Sunday lunch. Wigan, briefly in first place themselves in August but falling fast ever since, have now played the undisputed big four of English football in 18 games over the past three seasons and lost every one.' – *The Independent*
- 'Ferguson's United teams have never had trouble scoring goals since the dark days of the late 1980s but a string of 1–0 victories and a lack of a cutting edge in front of goal had cast doubts on the manager's transfer policy during the summer. Why spend more than £50 million on a winger and two midfield players when United needed a striker with the killer instincts of Ruud van Nistelrooy? Did he really need Owen Hargreaves? Was it worth gambling more than £16 million on Anderson's potential? The jury is still out on Hargreaves, who missed this game with a knee injury, but as far as Anderson is concerned, Ferguson appears to have struck gold.' – *The Times*

Wigan – the verbals

- 'When you consider we had 10 players missing by the second half, it was a fantastic performance. Once we were settled, we speeded the game up in the second half and played some very good football. I'm very happy with the squad I've got, and I think understanding is beginning to arrive.' – Fergie.

Match facts

United: Kuszczak, Pique, Ferdinand, Vidic (Anderson 21), Evra, Ronaldo, O'Shea (Simpson 30), Scholes, Giggs, Rooney*, Tévez (Nani 81)

Wigan: Kirkland, Melchiot (Hall 50), Boyce, Bramble, Kilbane, Scharner, Brown, Skoko*, Koumas, Olembe (Valencia 66), Bent [Hutchings]

FAPL 12.45 (Sky). Att: 75,300. Ref: M.Riley. Half-time: 0–0

*Yellow card

Other scores

Arsenal 3 (Van Persie 2, Senderos) Sunderland 2 (Wallace, Jones); City 3 (Elano 2, og) Boro 1 (Hutchinson); Bolton 0 Chelsea 1 (Kalou); Liverpool 2 (Voronin, Crouch) Spurs 2 (Keane 2)

League table

1. Arsenal 22 (8) 2. United 20 (9) 3. City 19 (9) 4. Liverpool 16 (8)…14. Wigan 8 (9)

Wigan to Villa

'The way he looks after himself, Ryan could go on for infinity.'

News

Kevin Reynolds, the drunk who punched Fergie at Euston, gets 15 months for assault. Giggsy agrees a new contract taking him to June 2009 and, surely, Bobby's record. United take 16-year-old Southend midfielder Medi Abalimba on trial. United sign Carlos Tévez's 17-year-old brother Miguel – a midfielder – on a two-and-a-half-year deal. And England qualify in style for Euro 2008 – or maybe not…

International Reds I

Rooney scores his first international goal for 11 months as England cruise past Estonia 3–0. Ferdinand is rested at half-time. Evra's France win 6–0 in the Faroe Islands. Ronaldo plays and Nani comes on as sub as Portugal win 2–0 in Azerbaijan.

Oh lordy, he's been sniffing the hairspray again

'I'm not at all bothered by what I've seen with Robbo [Paul Robinson]. He starts. He is our Peter Schmeichel' – Steve McClaren confirms he is bonkers as England prepare for the second leg of their crucial Euro double-header, against Russia.

England rumour of the week

From *The Times*:

'Russian fans have resorted to bizarre measures for success, hiring a voodoo priestess to curse three English players, the Tvoi Den newspaper reported Tuesday. Instead of using a voodoo doll, however, the fans used matryoshka dolls embossed with the pictures of Joe Cole, John Terry and Frank Lampard, the newspaper said.

"'They will have a problem with speech," the Haitian priestess said after cursing the players, Tvoi Den reported. "Apart from that the lads could unexpectedly have problems with their legs [apologies for the details] between their legs. Nothing serious. Simply some small discomfort, lethargy, ache and if all goes according to my plan, an itch."'

A curse that gives footballers itchy nuts eh? Not sure they'll feel the difference...

International Reds II

Rooney scores a cracking volley and then concedes a penalty that should never have been as England go down 2–1 in Russia (the winning goal comes courtesy of a mistake by 'our Schmeichel', Robinson). Ferdinand also features in a defeat that leaves England's Euro 2008 hopes hinging on Israel pinching a point off the Russians in the next game. Nani sets up Ronaldo's extra-time winner as Portugal scrape a 2–1 win over Kazakhstan. Fletcher makes his comeback from his fractured leg as Scotland flop 2–0 in Georgia. O'Shea plays 90 minutes as the Republic snatch a late equaliser at home to Cyprus.

International story of the week

Remember how Stephen Ireland lied about his 'dead' grandma when he withdrew from the Republic squad for the last round of international games? And then blamed it on his girlfriend's miscarriage? Well, it seems that something else might have been a problem.

From *The Times*:

'Newspaper reports in Dublin at the weekend claimed that the reason that Ireland put his international career on hold was that he had been mocked by his Ireland colleagues over an alleged hair transplant or his wearing of a hairpiece.

This taunting, it was said, degenerated into two team-mates pinning him to the floor and attempting to remove the "evidence". It is understood that Ireland's distress at the reports could shatter his recovery. "If this goes on, there's now a great fear that Stephen will retire from Ireland for good," a source said. Another source told *The Times* that it was "more basic ribbing but he took it really badly". The FAI denied that any bullying took place.'

News II

UEFA ban Dida for two matches for his disgraceful playacting at Celtic. Porthmadog sack Clayton Blackmore as manager after just four months (wonder if they couldn't afford the electricity – that tan doesn't look after itself). Sammy Lee is dumped by Bolton after just games, leaving the Premiership without a guinea pig look-alike.

United quotes of the week

- 'The way he looks after himself, Ryan could go for infinity. I just don't see any marked deterioration in the lad. He's 34 in November, and when a player gets to that stage you look to see if they have lost this or that. But there's not really been a downturn. He's unique.' – Fergie salutes United's most successful ever player.
- 'I haven't seen the rugby. I have been watching the rugby league instead.' – Rooney refuses to jump on the Rugby World Cup bandwagon. Top man.
- 'No disrespect to City but, in Manchester, Manchester United will always be top dog. As much as they want to believe it, it is not going to be.' – Even Joey Barton speaks sense sometimes.

Aston Villa 1 United 4   20/10/2007

Agbonlahor 13, Rooney 36, 44, Gardner (og) 45, Giggs 75

In the build-up to the egg-chasers' big night in Paris there was a lot of guff talked about rugby overtaking football as the nation's game. In 90 minutes at Villa Park – and 80 more in France – the argument was killed stone dead. While England and South Africa were preparing to swap up-'n'-unders and sweat, United were seducing all but ABUs with a symphony of high-speed passing, athleticism and skill. And they did it with Ronaldo on the bench and half a team back in Manchester. No wonder Fergie ended the night looking like he'd just got his hands on the Rock of Gibraltar's testicles…

Goal action

14 (0–1): Fair play to Villa. They really gave it a go, especially early on, and they probably deserved their early lead even if Agbonlahor's header from Young's left-wing cross should have been chalked off for offside against Moore.

36 (1–1): In retrospect, though, Villa might have been better off if the linesman had been doing his job. Agbonlahor's goal merely gets United in the mood. And when they finally start scoring, they find it difficult to stop. First Rooney capitalises on calamitous dithering by the towering Zat Knight to tap in Nani's low-speed centre at the far post…

44 (2–1): Then Tévez, who was brilliant all night, takes no fewer than five Villa defenders out of the game with one pass to Rooney in the box. A cushioned touch and controlled sidefoot later and Carson is picking the ball out of the net.

45 (3–1): A minute later it's game over. Pique's header is cleared off the line, Ferdinand mis-volleys the rebound towards goal and Gardner slices the ball, embarrassingly, in off the underside of the bar.

75 (4–1): After Reo-Coker was sent off for two yellows and Carson for chopping down Tévez in the box, United could have racked up a cricket score… if they'd fancied it. As it was they settled for just the one more. Minutes after Rooney sees his tame penalty easily saved by reserve 'keeper Stuart Taylor, Giggs cuts in from the right and sent in a pinball of a shot that ricochets off two Villa defenders and floats into the net.

What was good?

❂ Tévez: Diego Maradona once described Tévez as the 'Argentine prophet for the 21st century'. Now we're starting to see why. He's not as quick as Rooney or as good in the air. But his vision and work-rate are excellent, so is his attitude and he's a nightmare to knock off the ball. He's not the next Maradona, no way. But if you could cross Maradona with Mark Hughes...

❂ Rooney – back to his brilliant best (apart from his penalty).

❂ Tévez and Rooney – who said they couldn't work together?

❂ Fergie's tactics: As Kevin Nicholls could tell you, Fergie's got balls. And he proved it once again with his tactics here. With so many regulars missing through injury, many managers would have played it safe. Instead Fergie trusted Pique to cope with Agbonlahor's pace and Carew's brawn. He packed his midfield with artists rather than water carriers. And the 4–1 result was his reward.

What was bad?

❂ Not a lot – unless you had to watch this game on Setanta. I know they're new to this, but they aren't very good are they? I can't decide who's more annoying. The wet nobody who presents it, the new chubby-chinned version of Steve McManaman or the Andy Gray wannabe in the gantry (Craig Burley. Who? Exactly).

In fairness, though, they aren't as bad as the Beeb's mob. Who would you leave in a burning building the longest out of Lineker, Chiles, Lawro, that screaming harridan (Jacqui Oatley), the black Yoda (Crooks), Bright, Shearer and Peacock?

OK, it would be Poppins, of course it would. But there's not that much in it...

Quote of the day

'The myth about Tévez and Wayne not being able to play together was put to bed finally. We knew that as a team, but I think on Saturday they put it on show and their movement and awareness around each other was unbelievable.' – Rio raves about Rooney and Tévez too.

Match facts

Villa: Carson† 66, Mellberg, Knight (Taylor 67), Laursen, Bouma, Gardner (Maloney 53), Reo-Coker** 60, Barry, Young*, Agbonlahor, Moore (Osbourne 54) [O'Neill]
United: Van der Sar, Brown, Pique, Ferdinand, Evra, Nani*, Anderson, Scholes* (O'Shea 77), Giggs (Ronaldo 76), Tévez (Fletcher 73), Rooney
FAPL 17.15 (Set) Villa Park. Att: 42,640. Ref: R.Styles. Half-time: 3–1
*Yellow cards **Two yellow cards † Red card

Other scores

Arsenal 2 (Toure, Rosicky) Bolton 0; Everton 1 (Hyypia og) Liverpool 2 (Kuyt 2 pen); Middlesbrough 0 Chelsea 2 (Drogba, Alex); England 6 S. Africa 15

League table

1. Arsenal 25 (9) 2. United 23 (10) 3.City 22 (10) 4. Liverpool 19 (9)…9. Aston Villa 14 (9)

Villa to Kiev
'If anyone is to blame it is Gary Neville'

Blame culture

Amazing. Simon Barnes in *The Times* somehow blames Gary Neville for the disastrous form of 'our Schmeichel', Paul Robinson:

'The truth of the matter is, the reason he lost his nerve in the first place is because he was involved in an incident that wasn't his fault. That famous air shot against Croatia, when he kicked and missed…it wasn't his fault. If anyone is to blame it is Gary Neville, for propelling a back-pass in his direction.'

Next week, why Darren Fletcher's spots are to blame for global warming.

Love United, Love Glazers

Watch what you say about those lovely folk from Florida. From *The Guardian*:

'Disgruntled fans of Sheffield Wednesday who vented their dissatisfaction with the football club's bigwigs in anonymous internet postings may face expensive libel claims after the chairman, chief executive and five directors won a high-court ruling last week forcing the owner of a website to reveal their identity. The case, featuring the website *owlstalk.co.uk*, is the second within days to highlight the danger of assuming that the apparent cloak of anonymity gives users of internet forums and chatrooms carte blanche to say whatever they like.'

Though it's not all bad news. *The Guardian* continues:

'But the judge decided some fans, whose postings were merely "abusive" or likely to be understood as jokes, should keep their anonymity. The judge ordered that three fans whose postings might "reasonably be understood to allege greed, selfishness, untrustworthiness and dishonest behaviour", should be unmasked. Their right to maintain their anonymity and express themselves freely was outweighed by the directors' entitlement to take action to protect their reputation, he said.'

Insert your own Colleen joke here
'Wazza is one of those that goes on a mad goal spree, and long may it continue. He's in the groove. He's a spurter.' – Rio Ferdinand.

Stat of the week
More Scots played in the last round of Champions League matches than Englishmen – the Old Firm fielded 13 Scots between them, while Chelsea, Manchester United, Liverpool and Celtic fielded only 12 Englishmen (Arsenal, surprise, surprise, contributed 0).

In all, no fewer than 13 countries had more representatives than England in the European Cup, including Brazil (53), France (34), Italy (30), Spain (29), Argentina (20), Romania (16) and Turkey (15).

Spending for two
The Sun reveals that the Djemba twins have fallen on hard times:

'Ex-Man United ace Eric Djemba-Djemba, who made around £4 million from English football, has gone bust, it was revealed yesterday. The Cameroon international, said to owe cash to Aston Villa, another former club, has been declared bankrupt. His agent, Charles Collymore, said it followed "an accumulation of problems over a long time".'

Though life probably isn't that bad for the Djembas. His new contract at Qatar Sports Club is reported to be worth a cool £2.5 million a year.

It's long...but it's worth it
Jose Mourinho gets all creative as he blames a German beauty and an ugly Canadian for Chelsea's inability to assert themselves as one of England's great clubs:

'Most of the black community are fans of Arsenal, the Jewish community support Tottenham, in the most disadvantaged area of London they're fans of West Ham, and Fulham are a small club but with a strong nucleus of fans.

'And then comes Chelsea, a cosmopolitan club, with fans famous around the world, like Bryan Adams, Claudia Schiffer and Chelsea, the daughter of former president Clinton.

'And there's a common denominator among them all – they're foreigners, which fits in with the general profile of the fan of the club. Whoever is a foreigner and leads a life above the means of the average citizen is a fan of Chelsea because Chelsea have the most expensive tickets, the most expensive meals, their social life around the game is more important than that of other clubs.

'Because they have that spending power, the Chelsea fan is more "society" and, of course, that's reflected in the stadium, with the support they give the team.

'It's the soft sort of fan who doesn't get behind the team a lot, who don't organise themselves into fan groups, with the cheering on that is characteristic of the image of English football.

'They create a different atmosphere because a lot of our fans also go to the opera, the theatre, other types of shows that don't lend themselves to lots of shouting. That's the Chelsea fan.

'That's why Chelsea have some difficulty in asserting themselves as a great club of English football.'

Rumour of the week

'Wayne Rooney is going all intellectual – by studying for his GCSE exams in English and Maths. The football star takes regular lessons at home with a private tutor – and is also learning to play the guitar. It is the latest proof that Manchester United and England striker Rooney, 22, is turning into a bit of a TOFF.' – Yes, that's right, *The Sun* believes anyone taking a GCSE is a toff. Hilarious.

Kiev 2 United 4   23/10/2007

Ferdinand 10, Rooney 18, Rincon 33, Ronaldo 41, 68 (pen), Bangoura 78

Kiev coach Jozsef Szabo became an instant hero of the NWAF brigade when he blamed his players' wives and girlfriends for the team's poor start to the season – and ordered the squad to a training camp away from any distractions. But one thing became very clear in the first half of this game – footballers can be as celibate as they like off the pitch, but if they defend like Kiev did here they'll still get (you know the rest).

No matter how inept Kiev's defence was, though, this was still a triumph well worth noting. Kiev aren't in the habit of losing at home – only one English team, Liverpool in 2000, had ever previously won there. United aren't in the habit of scoring lots of goals in European aways either – last year they only scored four in the whole campaign. Plus they were missing no fewer than nine first-team regulars. In the circumstances, any win would have been good. Sticking four past the bowl-headed Shovkovskiy was that with bells on.

Goal action
With so many to get through, I'd best be quick:

10 (1–0): Ronaldo is fouled on the left, Giggs curls in the free-kick and Ferdinand climbs unopposed – like an actor in one of those Wickes 'Just the job' ads – to thump a header into the net.

18 (2–0): The first goal was made on the left, the second on the right. Brown feeds Ronaldo, Ronaldo feeds Brown back and Brown slips a perfectly weighted pass across the six-yard box. Rooney does the rest.

33 (2–1): United do a Kiev, allowing Rincon an even more free header than Ferdinand had enjoyed from a corner.

41 (3–1): Within minutes of getting back into the match, Kiev's defence is at it again, allowing Ronaldo a free header from Giggs's routine cross.

68 (4–1): United ease off after the break while Kiev step it up a gear. But it's United who strike next, Ronaldo netting from the spot after Tévez's cross strikes the Kiev full-back Gavrancic's arm. It's a harsh penalty (the handball might not have been deliberate or in the box) but a fair scoreline.

78 (4–2): At least Kiev can lay claim to the goal of the night, Bangoura slamming the ball low past 'keeper Van der Sar from the edge of the box.

Views from the broadsheets

☻ 'When Manchester United defeated Roma in their last Champions League tie it was their sixth 1–0 win in eight matches. "It's a disease, I'm trying to get a vaccine for it," said Sir Alex Ferguson. It appears an elixir has been found. This was the third successive match in which United have scored four goals. With a vibrant display of attacking football, aided and abetted by some diabolical defending, Ferguson's team moved to the brink of a place in the knockout stages.' – *The Independent*

☻ 'The last time United scored more than three goals on the road in Europe they went on to win the Champions League. There remains much to do before repeating that triumph but, to illustrate their creative potential, with better finishing last night they could have exceeded the six goals they put past Brøndby in Copenhagen nine years ago this week.' – *The Independent*

Match facts

Kiev: Shovkovskiy, Ghioane (Belkevich 45), Gavrancic, Diakhate*, Gusev, Yussuf, Nesmachniy, Correa (Rotan 83), Bangoura, Rincon, Shatskikh (Milevskiy 45) [Szabo]
United: Van der Sar (Kuszczak 80), Brown, Ferdinand, Vidic, O'Shea, Ronaldo, Anderson, Fletcher, Giggs (Simpson 80), Rooney, Tévez (Nani 72)
CLGF 19.45 (ITV). Att: 43,000. Ref: V. Kassai (Hungary). Half-time: 3–1
*Yellow card

Other scores

Roma 2 Sporting Lisbon 1; Besiktas 2 Liverpool 1; Arsenal 7 Slavia Prague 0; Chelsea 2 Schalke 0

League table

1. United 9 (3) 2. Roma 6 (3) 3. Sporting 3 (3) 4. Dynamo Kiev 0 (3)

Kiev to Boro

'A minute playing for United is worth 10 anywhere else.'

News

The Republic of Ireland win the fight with Northern Ireland to play United kid Darron Gibson…they also sack Steve Staunton as manager. Chelsea are fined £30,000 (that would be about 3p for you and me) for failing to control their players during the 2–0 defeat at Old Trafford. Sports Minister Gerry Sutcliffe throws out the latest campaign to bring back standing up at football matches, saying, 'I've not heard anything to make me change my mind.'

Nice try

'I am a strong football fan and I know there is strong support for the re-introduction of safe standing space. The all-seater rule was introduced following the tragic deaths at Hillsborough. But, in the cold light of day, taking into account all the studies that have been conducted, it is now thought that standing was not the problem. Rather, it was to do with allowing too many people into an area and the fencing that kept spectators boxed in. In practice, many fans stand anyway.' – How Labour backbencher Roger Godsiff reignited the standing debate.

Right or self-righteous?

Phil Hammond, chairman of the Hillsborough Family Support Group, predictably pours scorn on the plans:

'There's no such thing as safe standing. Once you have standing, you also have to put fences up, that is UEFA's law. It would take us back to fans being caged in football stadiums. It also leads to fans jumping into the standing areas, and that's when crushing is going to start. If those 96 supporters at Hillsborough had been seated, the tragedy wouldn't have happened.'

What's safe at rush hour but lethal at 3pm...?

...and 7 more 'standing' questions that never get answered:

- Why is it safe for people to stand at lower-League football matches, rugby matches, pop concerts and *Songs of Praise*...but dangerous to stand at modern Premiership stadiums?
- Why is it safe to stand on steep, packed escalators in shops and the Tube, but not safe to stand at Old Trafford when there are seats separating you from the people in front and behind?
- Why is it dangerous to stand at Old Trafford during unexciting moments in the game, but safe to stand, jump around and have dry sex with the bloke in front at moments of 'high excitement'?
- Why do safe standing areas work in Germany, but not here?
- Why not judge each stadium on its own merits rather than enforce a blanket ban on standing? Hillsborough was an accident waiting to happen. Old Trafford wasn't, even before the redevelopment. Remember, before Hillsborough, Old Trafford had welcomed more than 50 million fans over 78 years without any major problems.
- Of course everyone can understand why the Hillsborough groups oppose standing. But if a similar blanket ban had been used after the Kings Cross fire would we never have been able to use the Tube again?
- Why can't we as adults have the chance to make our own bloody minds up?

News II

After touting his job around since the start of the season, the classless Spurs board finally sack Martin Jol. In a final indignity Jol only found out he was getting sacked by text message during the UEFA Cup defeat by Getafe. Jol's replacement is £4.8 million-a-year Sevilla coach Juande Ramos. Coleen buys Wayne a Louis Vuitton manbag, a designer woolly jumper and a guitar signed by Noel Gallagher for his 22nd birthday (OK, it was a slow news week at OT).

Quotes of the week

- ☺ 'Happy Birthday Fatboy.' – What Noel Gallagher reportedly wrote on Rooney's birthday guitar.
- ☺ 'Happy Birthday k***head.' – What Noel Gallagher wrote on Gary Neville's birthday guitar in 2000. The old ones, eh?
- ☺ 'Professionally, it would be a logical choice, but my personal view is that he is the most insincere man I know in football' – Tony Cascarino doesn't mince his words after David O'Leary is touted as the new Ireland manager.
- ☺ 'A minute playing for United is worth 10 anywhere else.' – Danny Simpson makes the t-shirt sellers very happy indeed.
- ☺ 'I can't quite believe what is happening at the moment. I just seem to be walking around with a big smile on my face all the time. The manager knows I am there if he needs me, and I am chuffed to bits at the fact he is using me.' – Simmo's living the dream.

With friends like these

'Mad' Jens Lehmann loses it after being dropped by Arsenal:

'Wenger spoke of three world-class goalkeepers. One of them must be me. The other two have proved their class by winning titles? If I think about that, I can't recall any. I guess today you're nevertheless world class. I'm convinced that I'll be playing again. Almunia has not yet showed that he can win matches for us. I've experienced this situation before and know what the others are expecting from the goalkeeper. I can't imagine he'll be able to handle this.'

Quote of the week

'We went to the [training] base, because women in football are a scourge. They do not understand that men need to work, that they have a hard job to do.' – Kiev coach Josef Sabo, Mike Newell's favourite Ukrainian.

Gossip

United are strongly linked with moves for Mexican 'keeper Guillermo Ochoa and 17-year-old Partizan Belgrade prodigy Stevan Jovetic. *The Mirror* links us with Atletico Bilbao's 19-year-old midfielders Javi Martinez and Markel Susaeta. *The Sun* reckons we're set to fight it out with Liverpool for '£6.5 million-rated Monaco strike star Jeremy Menez, 20'

United 4 Middlesbrough 1   27/10/2007

Nani 3, Aliadiere 6, Rooney 33, Tévez 55, 85

Afterwards, Rooney said it was 'a real honour' to play in this United team. It was fast becoming a real honour to watch them too. Nani's opener was stunning. The goal that Tévez and Rooney cooked up between them was just breathtaking, a meeting of footballing genius. Was it only September that everyone thought those two were too similar to work well together? Was it only 6 October that United had scored fewer goals than anyone bar Derby?

Goal action

1–0 (3): Nani sometimes looks like he'd get knocked about by Luke Chadwick. But he's got a hammer of a right foot on him, and he wielded it to devastating effect here. Woodgate and Young allow the mini Ronaldo to saunter in from the left, he draws back his boot and, bang, Schwarzer is on his back and the ball is bouncing around in the net. The look on Schwarzer's face said it all. It was just like Frank Bruno's after he'd first met Mike Tyson's fist.

1–1 (6): Nani's goal would have knocked the fight out of many sides. But credit to Boro, they clear their heads and grab an equaliser with their first decent attack. Tuncay twists and turns past O'Shea on the right, and his inswinging cross is flicked into the net by Arsenal reject Aliadiere.

2–1 (33): The final score makes this game look like a mismatch. But make no mistake Boro brought their A-game to Old Trafford, and if it hadn't been for two bad Downing mistakes they might well have led at the break. First, the Boro winger heads Tuncay's enticing cross into the Stretford End. Then he takes an age to line up a clearance from inside his own area, Nani pinches the ball and Rooney's low drive does the rest.

3–1 (55): Remember the goal that Yorke and Cole conjured up in the Nou Camp in 98? Dummy, run, pass, run, cross, diving header. Amazing stuff. But in terms of footballing telepathy, this was every bit as good. Tévez volleys Anderson's clipped pass to Rooney. Rooney controls instantly with his right foot and, without looking, back-heels the ball into the space he somehow knows Tévez has moved into. Without having to break stride Tévez simply rolls the ball into the net.

4–1 (85): And the front two hadn't finished yet. Rooney charges 50 yards from inside his own half and threads a ball through to Tévez on the left. A twist, shot and high, looping deflection later and United history is made. For the first time since the very first title-winning season, exactly 100 years and one day ago, United had scored four times in four successive games.

Quote of the day

'It's brilliant to play in this team, a real honour. The way we play every week, fast and attacking, that's the football I want to be involved in. Hopefully, I can continue in this form. I try to score in every game, and it is brilliant playing with Carlos, he is a clever player, very intelligent. I think we both work off each other and are scoring goals together. It's good.' – Rooney explains why he'd never sign for Chelsea.

Understatement of the season

'I think they've probably got more attacking options this year.' – Good spot, Gareth Southgate.

Views from the broadsheets

- ☺ 'What, within reason, could be better? An autumn afternoon leaden enough to dictate that the lights shine down on lush turf, Old Trafford's customary full house and a performance from the visitors so spirited that Manchester United had to come up with a display featuring two candidates for goal of the season in order to defeat them.' – You get the idea the man from *The Sunday Telegraph* really enjoyed his afternoon out…
- ☺ 'Although Nani's, from long range before Middlesbrough had settled, was breathtakingly spectacular, it will take something very special over the next six months to take my vote away from the first of Carlos Tévez's pair. To say it was a stroked sidefooter after a one-two with Wayne Rooney would be (as J.B. Priestley might have put it) to call a violin so much wood and catgut. The move was all one-touch, apart from Rooney's preparation for a backheel, and so beautifully precise it might almost have been conceived as mockery of the notion that Tévez and Rooney cannot play together.' – And I mean really enjoyed it.
- ☺ 'Manchester United's attacking options start with the throwing arm of Edwin van der Sar, and continue through every fibre and sinew of the 10 men in front of him. They even scare teams when Ryan Giggs warms up on the touchline, or Louis Saha shifts position in his seat in the stand [though he'd probably pull something doing it, ed].' – *The Telegraph* was impressed too…
- ☺ 'If it wasn't Nani performing like a slighter Cristiano Ronaldo on the left, it was the real thing on the right; or else it was Wayne Rooney and Carlos Tévez carousing

through the centre. Anderson probed just behind and Owen Hargreaves anchored midfield and sprayed the ball around. It was magnificent stuff.'...Really impressed.

Strained link of the day

'Wayne Rooney was bought a guitar for his 22nd birthday last week, but the Manchester United forward will be hard pressed trying to strike a chord as sweet as his partnership with Carlos Tévez is at the moment.' – *The Times*

The Centurions

United have only previously scored four goals in four consecutive games once before, back in the first-ever Championship-winning season of 1907–08. Here's how they did it:

28/09/1907 Chelsea 1 United 4

Moger – Holden, Burgess – Duckworth, Roberts, Bell – Meredith (2), Bannister (1), J. Turnbull, A. Turnbull (1), Wall

05/10/1907 United 4 Forest 0

Moger – Holden, Burgess – Duckworth, Roberts, Bell – Meredith, Bannister (1), J. Turnbull (1), A. Turnbull, Wall (1) (+og)

12/10/1907 Newcastle 1 United 6

Moger – Holden, Stacey – Duckworth, Roberts (1), Bell – Meredith (1), Bannister, J. Turnbull (1), A. Turnbull (1), Wall (2)

26/10/1907 Blackburn 1 United 5

Moger – Holden, Burgess – Duckworth, Roberts, Bell – Meredith, Bannister, J. Turnbull (2), A. Turnbull (3), Wall

Match facts

United: Van der Sar, Brown, Ferdinand (Pique 73), Vidic, O'Shea, Ronaldo, Hargreaves (Fletcher 66), Anderson (Giggs 78), Nani, Rooney, Tévez

Middlesbrough: Schwarzer, Young, Woodgate, Wheater, Taylor, O'Neil, Cattermole* (Boateng 90), Rochemback*, Downing, Aliadiere (Hutchinson 56), Sanli (Lee 80) [Southgate]

FAPL 15.00. Att: 75,720. Ref: A. Wiley. Half-time: 2–1

*Yellow card

Other scores

Liverpool 1 (Gerrard) Arsenal 1 (Fabregas); Chelsea 6 (Drogba 2, Essien, J. Cole, Kalou, Shevchenko) City 0

League table

1. Arsenal 26 (10) 2. United 26 (11) 3. City 22 (11) 4. Chelsea 21 (11)...17. Boro 8 (11)

Boro to Arsenal

'The day I signed for Chelsea I just felt disgusted'

News

Edwin Van der Sar announces his plans to retire from international football after Euro 2008. Jaap Stam retires from all football at the age of 35. Chelsea recruit United fan Darren Campbell in a desperate attempt to make Andrei Shevchenko's shot legs go quicker (what are you doing son?). United sign 15-year-old Norwegian starlet Joshua King from Valerenga. Gerry Sutcliffe has a pop at the ticket rises at Old Trafford and the obscene wages of Premiership footballers, and he couldn't have got his timing any better...

So that's how much a long throw-in costs you these days

In the same week that Sutcliffe attacks Premiership wages, one of John Arne Riise's old payslips is splashed all over the internet. For a decent journeyman pro, the number of noughts in it is extraordinary.

In September 2006 Riise earned £140,000, made up of £120,000 basic salary, a £15,384 Champions League bonus, £4,000 appearance money and a £250 points bonus. Even after £55,000 was deducted in tax and £101 in meals and tickets, he had to scrape by on £82,413.67. It's a wonder the poor lad could even feed himself.

Quote of the week

'I've been very fortunate to play in some fabulous places. I've played in two World Cups, a European Championship, a Champions League Final. It's very difficult to compare those experiences. I used to play in front of 70,000 people for Bayern Munich. But I will say that I actually enjoyed watching the last 30 minutes against Middlesbrough after I'd come off. I leaned over to Giggsy and said "you must be so happy to have played here for your whole career". I think Old Trafford helps you feel very strong, and it's great to be a part of it.' – Owen Hargreaves is home at last.

The missing link

Question: What's missing from Gerry Sutcliffe's attack on Glazer rule (below)?

'This year Manchester United increased their season tickets by 13 per cent and said fans have to automatically buy European and Carling Cup games as well and that costs an extra £200 [£300 more like]. That's taking the game away from the ordinary grass-roots supporter. Ordinary working people who want go and see Manchester United face being priced out. There is a danger that there will be a move away from the game and we don't want to be in a position where people are alienated.'

Answer: That's right...Any sign that the government will be doing anything about it.

Maddening crowds

After Sutcliffe's comments become public, David Gill defends the indefensible:

'Our average increase was 10.78% and we think the prices between £25 and £45 are very fair in relation to other clubs such as Chelsea and keep us in touch with our grassroots supporters.'

Worse still, Fergie is at it too:

'Prices at Arsenal and Chelsea are obscene, almost double our prices. I object to the sports minister coming out with this stuff about ticket pricing and United. I thought that was unfair and inaccurate.'

'It's all a bit sad really. There was a time when Fergie would stand up for the rights of the fans. Now he seems happy to sit back or comply as his chief executive twists the facts (no mention of the ACS), ignores the wage gulf between Manchester and London and pretends that another 10 per cent season-on-season increase in an era of unprecedented TV income is somehow fair. Don't get me wrong. Every sane Red is immensely grateful for what Fergie has done for us. But it's no coincidence that you don't hear "Every single one of us loves Alex Ferguson" sung at Old Trafford these days.'

Unlikely revelation of the week

From Wayne Rooney's biographer Hunter Davies:

'Gazza used bad language all the way through, but Rooney never swore once. Tony Blair, you know, when the cameras are off him, swears all the time. But Rooney absolutely wouldn't. And you know why? Because his mother would have smacked him.'

Does Jeanette Rooney never watch telly then?

Quotes of the week

- 'I can't go on anymore. I'm disappointed in myself, but that's the way it has to be. There were many footballers more talented than me, but my commitment boosted my career. I wanted to win the Eredivisie title with Ajax.' – Jip Jaap Stam, a modest Dutchman.
- 'You and I both need a bigger club' – What Dimitar Berbatov allegedly told Martin Jol when the Dutchman announced his sacking.
- 'They are a brilliant team, and they have so many attacking players. Wow.' – Kolo Toure butters us up before the Emirates game.
- 'Is he [Sutcliffe] a United fan? Well, he'll not be coming back here again. He can go and join that mob who watch United FC.' – Fergie, the man of the people.

Revelation of the week

'The day I signed for Chelsea I just felt disgusted. I had no desire to be there. I did some absurd things just so that I wouldn't have to go to Chelsea. The medical was in a Paris hospital, and I clearly remember praying they would find a problem with my knee or something so the move would collapse.' – Didier Drogba launches a one-man campaign to get himself out of Chelsea.

Arsenal 2 United 2 03/11/2007

Gallas (og) 45, 90, Fabregas 48, Ronaldo 82

It's 21 years – give or take a weekend or two – since Fergie first sat on the bench for United and watched Big Ron's badly fuelled team get outrun and outplayed by Oxford. Much has changed since that first game at the dilapidated Manor Ground, not least for Oxford who now play their football in the Conference. But one thing that hasn't changed is Fergie's temper. He was fuming when Hogg, Duxbury, Davenport and Barnes folded at the Manor Ground. He was perhaps even more angry when his team of champions missed the chance to burst Arsenal's bubble here at the Emirates.

For 90 minutes the game had gone pretty much to plan. United, with Hargreaves and Anderson excelling as a midfield shield, had left Arsenal stuck in stereotypical mode – plenty of pretty passing but little penetration. The second half started badly with Fabregas's sloppy equaliser, but when Ronaldo finished off a French masterclass with eight minutes to go you can imagine what they were saying on the United bench. Keep it tight. Stop the crosses that allowed Arsenal to steal it at the death last year. Pick them off on the break. What the hell are you wearing shorts for, Mickey Phelan?

And then Clichy was allowed all the time in the world to send in a cross from the left. And we had to spend the rest of the weekend avoiding pictures of Arsenal celebrating like they'd just won the League, Grand National and European Cup. I love United, I really do, but considering the number of weekends they can ruin I'm sometimes envious of those who don't give a monkeys.

Goal action

1–0 (45): Brown outmuscles the pasty Hleb and slides the ball down the line for Ronaldo. Rooney beats Gallas to his low near-post cross, and his shot flicks off the Frenchman into the net.

1–1 (48): Sloppy. United make a mess of a throw-in near Arsenal's corner flag, which allows Arsenal to break. Eboue floats a hopeful ball into the box that Adebayor's telescopic right leg turns into a dangerous one. Van der Sar smothers his volley, but Sagna reacts quickest to hook the ball back to the unmarked Fabregas five yards out. With only Ferdinand to beat on the goalline, he was never going to miss.

2–1 (82): The move of the match. Saha, under heavy pressure near the left-hand corner flag, takes four Arsenal defenders out of the game with an exquisite reverse pass to Evra. As Almunia charges out of his goal, Evra coolly rolls the ball sideways for Ronaldo to tap in.

2–2 (90): First the good news. Van der Sar keeps out Gallas's close-range volley. Now the bad news. The ball's a good foot over the line when he does it. Even worse, the pesky linesman spots it.

Views from the Sundays

(Including the prediction of the day from *The Sunday Telegraph's* Patrick Barclay)

- ☻ 'You know Manchester United's title defence is going well when they descend upon London, earn a deserved draw with high-flying Arsenal and then complain as if they have somehow been short-changed. All that happened was that at the end of a frantic last quarter, Arsenal scored an equaliser that was both dramatic and deserved.' – *The Sunday Times*

- ☻ 'A game to stop the world, as Arsène Wenger had promised? Hmm. Perhaps not quite. Amid the recriminations there were too many comedy capers in front of goal for that. But by the end, it was one to stop the hearts of Wenger and Ferguson, who even in the collective experience of 30-odd years cannot have witnessed too many more dramatic denouements in this fixture. Wenger promised beforehand that this match would be a beautiful work of art. For sheer unpredictability it was a vividly entertaining abstract work, and one that will hearten their principal rivals, Liverpool and Chelsea, because of the manner in which both defences were found wanting at crucial moments' – *The Independent on Sunday*

- ☻ 'For all the beauty and the bravery of Arsenal's football, for all the doggedness that again made the 11th hour their finest, it is difficult to envisage their regaining the Premier League title this season. Not with this back five. Manuel Almunia is hardly the calibre of goalkeeper you need at the top level and the rest of the rearguard, while good to excellent individually, have yet to knit. Nor are the central pair of Kolo Toure and William Gallas particularly well equipped for an aerial battle. Manchester United possess a more mature and balanced side. As do Chelsea, for that matter.' – *The Sunday Telegraph*

The Emirates – the verbals

- ☻ 'I think we have thrown it away. At 2–1 you think you've won the game and for them to get a second goal when they did – for us to give it way in injury-time – it is very hard to take I can tell you. It is a fact that they got out of jail.' – You get the feeling Fergie's going to be clumsy with the dressing-room crockery…

- ☻ 'It seemed some of the Arsenal players thought they had won the game when the final whistle went. I am not sure we would have celebrated like that if we had just drawn at home.' – Giggsy makes a valid point.

- ☻ 'We had to fight. We said if we had to die we would die together on that field.' – The melodramatic William Gallas gives the first sign of the weirdness to come.

Match facts

Arsenal: Almunia, Sagna, Toure, Gallas, Clichy, Eboue (Walcott 74), Fabregas*, Flamini, Rosicky (Eduardo 80), Hleb (Silva 80), Adebayor [Wenger]

United: Van der Sar, Brown (O'Shea 71), Ferdinand, Vidic, Evra*, Ronaldo, Anderson (Carrick 76), Hargreaves*, Giggs, Tévez (Saha 76), Rooney

FAPL 12.45 (Sky) Emirates. Att: 60,161. Ref: H. Webb. Half-time: 1–0

*Yellow card

Other scores

Blackburn 0 Liverpool 0; Wigan 0 Chelsea 2 (Lampard, Belletti); Newcastle 1 (og) Portsmouth 4 (Pamarot, Benjani, Utaka, Kranjcar)

League table

1. Arsenal 27 (11) 2. United 27 (12) 3. Chelsea 24 (12) 4. Portsmouth 22 (12)

Arsenal to Kiev

'It's difficult to comprehend the journey I have made, but suffice to say it's been a fantastic journey.'

News

Rooney is named Premiership Player of the Month for October. Stoke's on-loan Red Ryan Shawcross wins the Championship version and Hughesie gets the manager award. Stephen Ireland celebrates his goal against Sunderland by dropping his shorts to reveal Superman pants. United kit man Albert Morgan has a Warhol moment at the Emirates. Fergie celebrates an extraordinary 21 years in charge at Old Trafford…

And you get the idea he's not going anywhere soon

'I guess I have to think about retiring at some stage, but I still have plenty of ambition. I'm proud of the current team – they need a little bit of direction at times but they're showing fantastic enthusiasm.

'The players clearly want to do well in the Champions League and if you are one of the best, you naturally look to spell it out with Cups and medals. Otherwise you are in danger of ending your career as a nearly man – and I don't think a single Manchester United player [or manager? ed.] wants that.'

Spot the difference

☉ 'Howard is without question the best referee in the League' – Sir Alex Ferguson raves about Howard Webb before the Arsenal match.

☺ 'I think Howard Webb has a great chance to be the top referee.' – After accusing Webb of 'favouring Arsenal', Fergie's praise isn't quite as effusive afterwards (from *football365.com*).

Albert gets his 15 minutes

From *The Mirror*:

'Kit man Albert Morgan had a hilarious confrontation with *Manchester Evening News* reporter Stuart Mathieson in the stadium's foyer as hacks tried to grab a few precious seconds with United players at the end of the match.

'Morgan told the bemused *MEN* man: "I'm not happy with your paper, by the way. Five pages on City. Five f**king pages! Even my missus has noticed it."

'"And what do we get?" He then held his fingers together to suggest a small amount of space. 'Mathieson replied: "Well, they talk to us. That's why."

'"They talk to us and you can never get anything out of United."

'Morgan disagreed, at which point Ryan Giggs walked by. Mathieson shouted out: "Ryan, any chance of a word?" "Not today," replied Giggs, striding on to the team bus.

'Morgan's was the only dry eye in the house.'

Quotes of the week

☺ 'I dated a girl from Manchester, and she showed me that steak pies and chips are very good.' – Steak pies, chips and breasts the size of Central Library. What was Ronaldo thinking splitting up with Gemma Atkinson?

☺ 'A Brazilian should be able to triumph in any club in the world, including this one, so I won't make any excuses. I am Anderson, not Veron or Kleberson. This is the difference. Perhaps I have arrived with more ambition than those two did.' – Viv's shaping up very nicely.

☺ 'Both of our goals were beautiful bits of play, but their [Arsenal's] goals were more scrappy' – So is Owen Hargreaves.

Once a Scouser...

'Portsmouth star Djimi Traore was marched off a training pitch by bailiffs yesterday – over £1,906 in unpaid council tax. Stunned teammates looked on as the heavies swooped, threatening to clamp his Range Rover unless he paid up. Traore, 27 – a Champions League winner with Liverpool in 2005 – had not paid a penny in tax on the posh harbour flat Pompey rents for him since last April. Portsmouth Council said he had ignored bills, reminders, a court summons and liability order' – *The Sun*

Anniversary quote of the week

'It's amazing to think I've been here for 21 years and difficult to comprehend the journey I have made, but suffice to say it's been a fantastic journey.' – Happy 21 years Fergie.

United 4 Kiev 0   07/11/2007

Pique 31, Tévez 37, Rooney 76, Ronaldo 88

When the Kiev of Shevchenko, Rebrov and Luzhny reached the semi-finals of the Champions League in 1999, Fergie reportedly feared meeting them in Barcelona more than Bayern. But time hasn't been kind to either Kiev or their famous old trio: Shevchenko, once the hero of the San Siro, is now little more than a rich man's plaything. Rebrov, who came on at half-time here, was finished as soon as he moved to Spurs. And Luzhny, who was last seen at Old Trafford on the wrong end of the famous Arsenal 6–1, ended up as manager of this bunch of no-hopers. There have been plenty of poor teams at Old Trafford in the Champions League, but I can't think of any that have been as negative, soulless and half-arsed as this.

Goal action

1–0 (31): A landmark moment for Pique, starting his first Champions League game. Ronaldo's free-kick ricochets off Carrick and Tévez and balloons up towards the young Spaniard who outmuscles his marker and heads in his first United goal.

2–0 (37): The capitalution begins. Tévez puts his foot down after winning the ball in the centre circle, plays a simple one-two with Rooney and sidefoots firmly past Shoykovskiy.

3–0 (76): Rooney said afterwards that Kiev's approach had left him bored. He must have enjoyed this bit though. Nani bends it in like Beckham from the right and Rooney volleys in unmarked.

4–0 (88): Ronaldo seals the win, and United's safe passage into the next round, by cutting in from the left at pace and lashing a low, diagonal shot into the far corner.

Views from the broadsheets

- 'United were efficient rather than irresistible, steady rather than scintillating, yet still tore Dynamo Kiev to shreds. With better finishing it could have been a repeat of Liverpool's eight-goal triumph over Besiktas at Anfield on Tuesday night. United had 23 shots, not that overexertion was required.' – *The Times*

☺ 'It said a lot about them that the Ukrainian players were taking souvenir snaps of one another before kick-off. There are not many duff teams in this competition but Kiev's record is so poor that the club badge could be a wooden spoon and the only surprise when United took the lead was that it was their first serious attempt at goal and it had taken half an hour to come.' – *The Guardian*

Kiev – the verbals

☺ 'They came here and did not want to play. I didn't really enjoy it. We got the win and are through, but we got frustrated and bored. It was like a training session as they had no enthusiasm to play. It wasn't enjoyable.' – Rooney's not happy.

☺ 'I know what Wayne means as it was a bit tedious at times. I think Kiev had come here determined not to be embarrassed.' – Fergie's not impressed either.

Pundit of the week

'Well that was a crap game, wasn't it?' – RTE's Bill O'Herlihy introduces the analysis of United's Kiev stroll.

Match facts

United: Van der Sar (Kuszczak half-time), Simpson, Vidic, Pique (Evans 72), Evra, Ronaldo, Carrick, Nani, Fletcher, Rooney*, Tévez (Saha 67)

Dynamo Kiev: Shovkovskiy, Fedorov, Vashchuk, El Kaddouri, Markovic, Diakhate*, Rotan (Rebrov 46), Correa*, Gusev (Rincon 46), Ghioane, Milevskiy (Bangoura 76) [Luzhny]

CL/F 19.45 (Sky). Att: 75,017. Ref: Jan Wegereef (Holl). Half-time: 2–0

*Yellow card

Other scores

Liverpool 8 Besiktas 0; Slavia Prague 0 Arsenal 0; Schalke 0 Chelsea 0

League table

1. United 12 (4) 2. Roma 7 (4) 3. Sporting 4 (4) 4. Kiev 0 (4)

Kiev to Blackburn

'Stay at home and vomit in your own living room'

News

United snap up Burnley's 14-year-old superkid John Cofie. The deal for the German-born Ghanian striker is reported to be worth up to £1.25 million. The Barclays curse strikes again as Rooney injures his ankle playing head tennis just minutes after picking up the

Player of the Month prize for October. A new book, *Celtic United*, once again accuses Liverpool fans of stealing *You'll Never Walk Alone* – the song was first sung by United fans as a tribute to the victims of Munich. Setanta fail in a bizarre request to move the Everton game to 8pm on Christmas Eve.

Worry of the week
Even Darren Anderton wasn't Sicknote at 22. Rooney's had three metatarsals already. And now this…

Quotes of the week
- 'I see similarities with me and Mark, aggression and determination, great quality.' – Fergie manages to praise Sparky and slap himself on the back all in the same sentence.
- 'I didn't know for certain Tévez and Rooney [would work], but I hoped.' – Fergie again.
- 'Playing in this team is a great privilege. This is such a great club, I am delighted to be able to extend my stay here. The fans and everyone at the club have been very special to me. I hope I can do my bit to bring the club even more trophies in the years ahead.' – Nemanja Vidic extends his contract by two years. Forwards across Europe weep.

Pah!
'Ideally, we would like every game to be at 3pm. Our commitment to the TV agreement means that isn't possible, but we always try to strike a balance for the sake of football fans.' – Premier League spokesman Dan Johnson talks rubbish – how many Old Trafford games kicked-off at 3pm on a Saturday in the first three months of 2007–08? One.

A life less special
Now he can no longer abuse fourth officials, take potshots at Arsene Wenger and wind up Scousers, it seems that Jose Mourinho has had to turn to other targets, in this case a classmate of his young daughter, Matilde.

The Telegraph reports from Setubal, near Lisbon:

'According to headmistress Isabel Simao, 12-year-old Pedro Farrim had upset Matilde after taunting her with the suggestion that her trophy-winning father was "not the best". The Special One sought retribution as he came to collect his daughter. Shocked parents at claimed he pulled Farrim's ears and hair in an ugly playground spat that reduced the boy to tears.

'Mourinho was later called to the private day school to explain his actions and was forced to write a formal apology to Pedro, his family and the school. The boy's father, Antonio Farrim, will not be pressing charges and was happy the situation has been resolved.'

Letter of the week

The *Elmundo Deportivo* newspaper clearly doesn't buy into the old cliché about Scottish fans being perfect guests abroad. This was the open letter they wrote to the visiting fans after negative Rangers went down 2–0 in the Nou Camp:

'Dear Rangers supporters, never come back to Barcelona again. And not because your players themselves aren't a legitimate team. No, it's not because of that – the Nou Camp frequently hosts teams who are lazy, boring, who only defend, who run and kick their opponents, and who shouldn't be in elite competition. On top of this, Rangers merely defend, run at the opposition and play dirty. Their defenders are butchers, their midfielders, heavy-footed; and their strikers just stand there like the furniture.

'But even apart from the footballing aspect, the best thing would be for Rangers never to return to Barcelona, because every time they do, they make a mess of the place. 35 years ago, you (the Rangers supporters) destroyed the seats at the Nou Camp. This time we have enjoyed no less than 48 hours of brawls, provocation, rackets, fights and common drunk women throughout the whole city, which you have fouled however you pleased.

'Stay at home and vomit in your own living-room, urinate in your sitting-room corners, fight with your neighbours, the Celtic supporters (who deserve a prize just for putting up with you) and foul the streets of Glasgow instead. Don't come back here again, because it is not a laughing matter. And, by extension, don't play in the Champions League either. You are not at that level neither in a sporting nor human sense.'

(If only Manchester City Council had heeded the warning.)

United 2 Blackburn 0   11/11/2007

Ronaldo 34, 35

Blackburn arrived at Old Trafford with seven wins and a Liverpool draw behind them. They'd also taken points off Arsenal at home and Chelsea away. So United couldn't have chosen much tougher opponents to face the day after Rooney forgot the golden rule of head tennis – don't mess with the stanchion. But the team was playing with so much confidence that the absence of one of the golden boys didn't really matter. The defence stood firm against Blackburn's early pressure, Ronaldo enjoyed a minute of mayhem and Dunn crossed Chris Foy twice too many. After that it was a question of how many more United would score, whether Ronaldo would score his first United hat-trick, and whether the guy in the row behind would stop giving his running commentary and go home early. Unfortunately, the answer to the third question was the same as the one to the first two. It's one of the big problems with all-seater stadiums – once you get stuck next to a moron, you stay stuck with them.

The minute that mattered

1–0 (34): Giggs, playing his best game of the season, sends over an outswinging corner from in front of the North Stand. Ronaldo – who's got to be the most dangerous winger in the air since Ian Ormondroyd was at his pomp – times his jump fantastically, flexes his neck muscles and powers the ball into the net.

2–0 (35): Emerton makes a mistake near the halfway line that would have been harmless against almost every other team. At Old Trafford it proves fatal. Saha instantly flicks on to Tévez, he scurries down the inside-left channel and curls over a low cross that Ronaldo dispatches past Friedel.

Views from the pressbox

⚽ 'United were not at their fluent best here but the result will serve as a statement of intent. This is clearly a side than can still flourish without Wayne Rooney, who is out for a month with ankle damage. Cristiano Ronaldo provided the bite more normally demanded of the England forward, taking his season's goal tally into double figures, to shrug the hosts out of their initial lethargy.' – *The Guardian*

⚽ 'If there was a sharp intake of breath around Manchester United's training ground on Friday, when Wayne Rooney twisted his right ankle during a game of head tennis, it cannot have taken long for a sense of calm to be restored. A quick look around the United dressing-room would indicate that it will tale more than a twisted ankle to throw their title challenge off course and, by the time Cristiano Ronaldo had scored twice in as many minutes at Old Trafford yesterday, they were coasting back to the top of the Premier League.' – *The Times*

☉ 'There is no stopping Ronaldo in this form. Rooney may be missed more by his country than he is by his club. The winger has scored 10 times in 15 United appearances this term, a record which suggests that Ferguson's pre-season demand that he improve on last season's tally of 23 may not be fanciful.' – *The Guardian*

Blackburn – the verbals

☉ 'I believe that this is the strongest squad I've ever had. So much so that I would be pushed to name my overall best team. We've got young players led by Wayne Rooney and Cristiano Ronaldo and more in the likes of Carlos Tévez, Nani and Anderson. In fact, it's difficult to know when to stop when talking about our important players.' – Fergie basks in the afterglow of United's latest victory (their 13th in the last 15 games, all won in the midst of a major injury crisis).

☉ 'This is what I have been working towards. I don't like the short-term fix. I prefer to see a pool of players emerge and develop into something special which, believe me, is what is happening at Old Trafford this season.' – Fergie again.

☉ 'If you give Manchester United your little finger, they'll take the whole hand. You could always come back with the scoreline at 1–0, but with 2–0 and 10 players it gets tough. Arsenal are a strong side, but United are better. Look at that team. They're incredibly strong.' – Morten Gamst Pederson rates us.

☉ 'I will not be attempting to bet anything with Cristiano this season unless it is 50 goals. Somehow I don't think he would accept that.' – Fergie makes a good decision.

Match facts

United: Van der Sar, Brown, Ferdinand, Vidic, Evra, Ronaldo*, Anderson, Hargreaves (Carrick 77), Giggs, Tévez, Saha (Nani 68)
Blackburn: Friedel, Emerton, Samba*, Nelsen*, Warnock, Bentley, Dunn 53**, Mokoena*, Pedersen, Santa Cruz (Derbyshire 78), McCarthy [Sparky]
FAPL 15.00. Att: 75,710. Ref: C. Foy. Half-time: 2–0
*Yellow card **Two yellow cards

Other scores

Liverpool 2 (Torres, Gerrard pen) Fulham 0; Portsmouth 0 City 0; Chelsea 1 (Drogba) Everton 1 (Cahill); Reading 1 (Shorey) Arsenal 3 (Flamini, Adebayor, Hleb)

League table
1. Arsenal 30 (12) 2. United 30 (13) 3. City 26 (13) 4. Chelsea 25 (13)...7. Blackburn 22 (12)

Blackburn to Bolton
'My dear, my penis is a mountain'

Off with their heads
England are given a surprise Euro 2008 lifeline as Israel beat Russia 2–1, meaning they only need a home draw in their final group game against already qualified Croatia to go through. But they then produce a display of quite exceptional ineptitude at Wembley to lose 3–2.

Which is bad news for landlords, peddlers of St George's tat and WAGs. And cracking news for five million Scots, 142 million Russians and everyone who wanted Steve McClaren to get the bullet. By 9am the next morning, the man who spent his Waterloo as England manager trying to protect his hair from the Wembley rain was gone.

Headline of the week
'The Wally In The Brolly' – *The Daily Mail*. Well, they did campaign for an English manager.

BBC unveils new comedy cast
It's...
Carson – Richards, Campbell, Lescott, Bridge – Wright-Phillips, Barry, Lampard, Gerrard, J.Cole – Crouch (subs: Defoe, Beckham, Bent)

Note there isn't a single United name in sight, or a Neville. The tabloids are going to have to work hard to pin the blame on us this time.

A man's word is his honour
'I'll bounce back. I'm not one to lie on a beach' – Sacked Steve McClaren speaking hours before, er, he flew out to his Caribbean holiday home. It was then reported that he used a chunk of his hefty pay-off to add a £1.9 million beach property to his property portfolio. It's a tough life being a failure.

Sweet FA
☺ 'I said right at the start I would live and die by results, and results haven't gone my way. In that sense we have failed.' – McClaren tries and, rather fittingly, fails to grasp what failure means.

- 'I don't think any of the Croatian team would get into our team.' – Michael Owen was clearly watching another channel.
- 'I would like to thank Steve for the work he has done since taking on the position last summer.' – FA Chairman Geoff Thompson speaks for the entire Russian nation.

Childish giggle of the week

The British singer who sang the Croatian anthem at Wembley falls victim to the mother, nay mountain, of all mistranslations:

'Tony Henry was trying to sing the national anthem in Croatian, but reportedly got the words wrong…The line in which Henry slipped up should have been "mila kuda si planina" (You know my dear how we love your mountains). But what he actually sang was "mila kura si planina" which means 'Dear Penis, you are a Mountain" or "My Dear, my penis is a mountain."' – Ananova.

Quiz question of the week

When was the last time England played a competitive game without a single United player in the line-up?*

Politician of the week

Step forward Roger Godsiff, who tabled this Early Day Motion the day after the Croatia debacle:

'This House…

- congratulates Croatia and Russia on qualifying for the European Football Championships from Group E.
- acknowledges that the Croatian team which beat England were far superior in technical ability, skill and commitment than the insipid and inept England team.
- notes that £747 million was spent on the new Wembley Stadium, but the match was played on a surface similar to those used by Sunday footballers on council pitches.
- thanks the efforts of the Israeli and part-time players of Andorra in trying to help England by doing their very best against Russia.
- commiserates with the fans who have spent large amounts of their hard-earned money following England during these Championships.
- believes that the over-paid, over-pampered and over-hyped English prima donnas from the Premiership who took the field against Croatia disgraced the England shirt once worn by legends such as Stanley Matthews, Duncan Edwards, Bobby Moore, Nobby Stiles and Bobby Charlton and recognises that they will no doubt be consoled by the thought that while they are watching the European Championships from their luxurious holiday destinations their celebrity lifestyles will be protected by them still receiving their vastly inflated wages, provided by Sky and Setanta television money,

*Answer: The semi-final defeat to Germany in Euro '96.

from clubs in a Premiership League, which is nothing more than a money-making machine for players, agents and entrepreneurial club owners which does very little for promoting the well-being of football in England either at the grass roots or international level.'

We're good, you're not

'In my heart I am disappointed, but I have to laugh at them because they would do the same to me if France had not qualified. I was singing "England, England" in the dressing room, which I found quite funny even if they didn't. I still can't quite believe it.' – Paddy Evra enjoys the Croatia result.

International Reds

Injuries and suspensions make it a slow week for international Red watchers. Ronaldo and Nani feature as Portugal get the 0–0 draw against Finland they need to make it to Euro 2008. Tévez is sent off playing for Argentina against Colombia. And that's about it.

News

Italian police shoot a football fan dead during a service station fight between Lazio and Juve fans. The shooting sparks riots by football fans across Italy and the postponement of matches involving Lazio, Inter and Milan. Steve Bruce is named as Wigan manager for a second time. Amusingly, the move initially looked in danger because of a dispute over Brucie's image rights. (It must be all those duvet covers he sells.) John O'Shea extends his contract to 2012. Youngster David Gray moves to Crewe on loan. And Red legends Mark Hughes, Nobby Stiles and Billy Meredith are inducted into the National Football Museum Hall of Fame.

What's he up to?

'We have tried to buy Anelka several times. He is a very talented player. You always assess players with pace and ability to score, and he comes into that category, and has done throughout his career.' – Fergie chooses the day before the Bolton game to go public with his admiration for Nikolas Anelka. Unfortunately, if it was an attempt to put him off his game, it didn't work...

Bolton 1 United 0   24/11/2007

Anelka 11

Bloody international breaks...

Before this latest one United had been rampant while Bolton had sunk so low they'd ended up hiring Gary Megson. And then this happens: Bolton get themselves pumped up, United look tired, Pique makes a complete hash of a routine header, Tévez misses an open goal from a yard and United lose at Bolton for the first time since the 1970s.

So what went wrong? Well, Fergie was right. The hapless referee, Clattenburg, had a shocker, particularly in the first half when he allowed Bolton to niggle and foul the life out of the game. It didn't help that United were missing Rooney, Ronaldo and half a dozen other players who would normally expect to feature either. But let's not get hooked on whinging about dirty northerners and injuries – leave that to Arsenal and Chelsea.

No, give credit where it's due. Bolton did a job on us. They gave us no space, they were well organised, they chased and harried and, every now and then, when they weren't trying to break Patrice Evra's legs, they even played a spot of football. I won't go as far as to say they deserved to win. They didn't. But they didn't deserve to lose either. Though if Anderson, who transformed the speed and flow of United's game when he came on, had been on for the whole 90 minutes, who knows...

The (three) moments that mattered

0–1 (11) – Campo chips a hopeful free-kick into the area, Pique mistimes his jump horribly and the ball falls to Anelka who swivels and scores from close range.

Off! (45) – Fergie gives Clattenburg a mouthful in the tunnel for not clamping down on Bolton's roughhouse tactics and gets sent to the stands. It's the only strong decision the referee makes all afternoon.

Miss! (74) – United blow their best chance. Evra, who was easily United's best attacker (and many Reds' pick for the Player of the Autumn), motors down the left and sends over a cross that Tévez somehow flicks wide from almost under the bar.

Views from the broadsheets

⚽ 'Ferguson's complaint was that the Bolton tactics were, at best, primitive and, at worst, dangerous. Others would argue that the reasons for United's poorest performance of

2007 stemmed from their inability to pass the ball with the usual zip, the debilitating effects of being without Wayne Rooney and Cristiano Ronaldo, the erratic finishing of Carlos Tévez and, in the absence of the injured Nemanja Vidic, Gerard Piqué making a pig's ear of some basic defending before Nicolas Anelka turned in the winning goal for Bolton.' – *The Guardian* blasts Fergie for using Bolton's tactics as an excuse. Then they make excuses (no Ronaldo, Rooney or Vidic) for him.

☺ 'Where Ferguson undoubtedly had a point – and it was one which had the poison removed by his admission that his team at no point deserved to win – was that if you invest in the finest talent…a little bit more official protection is not asking too much. Bolton's Kevin Davies, for example, did more than enough for a red card in a series of cynical assaults on Patrice Evra.' – *The Independent* says something far more sensible.

☺ 'A shambles, Sir Alex Ferguson called it. He was talking about the first half, which he claimed Bolton Wanderers, with the referee's help, turned into a kicking match, but from Manchester United's point of view he might have been talking about the whole afternoon – an undignified affair summed up by the sight of Ferguson banished to the stands and Edwin van der Sar anxiously wrestling the ball from Lofty the Lion, the Bolton mascot, as the clock ticked down.' – *The Times* leaves us with the great image of a 37-year-old multi-millionaire fighting with a life-sized cuddly toy.

The Reebok – the verbals

☺ 'I told him how bad he was and he didn't like it. Some referees don't like the truth. I thought we should have got more protection and it was becoming a shambles. But we can't say we deserved to win the game because we didn't make enough chances.' – Fergie explains why he was sent to the stands.

☺ 'It was a big fight. I received more tackles in one game than I've had in my entire life. It was the same last year, too. Davies kicked me then as well, and I said to him, "Why did you do that?" He said, "Because I don't like you." I didn't understand it. And today he did it again.' – I'm not sure Evra enjoys coming to the Reebok.

☺ 'We put them under pressure, we battled and we made it difficult for them. I don't understand what the problem is. We were right at them from the start but, in all honesty, I don't think there was a malicious tackle in the whole game.' – Andy O'Brien clearly can't see past his nose.

29 years of shame

This was United's first defeat at Bolton since Dave Sexton's side got thumped 3–0 on 22 December 1978. The team that lined up at Burnden Park that day was:
Bailey, B.Greenhoff, McQueen, Buchan, Connell*, Coppell, Macari, McIlroy, Thomas, J.Greenhoff, Ritchie (sub. Nicholl)

*21 year-old Irish left-back Tom Connell made his debut in this match. He only made one more appearance for United, at home to Liverpool. United lost that one 3–0 too.

Match facts
Bolton: Jaaskelainen, Hunt*, Meite, O'Brien, Gardner, Campo, Nolan* (McCann 83), Guthrie (Wilhelmsson 74), Davies* (Speed 70), Anelka, Diouf [Megson]
United: Van der Sar, Brown (O'Shea 88), Pique (Anderson 59), Ferdinand, Evra, Nani, Carrick, Hargreaves, Giggs, Saha, Tévez [Fergie† (half-time)]
FAPL 15.00 Reebok Stadium. Att: 25,028. Ref: M.Clattenburg. Half-time: 0–1
*Yellow card † Red card

Other scores
Arsenal 2 (Gallas, Rosicky) Wigan 0; Newcastle 0 Liverpool 3 (Gerrard, Kuyt, Babel); Derby 0 Chelsea 2 (Kalou, Wright-Phillips); City 2 (Petrov, Ireland) Reading 1 (Harper); Basically a terrible weekend.

League table
1. Arsenal 33(13) 2. United 30(14) 3. City 29(14) 4. Chelsea 28(14)…16. Bolton 11(14)

Bolton to Sporting
'I love to play for this club. It is a privilege to be a Manchester United player.'
That's somebody's daughter
The News of the World reveals how England players warmed up for the fateful Euro qualifier against Croatia:

'At a party thrown for Shaun Wright-Phillips's birthday in a Soho lapdancing club, an unnamed player had sex on a chair in the basement, SWP ended up in an "ugly scuffle" with a female guest who dared to take his picture (I hope she didn't rough him up too much)…

'…And John Terry p**sed on the floor.' Classy.

Justice for John
Forty-one years on, John Connolly becomes the third United player to win a World Cup-winners' medal after FIFA finally decide to award medals to squad members (before 1978 only players who actually played in the Final received a medal).

'It's justice for all those players,' said FIFA president Sepp Blatter, before racing off to check out the designs for the new refereeing kits.

OK, so that bit was made up. But I needed a link into this…

Storm in a D-cup

Brazilian lineswoman, Ana Paula Oliveira, causes a storm by stripping off for *Playboy*. I hope Wendy Toms doesn't get any ideas!

Quiz question of the week

Name the 11 English footballers who won a World Cup medal in 2007 (answers at the bottom for everyone else who can only think of Jimmy Greaves).

Quote of the week

'I love to play for this club. It is a privilege to be a Manchester United player.' – Paddy Evra rocks.

A bridge too far

Another amusing outburst from Chelsea's foreign legion. This time it's Florent Malouda's turn:

'Training sessions here are terrifying. They are just like matches, and you go flat out. During the actual games it is as though everybody's brains are switched off. People play by instinct, spontaneously, in the way they did when they first discovered football.' – Le whining begins...

'The people at Chelsea don't control what the players eat. You can help yourself to whatever you like, drink Coke or anything. It is a good job I have come over here at the age of 27 and so haven't been following the same diet as the rest of the club's players' – Oh Frank...

'I have only just had a phone line put in. Things are not as simple over here as they are in France. You can't just go to a shop and "bingo" they come round the next day to install your equipment. The traffic in London goes at a snail's pace at times, so sometimes I end up taking the Tube. If I don't want to spend my life stuck behind the wheel in traffic jams, I phone for a taxi to get me something to eat, or whatever. Or I'll hire a big chauffeur-driven car so I can take my kids out for a walk' – Heart bleeding for the £4 million-a-year man yet?

How many did you get?

The 'other' World Cup-winning XI from '66:

Jimmy Greaves (Tottenham), Jimmy Armfield (Blackpool), Peter Bonetti (Chelsea), Ron Springett (Sheffield Wednesday), Gerry Byrne (Liverpool), Ron Flowers (Wolves), Norman Hunter (Leeds), Terry Paine (Southampton), Ian Callaghan (Liverpool), George Eastham (Arsenal), John Connolly (United).

United 2 Sporting Lisbon 1   27/11/2007

Abel 22, Tévez 61, Ronaldo 90

For 90 minutes this was another of those instantly forgettable Champions League group nights. Sporting were good, but not that good. United were OK, sort of. But then came a soft free-kick, a stunning strike and a haughty shoulder-shrugging spree worthy of Eric the King. He plays on the left, he plays on the right…forget England, that boy Ronaldo was starting to make everyone look sh**e.

Goal action

0–1 (22): United never got out of second gear in the first half and were lucky to be trailing by just this one sloppy goal when it ended. Sporting full-back Abel smashes in a low centre from the right, Kuszczak, who had anticipated a cross, can't get back in time and the ball arrows past him at his near post.

1–1 (61): The game turned as soon as Fergie abandoned 4–5–1 at half-time, though it still took a fluke from Tévez to level things up. Ronaldo miscues a low shot across goal, the ball hits Tévez on the shin and cannons into the net.

2–1 (90): Despite United's second-half improvement, they never really looked like scoring again. But then Anderson wins a soft free-kick 30-ish yards out and to the left of centre, Ronaldo presses the ball into the ground, takes a couple of strides back and then smashes a fizzing, dipping free-kick over the wall and into the bottom right corner. Fergie called it a 'truly excellent goal, a marvellous strike'. Ronaldo – modesty personified – thought it was merely 'fabulous'.

Views from the broadsheets

- ⚽ 'The splendour of Ronaldo's goal did not, however, conceal the fact that United had produced a performance that for long spells must have dismayed their manager. Sporting, with only one away win in Europe's premier club competition since 1970, led 1–0 at half-time, as well as having a goal dubiously ruled out for offside, and Ferguson had strong words with his players to inspire a second-half revival.' – *The Guardian*
- ⚽ 'Of course, it had to be Cristiano Ronaldo's night. The Portuguese is currently in the form of his life and the piece of genius which delivered his side into the second round of the Champions League as group winners last night was one for his old side to

remember him by: a vicious, dipping 30-yard free-kick which clinched this tie four minutes into injury time.' – *The Independent*

✪ 'On scoring the goal that defeated Sporting Lisbon on his return to the Estádio José Alvalade in September, Cristiano Ronaldo suppressed his instinctive glee and bowed respectfully to the supporters who saw him take the first steps in his professional career. Back in his Old Trafford realm last night, having eliminated them from the Champions League with a spectacular stoppage-time free kick, he did what came naturally, offering a self-satisfied shrug that told his former teammates it was nothing personal, just a genius going about his business.' – *The Times*

✪ 'Fifteen years to the day after Eric Cantona walked into Old Trafford with the swagger that helped transform Manchester United from nearly men to English football's most dominant force, Cristiano Ronaldo paid homage to the Frenchman with a magic moment of his own to conform top spot in Group F with a stunning injury time free-kick against the club that set him on the road to stardom.

'All that was missing was the upturned collar, but Ronaldo's celebration, a knowing look and a shrug of the shoulders, was pure Cantona.' – *The Telegraph*

Sporting – the verbals

✪ 'We marginally won. I don't think we were a great deal better than them, but we certainly increased our game in the second half, with more speed and more tempo, and I think we might have edged it narrowly.' – Hmmm. I'm not sure about that Fergie. But a win's a win.

✪ 'I always try to score and I am happy, not just because it's Sporting – they respect me and I respect Sporting, but my colour now is red.' – Ronaldo in the good old days, before Real got to him.

✪ 'Anderson caught me and told me to do something for my mum, my family and I said OK. But my conscience is still the same and the people will understand.' – Ronaldo explains why he celebrated this time.

Match facts

United: Kuszczak, O'Shea, Ferdinand, Vidic, Evra*, Ronaldo*, Carrick, Anderson, Fletcher (Tévez half-time), Nani (Giggs half-time), Saha (Hargreaves 79)
Sporting Lisbon: Rui Patricio, Abel, Anderson Polga*, Tonel, Had*, Izmailov (Pereirinha 81), Joao Moutinho, Romagnoli (Vukcevic 67), Veloso, Purovic (Farnerud 81), Liedson [Bento]
CLF 19.45 (ITV). Att: 75,162. Ref: Claus Bo Larsen (Den). Half-time: 0–1
*Yellow card

Other scores
Kiev 1 Roma 4; Sevilla 3 Arsenal 0; Rosenborg 0 Chelsea 4; Liverpool 4 Porto 1

League table
1. United 15 (5) 2. Roma 10 (5) 3. Sporting 4 (5) 4. Kiev 0 (5)

Sporting to Fulham
'I'm in no doubt we'll take the lead at some stage.'

News
Ketchup-squirting United fans 'attack' a car carrying Joel and Bryan Glazer in Manchester city centre. Darren Ferguson is arrested on his dad's drive after a furious row with his estranged wife Nadine. Tévez reveals that a film (*Scarface*?) is in the works about his 'rags to riches' life. Harry Redknapp, bizarrely touted as the next England manager (on the basis that he's just about the only Englishman available), is arrested as part of the police's investigation into corruption in football.

Prediction of the week
'I'm in no doubt we'll take the lead at some stage.' – Lawrie Sanchez forgets that his main striker is called Shefki Kuqi as he looks forward to Fulham's trip to Old Trafford.

No wonder the prisons are so full
'They have to arrest you to talk to you, for you to be in the police station. I think that's the end of it, it didn't directly concern me.' – Harry Redknapp tries his best to distance himself from the corruption enquiries. Anyone convinced?

Conspiracy theory of the week
From Jamie Redknapp's brother, Mark, in *The Sun*:
'Someone is out to get my dad. Why is this happening now when the England job is vacant? There was no need for them to come around like this.'
So, let's get this straight. The police are so worried about Redknapp becoming England manager that they'd interrupt a major corruption investigation to blackball his reputation.

News II
Alex McLeish is given Brucie's old job at Birmingham. United's favourite manager Paul Jewell returns to football with Derby. Coleen runs up a £45.29 bill in a

Prestbury shop on 28 packets of crisps, a pasty, five fudge bars, two Rustlers chicken sandwiches, a pasty, Dairylea lunchables, a frozen chicken and beef dinner and a multi-pack of Red Bull (yes, *The Sun* really did think we needed to know that).

Quote of the week

'Tévez is like a son to me – from the moment I met him I have felt like that. I met him six years ago when he was at Boca Juniors, and instantly I could see he was going to be great. He reminded me of when I was his age – the hunger and the passion for the game. Every second he had a ball with him he was happy. He is a fantastic player. He is very strong on the ball and has amazing vision.' – Diego Maradona raves about United's best-ever Argentine.

United 2 Fulham 0 03/12/2007

Ronaldo 10, 58

At the end of this routine mismatch it was a toss-up who looked the bigger idiot. Lawrie Sanchez for coming out beforehand and predicting that his Fulham side would definitely take the lead, or Rob Stiles for booking Ronaldo for diving when it was blatantly obvious he should have awarded him a penalty – and the chance to complete his first United hat-trick. In the end Stiles just shaded it. Not giving the penalty was bad enough, but failing to send himself off (for denying United a clear goalscoring opportunity) was plain unforgivable…

Goal action

1–0 (10): Fulham have a habit of folding early at Old Trafford, and if Tévez had been sharper or luckier he alone could have scored three in the opening exchanges. Even so, United only had 10 minutes to wait for a goal. Steve Davis inexplicably heads the ball back into his own area after Giggs's corner is cleared. Vidic makes a nuisance of himself, the ball drops to Ronaldo and he lashes a blur of a half-volley past Niemi.

2–0 (58): After Tévez lets another hat-trick of chances slip by (no kidding, he could have had six by the break), United finally put the game to bed. O'Shea swings in a straightforward cross from the left, Ronaldo gets the run on Stevanovic and guides his header into the corner. Volleys, free-kicks, penalties, tap-ins, towering headers…even Kaka, the king to Ronaldo's prince (according to the latest world football awards), can't hurt teams in as many ways as this.

3–0 (65): F**k off Stiles, I'm giving it. Saha sends Ronaldo through, Niemi takes him out and Ronaldo tucks away his third from the spot.

Views from the broadsheets

- 'If there had to be a criticism, it was that Manchester United ought really to have won by a country mile. Two-nil scarcely reflected their superiority against a thoroughly outclassed Fulham side.' – *The Guardian* says it all in two sentences.
- 'Ferguson complained that United missed an uncommon number of chances and, on that front, it was hard to disagree. Tévez, alone, could have added six goals to the scoreline, even before half-time. Time and again, he carved Fulham open, only to be

frustrated by a storming turn from Niemi or a failing in the execution. It would be harsh to be too tough on the Argentina striker, though. For long periods, he was the most exciting player on the field.' – *The Times* on Tévez. I told you I wasn't exaggerating about the six.

☺ 'To place an accusation of fakery against a man, the referee should be absolutely sure. Styles appeared to be acting on no more than a hunch, and a rotten one at that, and it was no surprise that Sir Alex Ferguson was deeply unimpressed.' – *The Times* stands up for Ronaldo's honour after Stiles denies him his penalty and then, ridiculously, books him for diving.

Fulham – the verbals

☺ 'I'm in no doubt we'll take the lead at some stage'. – Lawrie Sanchez's pre-match prediction is definitely worth another viewing,

☺ 'The penalty-kick incident is a result of perceived idea of the referee that Ronaldo dives. Why would he dive? He's on a hat-trick. It was a ridiculous decision. His reputation from years ago is still playing on the minds of referees. It was a ridiculous decision. It is quite unfair because he is nothing like that now. He is more mature and a magnificent footballer.' – Fergie rages about Stiles.

☺ 'I was trying to do my job, he was trying to do his job, and I respect that. My feeling was that it was a penalty, but it was not the important thing tonight. The important thing was three points.' – Ronaldo turns the other cheek.

No sh*t

'Both players had upset tummies. If they hadn't run off pretty sharpish, the pitch may have had some unexpected fertilisation.' – Brian McClair explains why Ferdinand and Evra had to make quick exits in the second half.

Match facts

United: Van der Sar, Brown, Ferdinand (Carrick 75), Vidic*, Evra (O'Shea 46), Ronaldo*, Hargreaves, Anderson, Giggs, Tévez, Rooney (Saha 71)
Fulham: Niemi, Omozusi, Hughes, Stefanovic, Konchesky, Davies*, Davis, Murphy, Bouazza (Ki-Hyeon 71), Dempsey (Healy 64), Kuqi [Sanchez]
FAPL 20.00 (Set). Att: 75,055. Ref: R. Styles. Half-time: 1–0

Other scores

Villa 1 (Gardner) Arsenal 2 (Flamini, Adebayor); Liverpool 4 (Hyypia, Torres, Gerrard pen, Babel) Bolton 0; Chelsea 1 (J. Cole) West Ham 0

League table

1. Arsenal 36 (14) 2. United 33 (15) 3. Chelsea 31 (15) 4. Liverpool 30 (14)…14. Fulham 13 (15)

Fulham to Derby

'If Wayne can stay fit, he'll break every record at Old Trafford'

News

United agree to play a friendly in Saudi Arabia against Al Hilal Al Saudi FC in mid-January. Fergie says it's a good excuse for a mid-season break. Cynics say it's a good way for the Glazers to make £1 million. United are drawn against Villa in the third round of the FA Cup (again). Liverpool, Chelsea and Arsenal all get byes. Mancunian hero Ricky Hatton prepares to fight Floyd Mayweather in Vegas. United unveil their plans to mark the 50th anniversary of Munich. Highlights include a '50s-style kit for the derby and a permanent Munich exhibition in the South Stand tunnel (to be renamed the Munich tunnel).

What could possibly go wrong?

'Manchester United star Rio Ferdinand is collecting £4,000 from each player to organise the lads' Christmas party and rounding up 100 "gorgeous females" to keep them company on their drinking, lapdancing and gambling blow out.' – *The Mirror* reports on the players' plans to let their hair down at Christmas. It didn't take a crystal ball did it?

Smarting

'It's a great test for us…It should be another epic with a full house.' Martin O'Neill's excited reaction fools no one after Villa draw United in the third round of the Cup for the fourth time in seven years (actually, make that five in nine. United were drawn away at Villa the year we went to Brazil as well).

Denial of the week

'It's a number 24 but because there's a line underneath the numbers, at that angle on the film it does look like a 25. It's been verified by our competitions department. There's no mystery and absolutely no problems with the draw.' – The FA respond to viewers' accusations that ex-Arsenal player Sammy Nelson mistook ball number 25 for number 24 during the televised FA Cup draw. If it had been a 25, Villa would have played Middlesbrough in the third round and United would have travelled to Bristol City.

Quotes of the week

- ☻ 'I've had some great players here over the years – Bryan Robson and Roy Keane. But in terms of sheer ability and imagination, Cristiano is, without doubt, looking the best now' – Fergie gives Ronaldo the ultimate accolade.
- ☻ 'If Wayne can stay fit, he'll break every record at Old Trafford' – The Lawman follows suit.
- ☻ 'We looked lively before they scored their first goal.' – Robbo tries to take the positives from 3–0 home battering his Sheffield United side are given by Stoke. For the record, Stoke scored after 100 seconds.
- ☻ 'It became very obvious from the start that I was never going to be the best singer or the best dancer or the best actress. You know, I've never been that good at anything, to be completely honest.' – Posh Spice does herself a disservice. She's world-class at pouting.

Cowardy custard

'If you go to prison for defending yourself then, yes, I suppose I'll think about it. But I don't care. It doesn't scare me at all.' – Joey Barton comes over all macho when Gabby Logan quizzes him about the Ousmane Dabo court case. (Don't worry, the custard connection will make perfect sense in a page or two.)

Tough love

From *The Sun*:

'Neville Southall left his daughter in tears – after *SUING* her to get back £55,000 of his trophies. The ex-Everton and Wales goalie gave Samantha, 19, his FA Cup medal and other gongs, plus international caps and his MBE, when she was 10. But Southall, 49 – who yesterday starred in an England Legends charity game in Manchester – never meant for her to keep them, a judge heard.

'Sam, whose dad walked out on her and her mum a decade ago after a string of affairs, sobbed as a "saddened" judge at Liverpool's civil and family court ordered her to return the memorabilia. The hard-up law student was also told to pay £6,000 costs. She said: "I'm devastated – I idolised my dad. I don't know how I'll pay the costs." Southall, now thought to be living in Kent with a new love, was not at court. His lawyer said: "He is pleased the matter's been resolved."'

And you thought your old man used to give you a hard time! (from *football365.com*)

United 4 Derby 1 08/12/2007

Giggs 40, Tévez 45, 60, Howard 76, Ronaldo 90 (pen)

This was a funny old match. United won 4–1, but Derby seemed the happier side at the end. Maybe it was because they'd managed to hold their own for most of the first half. Maybe it was because they'd bagged themselves an away goal for the first time all season. Or maybe it was because United knew they'd missed an opportunity. If the pitch hadn't been trashed by 90 minutes of biblical rainfall, they might even have threatened the Ipswich 9–0.

The moments that mattered

15.00 0–0: Yes, it's true. United are playing at Old Trafford at 3pm on a Saturday. They must be playing someone crap…

15.40 1–0: After a low-key opening half-hour, United suddenly flick the switch. Ronaldo picks up a loose ball on the left corner of the box and fires in a shot that Bywater can only parry to the feet of Giggs. He can't miss, and he doesn't, in the process becoming only the 11th United player to score a century of League goals.

15.45 2–0: United's first goal was scruffy, their second made the dad of the year, Neville Southall, look like James Bond. Ronaldo confuses the Derby defence by side-footing a free-kick into the area rather than going for goal. Derby fail to clear, Tévez swings and misses but recovers instantly to sidefoot home.

16.20 3–0: Derby don't learn. They stand off Tévez in the area, and he scores his second with a crisp, right-to-left shot into the bottom corner.

16.36 3–1: Has a crap consolation goal ever been celebrated so manically? Van der Sar, his brain clearly short-circuited by all the rain, rushes out of his goal to try to intercept a ball he's got no chance of reaching. Mears crosses and Howard, sliding in with Vidic and Brown, scores one of the worst goals you'll ever see, the ball rebounding off the back and trickling over the line.

16.51 4–1: Ronaldo, the innocent victim against Fulham, gets his bad reputation back with an elaborate fall in the area. Tévez clearly fancies the chance of completing his hat-trick. Saha clearly fancies a confidence boost. But Ronaldo shrugs off both their claims and, after a trademark stutter, finds the bottom corner. Rooney congratulates him by slapping him on the cheek – lucky he didn't do that a year ago, the papers would have had field day.

And the good news doesn't stop when the final whistle blows. First Liverpool lose 3–1 at Reading. Then City go the same way as Ricky Hatton in Vegas. And finally Arsenal get turned over at Boro. That's right, the Invincibles, the bestest team in the world, ever, are beatable after all.

Views from the broadsheets

☉ 'The rain showed no sign of abating, the water rose hour by hour, 'til the only dry land was at Blackpool, and that was on top of the tower. No, not really.' – *The Observer* comes close to losing the plot…

☉ 'Derby were lucky. Their experience at the Theatre of Dreams was a wet one. They might have come up against Manchester United on a dry day in August, or in an exhibition game in January in Saudi Arabia. It is easy to understand why United go on such jaunts when you see the sort of weather they have to put up with at home, but though the conditions kept the score down, the home side's effort and application could not be faulted.' …but recovers to make a good point about the weather.

☉ 'Bottom of the League, battered and beleaguered, with the chilly fingers of relegation already closing round their throats, it says everything about Derby County's predicament that their overwhelming feeling after sieving four goals to Manchester United was not embarrassment, or foreboding, but relief that it had not been even worse.' – *The Guardian* explains why Derby were 25/1 to win this two-horse race.

☉ 'People do strange things when they are in shock and Derby's supporters celebrated as though it [Howard's goal] were a last-minute winner. It was a peculiar moment, watching 3,000 people writhing around in raucous glee when, in reality, Goliath was giving David a good pummelling. And the thought occurred: what will it be like when Derby actually win a game?' – *The Independent* reports on the strangest sight of the day.

Derby – the verbals

☉ 'We are Derby, we are crap' – Derby fans, singing near the rain.

☉ 'We've got it out of the way. We haven't been too humiliated. I thought we were OK for half-an-hour.' – With standards like that, it's no wonder Paul Jewell's managerial record against United stands at no wins, no draws, eight defeats (with a goal difference of –21).

✪ 'It would have been a bonus had we got anything here. Like a corner. But we didn't throw in the towel and we scored a goal. I think there'll be a public holiday in Derby now.' – Incredibly, Jewell manages to leaves the scene of his latest humiliation with the aura of a winner.

✪ 'I was surprised there was no announcement. Maybe no one knew but I certainly did. It's a fantastic achievement, absolutely marvellous.' – Fergie raves about Giggs and chastises cheesy Alan Keegan.

✪ 'He will be appreciated more when he's retired. He's respected a lot more in foreign countries than in this country. It's a shame we're not appreciating a player who's been the most successful footballer of our generation, probably.' – Rio Ferdinand is understandably outraged by the lack of recognition Giggs gets when the greats of the modern game are discussed. All of the Giggsy-grumblers at Old Trafford and beyond won't know what they've had till he's gone.

Match facts

United: Van der Sar; Brown, Ferdinand (O'Shea 71), Vidic, Evra, Ronaldo, Carrick, Anderton (Fletcher 62), Giggs (Saha 64), Rooney, Tévez

Derby: Bywater, Griffin*, Moore, Davis*, McEveley (Howard 46), Leacock, Oakley, Fagan (Mears 46), Barnes (Teale 61), Pearson, Miller [Jewell]

FAPL 15.00. Att: 75,725. Ref: C. Foy. Half-time 2–0

*Yellow card

Other scores

Middlesbrough 2 (Downing pen, Tuncay) The Invincibles 1 (Rosicky); Chelsea 2 (Shevchenko, Lampard pen) Sunderland 0; Reading 3 (Hunt pen, Doyle, Harper) Liverpool 1 (Gerrard); Spurs 2 (Defoe) City 1 (Bianchi); Hatton k'o'd by Mayweather in 10.

League table

1. Arsenal 37 (16) 2. United 36 (16) 3. Chelsea 34 (16) 4. Liverpool 30 (15)...20. Derby 6 (16)

Derby to Roma

'We're not as good as we think we are. We need to go out there and prove that.'

News and gossip

Sporting Lisbon declare Queiroz 'persona non grata' after he confirms that United are tracking midfielder Miguel Veloso. Giggsy receives his OBE from the Queen. City fan Ricky Hatton is outclassed by Floyd Mayweather. The rumour-mill links United with Valencia forward David Villa, Villa's Agbonlahor, Ronaldinho (don't hold your breath) and Bayern right-back Willy Sagnol.

Fighting Lisbon

- ⚽ 'The scouting department is everywhere, and it would be ridiculous to say that good players are not referenced. Veloso, Moutinho, Quaresma, Bruno Alves, Bosingwa – all have been watched by us. Do we want to get these players? Of course, everyone does; however, we can not work with 200 players!' – Queiroz unwittingly sparks a civil war.

- ⚽ 'I can only regret Queiroz's declaration about Veloso. Queiroz made unacceptable insinuations.' – Bish. Sporting president Filipe Soares Franco lands the first blow.

- ⚽ 'The club president is just trying to deflect away criticism of his team after we beat them.' – Bash. Carlos counters with a low one.

- ⚽ 'We are the major Portuguese sporting strength, and Carlos Queiroz is now persona non grata at Sporting. People have the right to express themselves, but he did too much and attacked chairman Filipe Soares Franco. The club do not want to waste time on this person.' – Bosh. Sporting hit back.

- ⚽ 'The Sporting President accused me of trying to approach a player [Veloso] illegally and having a low moral and ethical code. His declarations must be clarified and investigated as it's the first time that a president of another club visits Manchester and publicly accuses a member of the club hierarchy of trying to illegally approach a player.' – Carlos goes toe to toe.

- ⚽ 'It is unfortunate the president has said this and it is more unfortunate that he has chosen Carlos as his target. Carlos is not in the field of doing these things. His behaviour is impeccable and I feel the president should retract his comments.' – Fergie backs his man up…

- ⚽ 'We have never been interested in Veloso at any stage. He is not what we need. We have six midfield players so why should we be interested? Why should we bother about tapping a player we are not interested in?'…and then makes what's known as a Freudian slip.

Every loser wins

Steve McClaren may have failed spectacularly in his job but he did at least end the year with a trophy, picking up the Plain English Campaign's 'Foot in Mouth Award' for these trophy-winning quotes:

- ⚽ 'Wayne Rooney is inexperienced, but he's experienced in terms of what he's been through.'

- ⚽ 'We're not as good as we think we are. We need to go out there and prove that.'

- ⚽ 'It was a no-win situation for everyone. We knew we had to win, and we did.'

Previous winning entries for the 'Foot in Mouth Award' include:

☺ 'I love England, especially the food. There's nothing I like more than a lovely bowl of pasta.' – Naomi Campbell, 2006.

☺ 'I could not fail to disagree with you less.' – Boris Johnson, 2004.

☺ 'Reports that say that something hasn't happened are always interesting to me, because as we know, there are known knowns; there are things we know we know. We also know there are known unknowns; that is to say we know there are some things we do not know. But there are also unknown unknowns — the ones we don't know we don't know.' – US Secretary of Defense, Donald Rumsfield, 2003.

☺ 'I know who I am. No one else knows who I am. If I was a giraffe and somebody said I was a snake, I'd think "No, actually I am a giraffe."' – Richard Gere, 2002.

Bonjour la!

A nice Scouse mickey-take from *The Guardian* on the eve of Liverpool's Champions League decider in Marseille:

'In their determination to prove that their idols will never walk anywhere alone, Liverpool fans have often gone to great lengths. Some of them have even been known to go so far as to buy tickets from licensed vendors. Others traditionally nab blags from shifty scallies, then blame the ensuing anarchy on bad policing, which is a lot like lumberjacks slagging off trees for failing to elaborate an effective strategy for dealing with axes.

'What they have never done – until now, according to reports in France ahead of tomorrow's Big Cup clash with Marseille – is knock up 1,000 counterfeit stewards' bibs in the hope of sneaking, clad in these fluorescent fakes, into their team's most high-profile match of the season before cunningly fobbing off any inquiries with high-pitched cries of "bonjour la!".'

I love it when a stereotype comes together Part II…

While Liverpool were winning in Marseille, burglars were breaking into Steven Gerrard's home in Formby. Bizarrely, it was the sixth time in just 18 months that a Liverpool player had been targeted by burglars while he was playing away. Is that why Benitez is so obsessed with squad rotation?

Roma 1 United 1 12/12/2007

Pique 34, Mancini 71

Once again a match between an English side and a Roman one is overshadowed by events off the pitch (not that this dead rubber took much overshadowing). And still there are no signs of UEFA throwing Roma, and their knife-happy fans, out of Europe. Perhaps the authorities thought that 'British hooligans' had stabbed themselves outside the Stadio Olympico again...

The moments that mattered (not a lot)

34 (1–0): The last time Fergie put his trust in the kids, they lost at home to Coventry. So there was a definite sense of foreboding as United took to the field with their least experienced defence for years. As it turned out, there was no need to worry. For an hour United were more controlled and fluent than a half-interested Roma. And they fully deserved the lead given them by Pique's thumping header from Nani's left-flank corner...

71 (1–1): ...but Roma were a different team once Vucinic, who had scored the winner in United's previous visit to Rome, came on. And it was only a matter of time before they equalised, Mancini stepping inside Brown and curling an excellent shot past Kuszczak.

Most predictable news of the night

United's return to Rome is scarred by violence, with five Reds stabbed and six more arrested after skirmishes with Roma's Ultras before the game. It wasn't all bad news though. At least the police didn't join in as much this time.

View from the pressbox

'On a night when AS Roma's supporters should have hung their heads in shame again, at least Manchester United's youngsters could hold theirs high. The violence that marred the previous meeting between the teams at the Olympic Stadium eight months ago resurfaced before kick-off, but for all Sir Alex Ferguson's dismay at a situation he had hoped would be averted, the manager's overwhelming feeling was one of pride at the impressive manner in which his emerging players acquitted themselves.' – The man from *The Times* is impressed. Are the kids alright after all?

Roma – the verbals

- ✪ 'We gave the ball away too often in the second half and you can't do that in Europe. You have to be more careful and the youngsters have learned that tonight. They have shown, though, that they have the temperament and the ability to play for us, however.' – Fergie puts the Coventry game to bed.
- ✪ 'These people are sick.' Roma coach Spalletti condemns the violence...
- ✪ 'There's little to say. I am disappointed that incidents have happened again. But this is a common phenomenon in football and does not only involve Roma.' ...But the shameless Roma MD Rosella Sensi still refuses to admit that her club's hooligans are any worse than any others.
- ✪ 'Roma should be banned from these competitions. They should not be allowed to enter from the start because the authorities are not able to look after the people who come to their city to watch football.' – Councillor McLuckie, chairman of Cleveland Police Authority, gets it spot on.

Rant of the night

Forget Istanbul, Moscow or Kracow. Rome now has a rock-solid case for being named the hooligan capital of Europe. The last four visits by English sides have resulted in an alarming number of fans spending time in local hospitals. Aggro at Serie A games is commonplace, there was a riot when that Lazio fan was killed by the police. Crossing the Pont Duca D'Aosta bridge is an open invitation for a be-scarved mummy's-boy to stab you in the buttocks. So what do UEFA do? Ban Roma from Europe? Make them play behind closed doors? Rename hooliganism the 'Italian disease'?

Do they hell. They give the Olympic Stadium the Champions League Final for 2009. If the same people had been in charge 20 years ago, Juve fans would have been blamed for Heysel...and the 1986 Final would have been played at Anfield.

Match facts

Roma: Doni, Cicinho, Ferrari, Mexes, Barusso* (Giuly 62), Antunes, Pizarro, Esposito (Vucinic 62), Taddei (De Rossi 46), Mancini, Totti [Spalletti]

United: Kuszczak, Simpson, Pique, Evans, O'Shea (Brown 54), Eagles, Fletcher, Carrick, Nani, Saha, Rooney (Dong 71)

CLGS 19.45 (Sky1) Stadio Olympico. Att: 30,000. Ref: M.Hansson (Swe). Half-time 1–0
*Yellow card

Other scores

Sporting Lisbon 3 Kiev 0; Arsenal 2 Steaua Bucharest 1; Chelsea 0 Valencia 0; Marseille 0 Liverpool 4

Final Standings:
Group F: 1. United 16 pts 2. Roma 11 3. Sporting 7 4. Dinamo Kiev 0
Group A: 1. Porto 11 2. Liverpool 10 3. Marseille 7 4. Besiktas 6
Group B: 1. Chelsea 12 2. Schalke 8 3. Rosenborg 7 4. Valencia 5
Group C: 1. Real Madrid 11 2. Olympiakos 11 3. Werder Bremen 6 4. Lazio 5
Group D: 1. Milan 13 2. Celtic 9 3. Benfica 7 4. Shakhtar Donetsk 6
Group E: 1. Barcelona 14 2. Lyon 10 3. Rangers 7 4. Stuttgart 3
Group G: 1. Inter 15 2. Fenerbahce 11 3. PSV 7 4. Spartak Moscow 1
Group H: 1. Sevilla 15 2. Arsenal 13 3. Slavia Prague 5 4. Steaua Bucharest 1

Roma to Liverpool
'You must be f***ing joking. I'm not a sadist!'

News
Fergie gets a two-match touchline ban for abusing Mark Clattenburg at Bolton. He's also fined £5,000. Fabio Capello is named as the new England manager. Bizarrely, the FA agree to pay him £6.5 million a year – £2.5 million more than even Sven got. United kids beat Brighton 2–1 in the FA Youth Cup.

Warming up for Anfield
- 'You must be f***ing joking. I'm not a sadist!' – Fergie struggles to choke back the vomit after being asked if he would like to see Liverpool win the League.
- 'How does relegation sound? Bloody hell.' – Fergie still can't believe he's been asked such a ridiculous question.
- 'I still enjoy beating Liverpool more than any other club, that's for sure.' – Fergie warms to the theme...
- 'In terms of success, winning the League is without question the barometer of our game. We have won the FA Cup more times than anyone, and you get a certain pride in that. Liverpool have won the title more times than anyone, and they'll be proud of that. I hope, before I leave, we can get to that position.' ...and gives a hint of what drives him on (there are just three to go).

Non-Fergie Quotes of the week
- 'If Steve McClaren said to me the grass is green, I would go out and check. He can be charming, but he had this streak of ambition that was absolutely bloody ruthless, and you can't go through life always trying to achieve your ambitions at the expense of others.' – Boro chairman Steve Gibson kicks a man when he's down.
- 'I have, somewhat bizarrely, played more training sessions with England at left-back

than in goal.' – West Ham 'keeper Robert Green gives a hint of what McClaren was doing wrong.

☺ 'You've got to pay the going rate.' – Trevor Brooking tries, and fails, to justify Don Capello's enormous salary. The second highest-paid manager in international football is Guus Hiddink on approximately £2 million a year.

☺ 'I am, like all Italian fans, proud to see the country who is the mother of football resort to an Italian coach. It means Italy is number one, both at international and club level. I discovered him as a coach so it's no mystery that I think very highly of him.' – Silvio Berlusconi gives himself a standing ovation after giving English football a kick in the ribs.

Number of the week

£20 million – what *The Independent* reckons Fergie could lose on the Rock of Gibraltar over the next decade. When the row over the ownership of the horse was settled, Fergie opted for a one-off payout of £2.5 million. But if he'd taken Magnier's offer of four stud nominations a year he could potentially have pocketed £2 million a year.

Memo to Frankie

The Mirror reports on an interesting idea from Austria:

'Austria coach Josef Hickersberger's team is so bad their fans want them to pull out of Euro 2008 to stop them bringing shame on the country. Fans have launched an internet petition on the website *www.rueckgrat.cc* which has collected 20,000 names asking for the co-host nation of next year's European Championship not to play in the tournament.

'Organiser Michael Kriess insisted that playing in Euro 2008 would be "an insult" to the whole country as their team has slipped to 88th in the FIFA rankings, and the website says the team leaves every fan "depressed". The campaign is entitled Osterreich zeigt Ruckgrat – Austria Shows Backbone – and its catchphrase is: "Let's Not Embarrass Ourselves".'

Sounds like something that could catch on at Eastlands.

Liverpool 0 United 1   16/12/2007

Tévez 43

Some day United will go to Anfield and give them an absolute spanking – the sort of humiliation that will send the locals scurrying back down their rat holes for good. Some day Scousers will go to a United match and not throw burgers, phones or (this year's choice) golf balls at Neville or Rooney. Some day someone will explain how the Premier League can fix Grand Slam Sundays for Sky but can't give any help to the clubs when they need it (who thought it would be a good idea for United to play City on the Munich anniversary?). Or how Liverpool got the City of Culture gig. But until that day, we'll all happily take more afternoons like this. To paraphrase Fergie's classic quote from the days of Calamity James, it's great to see empty seats at Anfield at lunchtime.

The formula for this year's Anfield win was the same as it's been for years. Keep it tight at the back. Watch out for Gerrard – and, this year, Torres. Take any chances that do come. And once you're ahead, get something in the way of Liverpool's barrage of hopeful long balls and even more hopeful long-range shots. As usual, Benitez argued afterwards that Liverpool controlled the game and were unlucky to lose. But while he had a case last year when United more or less got away with daylight robbery, he didn't this. United didn't create many chances to add to Tévez's close-range opener. But against this Liverpool team, who only looked like scoring when Van der Sar lost his bearings, one goal was always going to be enough.

The moments that mattered
VAN DER SAR – DUDEK MOMENTS! (27 and 30): Liverpool only come close to scoring twice, and both times Van der Sar creates the chance. First he comes for a Gerrard corner, collides with his defenders and is rescued, first, by Anderson's clearance and, then, by Torres's headed miss. Then he comes for a Gerrard free-kick, runs straight into Ferdinand and is rescued by Evra, who reacts faster than Kuyt as the ball bounces towards the empty goal.

TÉVEZ! GOAL! (43): Giggs takes a corner from the right at the Kop end, rolls the ball to the unmarked Rooney at the edge of the box and his low first-timer is converted from close range by the unmarked Tévez. It's a well worked goal from United's point of view. It's a terrible one from Liverpool's. Though it's not the first time that Benitez's flawed zonal marking system has gifted United a goal. I reckon six of the eight goals United have put past Liverpool since he arrived have come from set plays.

ROONEY – MISS! (78): Rooney misses a glorious chance to finish the match, shanking the ball wide under no pressure after Ronaldo's break and cross from the left.

Views from the broadsheets

- ☉ '[Benitez said] this result was hard on Liverpool. It was not an argument even the most rabid Koppite would try to make. While United were impeccable at the back, especially Rio Ferdinand and Nemanja Vidic, and solid in midfield with Owen Hargreaves and Anderson, Liverpool simply lacked a viable plan to win the match.'
  – *The Independent*
- ☉ 'Carlos Tévez's decisive goal was, in the words of the Liverpool manager, a "lucky" goal that United would only have been able to pull off "once in a hundred times". But even a Texan multi-millionaire with a background in baseball would have been able to spot the flaws in that argument. As the home crowd found it harder to contain their groans and complaints, the painful truth was taking shape that United look a lot further ahead of Liverpool than the nine-point gap that separates them in the Premier League.'
  – *The Independent*
- ☉ 'Accents have changed in the corridors of power at Anfield but its anguish sounds the same. On Saturday Alex Hicks, son of the Texan millionaire and Liverpool co-chairman, Tom, proposed to his girlfriend Portia Tuma [yes, really] when he reached the centre circle during a private tour of the stadium. Twenty-four hours later Liverpool's players were also on their knees posing serious questions, none of them related to love.' – *The Guardian*

Image of the day

'The middle-aged men were standing and screaming at each misplaced pass and referring decision, their faces contorted by the frustration of seeing the game drain away. It was the sight and sound of history repeating.' – *The Telegraph*

Liverpool – the verbals

- ☉ 'I think we were in control but did not create much. We had enough chances and it is important to score first and they did.' – Benitez. Are you sure man?
- ☉ 'A marvellous day for us. In terms of playing football, we were the better team.' – Fergie.
- ☉ 'We are not lucky and they were lucky' – Benitez again. Does he really believe this rubbish?

Numbers of the day

0 – the number of Liverpool players who have scored League goals against United under Benitez (O'Shea scored an own-goal in 2004).

4 – the number of successive clean sheets United have kept at Anfield, equalling Everton's 97-year record.

9 – how many points Liverpool ('it's our year you know') find themselves behind United.

10 – how many points Liverpool ('it's our year you know') find themselves behind the leaders, Arsenal.

50 – the number of times Fergie has managed United against Liverpool. His record now stands at 23 wins, 13 draws and 14 defeats.

Match facts

Liverpool: Reina, Arbeloa, Hyypia, Carragher, Riise (Aurelio 80), Benayoun, Gerrard*, Mascherano*, Kewell (Babel 65), Torres, Kuyt (Crouch 73) [Benitez]
United: Van der Sar, Brown*, Ferdinand, Vidic, Evra*, Ronaldo, Hargreaves, Anderson* (O'Shea 90), Giggs, Rooney, Tévez (Carrick 83)
FAPL 13.30 (Sky) Anfield. Att: 44,459. Ref: M. Halsey. Half-time: 1–0
*Yellow card

Other scores

Arsenal 1 (Gallas) Chelsea 0, City 4 (og, Bianchi, Etuhu, Vassell) Bolton 2 (Diouf, Nolan)

League table

1. Arsenal 40 (17) 2. United 39 (17) 3. Chelsea 34 (17) 4. City 33 (17)…5. Liverpool 30 (16)

Liverpool to Everton
'I bet you two were naughty together at uni.'

News

Ronaldo comes third behind Kaka and Messi in the FIFA World Player of the Year awards. City get dumped out of the Carling Cup by 10-man Spurs at home. Incredibly, it's their 69th unsuccessful Cup campaign on the spin. And the United Christmas do in Castlefield gets horribly and spectacularly out of hand. Bystanders talk of roasting, groping, fighting and Van der Sar dancing. Much worse, one female partygoer (falsely) accuses Jonny Evans of rape.

Now what could possibly go wrong?

Famous footballers + £4,000 kitty each + 100 hand-picked 'glamour' girls + 18-hour session + a booked-out city-centre hotel…

Prediction of the week

'P***ed-up bird falls out with her boyfriend and allegedly f***s off upstairs with a player, only to cry rape when he later asks her where she's been? I tell you what. If that f***er ever comes to court then my cock's a carrot.' – *Red Issue's* Mr Spleen.

Front page headline of the week

'Fergie bans Xmas' – *The Daily Mirror*

Question of the week

What happened to going to a quiet boozer in Bowden or Hale?

Roasted

United players were given plenty of grief following the Christmas party. And rightly so. They play for United, the biggest club in the country, nay the world. And, like it or not, as soon as you sign for United, you agree to uphold the club's good name every minute of the day. But what was striking about the flak that flew in the press was how much of it was aimed at the girls at the party, the same girls who left crying how terrible it had been.

The Times's India Knight gets it just about right, labelling the WAG wannabes 'free prostitutes'.

Famous person alert

'I have nothing to say about the events of the week. Why would I say anything? Alex Ferguson has been dealing with situations like this for 21 years – and I know exactly what we do. I will not be guided or instructed by anyone.' – Oh no, Fergie's started talking about himself in the third party.

United 2 Everton 1

23/12/2007

Ronaldo 22, 88 (pen), Cahill 27

I first went to Old Trafford the day that Norman Whiteside scored his first-ever United goal. In all the years since, I've seen and heard a lot of things: I've seen Peter Schmeichel score a header. I've seen Miss Manchester United's swimsuit go see-through in the rain. I've seen Kiddo go berserk on the pitch. I've seen Giuliano Maiorana run rings round Lee Dixon. I've seen 32,000 watch Eric in the reserves. I've heard the tough guy next to me scream out after being hit by an object thrown by Leeds fans…and seen the sheepish look on his face when he realised he'd actually been struck by a mini pack of M&Ms. I've seen Ronaldo (the other one) get the ovation of a lifetime. I've seen Terry Gibson score his one and only goal. I've seen Van Basten, Gullit, Maldini, Zidane and Ralph Milne. I've seen Jose Mourinho sprinting down the touchline. I've seen Brian McClair score a hat-trick. I've seen Dennis Bailey do the same. I've heard a white-haired granny call Michael Owen a 'little c***'. I've seen Lee Sharpe do his Elvis impression. I've seen Martin Keown pull his monkey move on Ruud. I've listened to Alan Keegan, Tom Tyrell and Keith Fane. I've seen Michael Knighton juggle the ball in his kit. I've heard Posh and Scary Spice get booed. I've seen Wigan beat St Helens. And Eubank draw with Benn. I've seen Denis Irwin start a mass brawl. I've seen David Busst snap his leg. I've seen United win the League. I've seen Arsenal do the same. I've seen both Nevilles score. I've seen John Virgo, Christopher Eccleston and Ian Brown. I've heard the Stretford End tell Fergie to sign Prunier. I've seen Ronnie Whelan score for us from 40 yards. I've seen United score nine. But in all those years I had never seen United score a penalty to win a game right at the death.

Well, thanks to Stephen Pienaar, I have now…

Goal action

1–0 (22): Everton arrived at Old Trafford as the other in-form side in the division, having won 11 of their last 13. But there's 'in-form' and then there's the form Ronaldo is in at the moment. After an opening 20 minutes, memorable only for a series of ugly fouls, he cuts back onto his left side and sends in a 20-yarder that flicks off Carsley's toe and loops and curls past Howard.

1–1 (27): Everton get back into the game quickly, taking advantage of Simpson's nerves and Ferdinand's unexpected absence (see below) to score an annoyingly simple equaliser. Pienaar swings in a right-footer from the left and Cahill, who's superb in the air, wins his mismatch with Evra to beat Kuszczak.

2–1 (88): United dominate the rest of the match and play some decent stuff, but with Rooney and Tévez only turning it on in short bursts Everton don't really look like conceding again. But then Pienaar succumbs to a moment of madness, flicking out his back leg as Giggs meanders into the area. Giggs tumbles over, Webb points to the spot, Moyes sinks to his knees with his head in his hands and Ronaldo makes sure a bittersweet week for United ends on a high.

Views from the broadsheets

⊙ 'It was enough to spoil any Evertonian's Christmas. Even their best-laid plans could not take into account the madness of one man or, for that matter, the brilliant improvisation of Ronaldo whose two goals make it 16 for the season. Whether it is a late dramatic penalty to win the match or a fabulous curled goal in the first half, he retains the ability to dominate the key moments of games. The wink at the television cameras on full-time was the look of the man who knows that he is getting all the best lines at the moment.' – *The Independent*

⊙ 'Cristiano Ronaldo is becoming so accustomed to scoring decisive goals for Manchester United he has taken to celebrating with the kind of expression first patented by the Fonz in Happy Days. You know the look: a mixture of smug satisfaction and bristling Cantona-esque indifference. Ronaldo has it to a T, putting it into practice once again after his 15th and 16th goals of the season ensured the club that put the X into Xmas party ended a difficult week on a happy note.' – *The Guardian*

⊙ 'Until Manchester United told the television company responsible where to go, this match was to have been played at 8pm tonight and Steven Pienaar will be grateful for that. Pienaar is a committed Christian and to have spent the precious hours when Christmas Eve blurs into Christmas Day asking himself why he made the challenge that cost Everton this match would have been especially cruel.' – *The Telegraph*

Seeing ghosts

The broadsheets compete for the David Moyes analogy award:

⊙ 'As the referee Howard Webb reached for his whistle, David Moyes could be seen placing both hands over his eyes in the manner of a child entering a fairground ghost train.' – *The Guardian*

⊙ 'As the winning goal was dispatched, David Moyes looked like a man who had just been told a faulty Christmas light had burned his house down bent at the knees in agony, his head in his hands.' – *The Independent*

Personally, I reckon he looked more like Moe from the Simpsons…after Homer told him he'd given up the booze.

Carrying the can

The Guardian speculates:

'Was it coincidence that Ronaldo was the one player to miss the now infamous Christmas party? It probably mattered little, but it did add to the script of another perfect day for United's number seven, one in which the party organiser and serial bird-brain, Rio Ferdinand, was notable by his absence. United are famously economical with the truth when it comes to these matters but the official line was that nothing should be read into it and that Ferdinand simply had a gashed leg. True or not, Ferdinand made a point of his own – watching the match in the next seat to Jonny Evans, the 19-year-old who has been bailed by police over allegations of rape.'

Match facts

United: Kuszczak, Simpson (O'Shea 46), Brown, Vidic, Evra*, Ronaldo, Carrick (Saha 71), Anderson* (Fletcher 86), Giggs, Rooney*, Tévez

Everton: Howard, Hibbert*, Yobo, Jagielka, Lescott, Carsley, Cahill* (Anichebe 85), Neville, Pienaar*, Yakubu (Gravesen 76), Johnson [Moyes]

FAPL 12.00 (Set). Att: 75,749. Ref: H. Webb. Half-time: 1–1

*Yellow card

Other scores

Liverpool 4 (Torres 2, Benayoun, og) Portsmouth 1 (Benjani), Arsenal 2 (Adebayor, Bendtner) Spurs 1 (Berbatov), Blackburn 0 Chelsea 1 (J. Cole)

League table

1. Arsenal 43 (18) 2. United 42 (18) 3. Chelsea 37 (18) 4. City 34 (18)…6. Everton 30 (18)

Everton to Sunderland

'Everything's been so positive and smooth. Apart from, obviously, the season.'

News

United announce the surprise signing of Angola striker Manucho from Angolan side Petro Athletico on a three-year contract, subject to a work permit. On the face of it, it's the least exciting forward signing since Dong. After all, Manucho – real name Mateus Alberto Contreiras Goncalves – is 24 going on 25*, he's never played outside Angola and he's not even a regular in the Angolan national team. But Fergie and Carlos have been on a roll in the transfer market recently. And it wouldn't take long – six weeks and four African Cup of Nations games, in fact – for the Manucho deal to start looking like another bargain in the making…

On a roll

Fergie's buys since the Kleberson-Bellion-Djembas debacle of 2003:

2007 – Hargreaves, Nani, Tévez, Anderson, Manucho

2006 – Evra, Vidic, Carrick, Kuszczak

2005 – Van der Sar, Park, Foster

2004 – Dong Fangzhou, Saha, Rooney, Smith, Heinze

A goal machine

☺ 'He's a very quick, aggressive forward, a big lad about 6ft 2in. We've had him on trial for three weeks and he's done very well. We're delighted to have made an agreement with his football team.' – Fergie introduces his latest African signing. At least Manucho can't be worse than the last one. Can he?

☺ 'I have been a fan of Manchester United from when I was very young. I am very happy to be here and I have worked very hard to make my dream a reality. I have found the adaptation easy because all the players have given me their support…and players like Cristiano Ronaldo, Nani and Anderson all speak my language.' – Be careful what support those three pups offer you Manucho. No one wants to see grainy pictures of your bum splashed all over the News of the Screws.

Rumour of the week*

It is notoriously difficult to tell the exact age of African footballers. Kanu is rumoured to be heading for his mid-40s. Roger Milla was meant to be older than Nelson Mandela. And Manucho? Well, if you believe this quote from *Allafrica.com* (at a time when Nigeria were bidding for his services), he'll soon be challenging Billy Meredith as the oldest-ever outfield Red:

'The Nigerian coach, Augustine Eguavoen, called me a few times. He said he promised to have faith in me and to give me playing time, but there was some pressure from him and other members of the Nigerian FA for me to not be true about my age – 30 wasn't a very good age if I ever wanted to play in Europe. But I don't believe in lies so in the end the choice was made for me. God wanted me to play for Angola.'

Number of the week

£1 million – How much Fergie fined his players for the Christmas party debacle (according to the *News Of The World*).

Quote of the week

'Everything's been so positive and smooth. Apart from, obviously, the season.' – Excellent stuff from David Beckham. So his move to LA Galaxy has gone swimmingly, apart from all the pesky football.

Sunderland 0 United 4   26/12/2007

Rooney 20, Saha 30, 86 (pen), Ronaldo 45

Keano's magic, every Red knows that. But his team isn't, not yet anyway. If United hadn't come over all compassionate in the second half, Sunderland would have got the sort of treatment their boss used to dish out to Munich-spouting Blues. Even so, United still strolled to their second biggest win at Sunderland ever and their biggest win at a Stadium of Light (how did Sunderland have the nerve to call it that?) since El Beatle was born...

Goal action

1–0 (20): Keano's had £40 million available to spend on new players. And even his biggest fan would have to say he's spent it strangely. So far he's brought in an odd mix of ageing Treble winners, Championship journeymen and ex-United reserves. Two of the latter – McShane and Higginbotham – lined up in central-defence here, and they just had no answer to the pace and movement of United's front six. The first goal was all too easy. Brown slips a simple ball down the middle, Rooney races onto it and scores his first goal for two months.

2–0 (30): Game over. Rooney moves out to the left, shifts the ball on to his right foot and delivers towards Saha who gratefully ends his own drought, which stretched back to Chelsea in September, by guiding a smart volley past Gordon.

3–0 (45): Yorke fouls Fletcher just outside the 18-yard box and slightly to the right. Ronaldo steps back and does something amazing from a free-kick. Again.

4–0 (86): United clock off for most of the second half, but they do manage a late fourth, Saha – yes, he made it through an entire game – scoring from the spot after Collins brings down Nani.

Views from the broadsheets

⚽ 'When asked what advice he would give him now he was a manager, Sir Alex Ferguson replied that Roy Keane should get used to losing. But he would not be used to losing like this, with his opponents using the final 45 minutes as a training exercise. He has been beaten before, he has been relegated before, but Keane has rarely been humiliated like this.' – *The Telegraph*

☻ 'Sir Alex Ferguson does not really do sympathy but there seemed a look of genuine concern in the Manchester United manager's eyes as he put an arm around Roy Keane at the final whistle. With the visiting fans, somewhat insensitively, chorusing "Keano, Keano, give us a wave" Ferguson treated United's former captain to, by his brusque standards, a warm embrace.' – *The Guardian*

☻ 'There were times when Manchester United's superiority over Sunderland made the neutral wince, so God only knows how Keane felt as he stood, arms folded, on the touchline.' – *The Independent*

Quote of the day
'We were outclassed, it was a harsh lesson, and it's not a very nice feeling. We're in a sticky patch.' – Keano.

Roker four
This was only the third time United had scored four times at Sunderland. The others were:

Sunderland 2 United 4 – 30 Nov 1929

Steward, Moore, Dale, Hilditch, Taylor, Wilson, Spence (2), Hanson (1), Ball (1), Rowley, Thomas

Sunderland 1 United 5 – 11 Nov 1981

Bailey, Gidman, Moran (1), Buchan, Albiston, Coppell, Robson (1), Wilkins, Moses, Stapleton (2), Birtles (1)

Match facts
Sunderland: Gordon, Whitehead*, McShane*, Higginbotham, Collins, Chopra (O'Donovan 86) Yorke (Richardson 61), Etuhu, Wallace (Leadbitter half-time), Jones, Waghorn [Keane]
United: Kuszcak, Brown, Ferdinand, Vidic (Pique 74), O'Shea, Ronaldo (Park 58), Fletcher*, Carrick, Nani, Rooney, Saha
FAPL 15.00 Stadium of Light. Att: 47,360. Ref: U. Rennie. Half-time: 0–3
*Yellow card

Other scores
Chelsea 4 (Shevchenko 2, Alex, Ballack) Aston Villa (Maloney 2, Laursen, Barry); Portsmouth 0 Arsenal 0; Derby 1 (McEveley) Liverpool 2 (Gerrard, Torres)

League table
1. United 45 (19) 2. Arsenal 44 (19) 3. Chelsea 38 (19) 4. Liverpool 36 (18)… 19. Sunderland 14 (19)

Sunderland to West Ham

'When it comes to Alex Ferguson I just want to thank the Lord.'

News

Joey Barton will spend New Year's in prison (insert your own 'with the family' line here) after being arrested for assaulting late-night burger eaters outside a Liverpool city-centre McDonalds. The four United fans jailed for their part in a fight with Roma fans in December are to remain in prison in Italy while they wait for their appeal hearing. United reserve Adam Eckersley doesn't get sent to prison, but he does get sent to Division Two no-hopers Port Vale on loan, which, in football terms, might just feel like the same thing.

Higher power

Football365.com pounces on the Barton news, reflecting on the recent interview that Saint Joseph did with the BBC:

Among other things, Joey revealed a hitherto unknown theological bent, claiming that no mortal on this earth could pass judgement on him:

'I don't think I'll ever be judged on this earth,' he said.

Well, we think the Liverpool Magistrates court might want a say, but go on Joey...

'Whatever higher power it is, when you finally meet him you've got to answer for every decision you've made. I believe I can stand in front of my maker and say, "Yeah, I did this for this reason, that for this reason."'

Hmmm. Hate to break this to you Joey, but we reckon you've got some explaining to do at the pearly gates.

Quotes of the week

- 'People want to keep beating me with a big stick that I'm a bad boy. I'm not a bad boy. People who know me, whose opinions I respect, know what kind of person I am.' – Let's think about that Joey: you're due in court in the summer for beating up your teammate Ousmane Dabo, you've tried to put out a cigar in the eye of City youth-teamer James Tandy, you've gotten involved with a 15-year-old Everton fan in Thailand, you bit Richard Dunne when he tried to intervene – it's not looking good is it?

- 'The CCTV clearly shows Mr Barton involved in altercations with members of the public going about their business. He was seen pacing around Church Street and lashing out indiscriminately at people walking around and standing around.' – A picture of a charming man. By the CPS's Jayne Hughes,

☺ 'I am moving to London and I'm going to play for Man Utd. I can say 90 per cent has been done but it's left with a little.' – Something tells me Ramsford Osei, Ghana's top goalscorer in the 2007 Under-17 World Cup, hasn't been doing his homework.

Chase me, chase me

Ayr United midfielder – and former Chelsea youth-teamer – Ryan Stevenson tells *The Daily Record* about life with John Terry. And it seems that the serial referee-botherer has got a homo-erotic side:

'He was crazy, a livewire. I can't forget my introduction to the Chelsea dressing room in my first pre-season when I arrived back from training knackered and went for a shower. The YTS dressing rooms were small, with only five of six us changing together. Sure enough, the rest of the lads then burst through the door with John leading the charge, whipped off my towel and battered me with their flip-flops.'

Silly top-100 list

The list ranks Gary Neville as the 86th greatest player and manages to leave out Best, Law and Cantona. The Association of Football Statisticians (boy, you can imagine a night out with them) gave points for goals scored by forwards and clean sheets for defenders, for every Cup won, for being captain and also for the level they played at.

Top 10: Pele, Ronaldo, Romario, Figo, Zidane, Maradona, Mattheus, Muller, Beckenbauer, Cafu.

And here come the Reds:
23 Charlton, 36 Schmeichel, 44 Beckham, 62 Giggs, 67 Blanc, 86 G. Neville, 89 Scholes, 91 Robson, 92 Keane, 94 Larsson, 98 Van der Sar.

Quote of the week

'When it comes to Alex Ferguson I just want to thank the Lord. Whatever may happen in the future, I have been trained by Alex Ferguson.' – Paddy Evra wins the brown-noser of the year award.

West Ham 2 United 1   29/12/2007

Ronaldo 14, A. Ferdinand 77, Upson 82

Watching Alan Curbishley stand in front of the media, it's hard to believe that he could ever inspire a team of multi-millionaire footballers. He carries the air of someone who is well acquainted with disappointment – the sort of bloke who expects to get hit every time a pigeon empties its bowels. His interviews are usually laced with whines, excuses and more whines, and his default expression (a sort of Hoddlesque squinting scowl) makes him look like a Scouser trying to pass gallstones.

But there is more to Curbishley – and his teams – than moans and excuses. On their day they can be tough opponents. Unfortunately for United, this was one of those days. West Ham were in their faces right from the start, they hassled and harried the superstars into anonymity and then their six-footers punished United's previously unseen fallibility in the air. United should have won the game – if Ronaldo had scored his penalty, there would surely have been no way back – but no one, not even in the away dugout, could argue that West Ham deserved the points.

Match action

1–0 (14): United didn't play well all afternoon. In fact, they played like they'd spent the time since Sunderland overdoing the sprouts and sherry, but they did break out of their lethargy long enough to score a classy breakaway goal. Tévez finds the sprinting Saha, Saha finds the sprinting Giggs, and his precision cross from the left finds Ronaldo's head.

2–0 (66): Ronaldo confidently strokes home his penalty after Spector handles in the area. Hang on a minute, he's put it wide. Still, it shouldn't matter. United only have to deal with the hopeful crosses coming into the area and they'll be OK. Hang on another minute…

1–1 (77): Noble's corner-kick from the right is headed in powerfully by Anton Ferdinand.

2–1 (82): Noble's free-kick is headed in, with a sense of inevitability, by the bearded Upson. When was the last time someone with a beard scored against United? Actually, when was the last time someone with a beard – a proper beard, Gary – scored for United? Was it Birtles? I don't know. What I do know is that this is the sort of game Chelsea would never have lost. That United had thrown away three points on a day when both their rivals would win.

What was good?

✪ The warm reception the West Ham fans gave Tévez.

What was bad?

✪ The warm reception the West Ham fans gave Tévez. It turned a lion into a pussycat.

Views from the broadsheets

✪ 'Who needs Carlos Tévez? It's as though the sight of their returning hero yesterday was all the Hammers needed to rekindle some of that Argentine fire from last season when they did the double over United. The two goals in the last 13 minutes with which they won the match – both headers from set-pieces by Anton Ferdinand and Matthew Upson – may not have been in the Cristiano Ronaldo class, but they were too good for a United side who were well below their best and without Wayne Rooney, not that that should be seen as an excuse.' – *The Telegraph* (by the way, why can't we use injuries as an excuse? Everyone else does.)

✪ 'It is there for all to see because while Rio Ferdinand and Nemanja Vidic are fine players, they do not dominate set-pieces, and you badly need strong, commanding centre-halves in those situations to get things sorted out, to get up, attack the ball and clear the danger.' – Don Howe overreacts to the two West Ham goals in *The Telegraph*. I know he had an off day here, but Vidic not strong and commanding? Are you sure Don? He'd skin his nan if it meant winning a header.

West Ham – the verbals

✪ 'If we'd scored our penalty it would have killed the game. I couldn't see it happening I must say, but if you're losing goals from set-pieces you're not at your best. They are a very competitive team, West Ham. They were always about us, tackling everywhere.' – Fergie thinks West Ham have been obscene again.

✪ 'I had 16 fit players today and I've now got 14. There's a walk to this room with pictures of the current squad on it, I think I've got a wall and a half out injured. At the end I've got a right-back playing wide right and a left-back playing wide left, everybody else is mucking in. I think it's just a fantastic result for us.' – Curbishley even whines when he's winning.

Don Howe stat of the day

Fifty-five per cent of the goals United have conceded in the Premier League have been headers. And 73 per cent of the goals conceded have come from crosses (the average is just 36 per cent). Both figures are the highest in the division.

Match facts

West Ham: Green, Neill, Spector, Upson, McCartney, Solano (Pantsil* 49), Parker (Ferdinand 55), Mullins*, Noble, Ljungberg (Ashton 70), Cole [Curbishley]

United: Kuszczak, Brown (O'Shea 89), Ferdinand, Vidic, Evra, Ronaldo, Hargreaves (Nani 80), Fletcher, Giggs, Saha, Tévez (Anderson 64)

FAPL 15.00 Upton Park. Att: 34,966. Ref: M. Dean. Half-time: 0–1

*Yellow card

Other scores

Everton 1 (Cahill) Arsenal 4 (Eduardo 2, Adebayor, Rosicky); Chelsea 2 (Essien, Kalou) Newcastle 1 (Butt); City 0 Liverpool 0

League table

1. Arsenal 47 (20) 2. United 45 (20) 3. Chelsea 41 (20) 4, Liverpool 37 (19)…10. West Ham 29 (19)

West Ham to Birmingham

'Technically he is the worst player I have ever seen in my life – and he knows it.'

Do you reckon Nani and Anderson have moved out?

'Soccer ace Cristiano Ronaldo is hooked on a new game – the grannies' favourite, BINGO. But Manchester United fans won't find the wing wizard shouting "House" down the local bingo hall. Instead the 22-year-old plays at home after being given a DVD version as a Christmas present.' – *The Daily Star*

Pass the remote

Rio's setting up a Rap Idol fundraising competition with a 'stack of celebrities' including Jordan, Chris Moyles, John Barnes, Shane Richie and Coleen McLoughlin. And you thought his *World Cup Wind-Ups* show was a bad idea.

Spare a thought for Parky

'If the fans sing your name then you should be happy, but the song they sing about me at the moment has some very strong words. It mentions killing people and maybe that is because of the country I am from and what happened there in the past.' – Nemanja doesn't like his song.

Fact of the week

Colleen is now reportedly earning more than Wayne. Mad isn't it?

Quote of the week

'Technically he is the worst player I have ever seen in my life – and he knows it. He has no skill at all. We all have more skill than him.' – Benni McCarthy on Robbie Savage.

Remember them?

Red Issue brings us an amusing insight into life at Elland Road:

'You sad bastards: Leeds United's match programme refuses to acknowledge their 15-point deduction and thus prints its Third Division table with Leeds at the top. You wouldn't be surprised if they started listing themselves as 1975 European Champions at this rate.'

United 1 Birmingham 0   01/01/2008

Tévez 25

If Fergie hadn't opened his mouth afterwards, this would have been filed away as one of those non-event games that you're just happy to win. Unfortunately Fergie did open his mouth and then stuck both feet right in it. He used to be able to get away with having a go at the fans for being quiet. After all, he was normally right. We do have an important role to play in lifting the team, and we're often guilty of turning up on matchday and just waiting to be entertained. But times have changed at Old Trafford. This time, Fergie's comments were met with genuine anger rather than resolve or indifference. If anyone was looking for confirmation of how badly Fergie had trashed his relationship with the fans in the four years since the Rock of Gibraltar affair, this was it...

Quote of the day
'The crowd were dead. That was the quietest I've heard them here. It was like a funeral it was so quiet.' – Has Fergie never been to Old Trafford on New Year's Day before?

The moment that mattered
TÉVEZ! GOAL! (25):
Alex McLeish summed up the game brilliantly by likening it to a 'water pistol against a machine gun'. But he wasn't anywhere near as accurate when he claimed that his Birmingham side had created 'as many opportunities as I've seen a team have against United for a long time'. Of course you worry that something freakish is going to happen when it's only 1–0, but in truth United were really comfortable winners. And the goal itself was good enough to win any game, even if it would be unfairly overshadowed by the bizarre celebration that followed it.

Fergie called the goal 'fantastic, absolutely superb', and this time he picked his words just right. Carrick fires a low ball at Tévez, who plays in Ronaldo – and takes out two Birmingham defenders – with a deft flick over his head. Ronaldo takes two touches to control and then, just as the move looks like stalling, sends Tévez racing clear with a brilliant backheel. Tévez bulldozes his way into the area, rolls the ball inside the far post and, after rummaging in his shorts, pulls out a dummy and sticks it in his mouth – a tribute, apparently, to his young daughter, Florencia.

View from the broadsheets

☻ 'In a season which has already revealed the colour of Stephen Ireland's Superman underpants, Manchester has come to expect some originality in its goal celebrations. Carlos Tévez opted for a pink dummy, whipped from his shorts and placed in his mouth after he had scored the goal which restored some order for Manchester United. For pure impact value, hardly in the same League as dropping your shorts but a welcome shaft of colour on an afternoon which even Sir Alex Ferguson said he had found funereal.' – *The Independent*

Match facts

United: Kuszczak, O'Shea, Ferdinand, Vidic, Evra (Brown* 84), Ronaldo, Anderson, Carrick, Nani, Park (Hargreaves 75), Tévez (Saha 71)
Birmingham: Maik Taylor, Kelly, Jaidi, Ridgewell*, Queudrue*, McSheffrey (De Ridder 67), Nafti* (Palacios* 81), Muamba, Larsson, Jerome (Forssell 67), O'Connor [McLeish]
FAPL 15.00. Att: 75,459. Ref: P. Walton. Half-time: 1–0
*Yellow card

Other scores

Arsenal 2 (Eduardo, Adebayor) West Ham 0; Fulham 1 (Murphy pen) Chelsea 2 (Kalou, Ballack pen)

League table

1. Arsenal 50 (21) 2. United 48 (21) 3. Chelsea 44 (21) 4. Liverpool 37 (19)…15. Birmingham 19 (21)

Birmingham to Villa

'The only atmosphere we've got is one where we're a little bit frightened of losing £1,000 for the season ticket we've paid for.'

Prawn again

IMUSA's Colin Hendrie comes out fighting after Fergie's attack on the fans:

'You can't stand up to make a noise. If you try to stand up, you've got stewards who are ejecting you, they're taking your season ticket away from you. It's almost like a police state in a football ground now and if you do stand up, people will take your arm, put it behind the back of your neck and throw you out of the ground.

'Under those circumstances, what atmosphere does he [Fergie] want? The only atmosphere we've got is one where we're a little bit frightened of losing £1,000 for the season ticket we've paid for.

'A lot of people are pretty upset [about Ferguson's comments], because it shows a lack of understanding about what it's like to be a football fan in 2008.'

What do you expect?

'Sir Alex Ferguson complained last week that the atmosphere at Old Trafford was like being at a funeral. Well, when you lose 5,000 of your hard-core fans because you sell out to debt-ridden owners, put your admission prices up, flood the place with corporates, reduce the allocation for away fans, widen the divide between the players and the public, allow your stars to blow £4,000 each on a party, tell your stewards to act like the Stasi and slag off what's left of the loyal supporters, what do you expect?' – Of all the column inches used up on this subject in the days that followed Fergie's outburst, *The Mirror's* Oliver Holt comes closest to hitting the nail on the head. Though he could also have said:

'And when you fill the Stretford End, the heart of Old Trafford, with corporate seats, when you pack the place with day-trippers rather than young singers, when you tell fans to go and support Chelsea, when most games kick-off at fan-unfriendly hours, when you kill any pre-match atmosphere by sticking on the tannoy at full blast and playing that ridiculous Premier League anthem, when no thought is given to the acoustics of the stadium, when fans are still struggling with their New Year's hangovers, when you're fed a diet of weakened teams…you're not exactly going to get a repeat of Barcelona '84 are you?'

In goes the other foot

Fergie takes the paper cut he made with his attack on the fans and pours vinegar on it by launching into a fawning appraisal of the Glazer regime:

'At a number of clubs there have been problems with friction between managers and owners. But you can see how smoothly the United ship is running as far as that is concerned, despite early hostility over the Glazer family's ownership. Those protests were unfair because they weren't given a chance, but the Glazers kept their cool and our owners have been nothing but supportive.'

Let's not mention the debt eh?

Finally, moving on from Fergie's bad week…

'Stingy Liverpool have refused to donate their gate money to cash-strapped FA Cup opponents Luton. The League One minnows are in administration. And the hard-up Hatters could go bust if they do not find a buyer by 5pm on Monday. Luton asked the Kop giants to give up their share of today's third-round gate, which is around £200,000. But their appeal was snubbed.' – *The Sun* reveals no pity from the self-pity city.

Rumour of the year (OK it's only the first week in January but...)

'WEEPING Joey Barton is struggling to handle tough prison life despite his hardman image. The 25-year-old soccer star – involved in a series of scrapes on and off the pitch – is living in constant terror of being attacked behind bars. He has been heard sobbing in his cell after jail tough guys branded him a "scumbag". And Barton has spent much of his prison cash allowance buying cigarettes, custard, coffee, tobacco and rice pudding for other lags to make sure they leave him alone.' – *The Sun*

Question of the week

What kind of prison 'tough guy' can be bought off with rice pudding?

Aston Villa 0 United 2   05/01/2008

Ronaldo 81, Rooney 89

A crowd of just 33,000 for a big Cup tie, and 7,500 of them were from the other team. It seems that Villa and their legions of fickle fans got the wrong kick-off time again. Then again, you maybe can't blame them for letting BBC pick up the tab for this one. United have got the Indian sign over Villa. At Villa Park in the Cup they're nigh on unbeatable. If every bone in your body was screaming that your team was going to get a seeing to, what would you do?

OK, you'd go and support your team. But the Villa fans who stayed at home ended up making the right call. When Villa got spanked 4–1 in October, they at least gave it a go. This time their sole tactic seemed to be to bore everyone to death and sneak a goal from a set piece.

Needless to say, it didn't work. United cruised through the opening 70 minutes and then, just as the tie seemed to be heading for Old Trafford, Rooney came on and took Villa to the cleaners. Ronaldo scored the crucial opener, bursting past the dozing Bouma to bundle Giggs's low centre over the line. Rooney then crowned his golden cameo with a beautifully taken second, running half the length of the field to support Ronaldo and then thrashing a difficult bouncing ball past Carson.

Views from the broadsheets

⚽ 'Wayne Rooney has never been slow to grasp the idea that first impressions count. Those who can recall his opening appearance for Manchester United, when he scored a hat-trick against Fenerbahce, will remember Sir Alex Ferguson admitting that it was as good a debut as any he had seen. There was not the time to reach those exhilarating heights here, but Rooney needed only 20 minutes to overshadow the nine other England hopefuls* on show.' – *The Guardian*

⚽ 'If Capello's English lessons are on schedule, he must have been amused by the wit and jollity those much maligned United fans brought to the party, too. Always at home at Villa Park, the travelling supporters first derided the home fans for not taking all their tickets (there were a few empty seats at the Holte End) then decided their manager was not making enough noise. "Fergie, Fergie give us a song" was followed by "Can you hear Fergie sing? Noo-oo".' – *The Observer* is impressed with the Red Army's response to Fergies 'funeral' comments.

(*the England references are there because Capello was watching his first game as England manager.)

Villa Park – the verbals

- ☻ 'What happens is we play Manchester United, we put big effort into it and they beat us.' – Somebody get hold of Martin O'Neill's belt and laces. Just in case.
- ☻ 'Wayne Rooney is a golden player.' – John Carew is impressed.
- ☻ 'It was great to have 7,500 of our fans making themselves heard. When the fans are behind us like that, we do not let them down.' – Hmmm. Not entirely sure about that Fergie. What about Real Madrid in 2000…Bayern 2001…Leverkusen 2002…Porto 2004…Milan 2005…?

Match facts

Villa: Carson, Mellberg, Laursen, Davies, Bouma (Gardner 83), Petrov (Maloney 75), Reo-Coker, Barry, Young, Carew (Moore 64), Agbonlahor [O'Neill]

United: Van der Sar, Brown, Ferdinand, Vidic, Evra, Ronaldo, Carrick, Anderson, Park (Rooney 70), Saha (Hargreaves 79), Giggs (O'Shea 90)

FAC3 17.15 (BBC) Villa Park. Att: 33,630. Ref: M. Atkinson. Half-time: 0–0

Other scores

Burnley 0 Arsenal 2 (Eduardo, Bendtner); Chelsea 1 (og) QPR 0; Everton 0 Oldham 1 (McDonald); Luton 1 (Riise og – and it wouldn't be the last!) Liverpool 1 (Crouch); West Ham 0 City 0

Villa to Newcastle

'We all make mistakes. Mine was making my £20 notes an inch too big.'

News I

United release their latest financial results. And at first glance they look mightily impressive. A gross turnover of £245 milion (second only to Real Madrid's £261 million), profits up 93 per cent to £59 million and new market research showing that they have a third of a billion supporters. But once you deduct the tax and the reported £42 million interest the Glazers make us pay then United's profits are slashed to just £289,000. Mickey Thomas reckons his old printing machine used to bring in more than that every three weeks…

Dirty cash

'Wayne Rooney's on a hundred grand a week. Mind you, so was I until the police found my printing machine.

'We all make mistakes. Mine was making my £20 notes an inch too big.' – Mickey T. reminisces.

News II

Tony Coton is forced to retire from his role as United goalkeeping coach because of a chronic knee problem. Newcastle sack Sam Allardyce. And that's only the start of the fun. United announce a summer tour of South Africa. Lee Martin (jnr) joins Sheffield United on loan. Supposed United target Nicolas Anelka joins Chelsea for a hefty £15 million. Real make another blatant attempt to unsettle Ronaldo. When will UEFA stop them?

Quotes of the week

- 'They (Real) do not know what respect is. They don't respect anyone but themselves.' – Fergie picks a better target for his angst this time.
- 'When you consider I came from Leeds and the clubs' supporters are not exactly the best of friends, it was a big thing for them to accept me the way they did.' – Alan Smith shows his appreciation for United fans before his fateful return to Old Trafford.
- 'The highlight of my time has to be the Champions League Final success. But I am not talking about the game itself. What was even better than that was the homecoming. Sir Alex let me ride on the open-top bus and I still get goose pimples when I watch it now. To witness the noise, people hanging out of windows, up drainpipes, over bridges was unbelievable, the one highlight I will never ever forget.' – Departing coach Tony Coton reminisces on his decade as a Red.

Rumour of the week

'Devout Scientologist Tom Cruise plans to build a $10 million bunker under his Telluride, Colorado, mansion. Equipped with a high tech air-purifying system, it's a self-contained underground system where up to 10 people can survive for years. Apparently, Scientologists believe that the evil deposed galactic ruler Xenu is set to attack Earth, and they'll need a safe place to survive' – *Star Magazine*

I wonder if Becks has baggsied a place...

United 6 Newcastle 0 15/01/2008

Ronaldo 49, 70, 88, Tévez 55, 90, Ferdinand 85

There was a time when City were the undisputed kings of the cock-up. At this stage of the season, though, it was just no contest. Newcastle have achieved the impossible and become even more amusing than City. Here are just a few reasons why:

Their fans are hilarious. They trademark themselves as the best around (the best in their one-club town more like) but in reality constantly undermine the team with their delusional demands for success and style. And what's so special about fat men taking their shirts off in the winter?

Their chairmen are hilarious. Freddy Shepherd, for example, slagged off Shearer and the tat-hungry Toon Army and used unfortunate prostitutes. His replacement, Mike Ashley, arrived with a reputation as a recluse but now sits with the fans and generally acts like a bar-coded Michael Knighton (minus the juggling, of course).

Their transfer policy is hilarious. Plan A is to get the biggest name they can, no matter how knackered (Smith, Owen) or unsuitable (Barton, Bowyer) they are. Plan B is to get the next biggest name they can, no matter how knackered or unsuitable they are. Plan C is…you get the drift. Their sponsors are hilarious. Northern Rock… how fitting can you get?

The way they treat their managers is hilarious. First they dump Ruud Gullit for daring to drop Mary Poppins. Then they get rid of Bobby Robson for 'only' getting them in the Champions League for two seasons in a row. Then they hire the disastrous Graeme Souness and stick with the hapless Glenn Roeder. And when they finally make a sensible decision, bringing in the pragmatic and proven Sam Allardyce, they get rid of him after just eight months.

The timing of Allardyce's sacking couldn't have been any better as far as United were concerned. Newcastle had no leadership from the dugout, they had no leadership on the pitch, and they would have been buried by the break if Rooney had brought his shooting boots and Styles had awarded stonewall penalties for fouls on Ronaldo and Giggs. Two goalline clearances in as many second-half minutes raised the question whether it was going to be one of those days, but when Ronaldo rolled in his clever free-kick, the floodgates opened. Tévez and Ronaldo made it three with 20 minutes left, and by the time Styles put Newcastle out of their misery United were looking like scoring with every attack. If the game had lasted just a few minutes longer they may well have equalled the Ipswich 9–0. As it was, Newcastle became the first major side I've seen crawl out of Old Trafford seriously relieved to lose 'only' by six.

UNITED 6 NEWCASTLE 0

The Six Pack

1–0 (49): Alan Smith commits what looks like a phantom foul on Ronaldo on the edge of the box. Ronaldo picks himself up, acts like he's going to blast a dipper over the wall, and then coolly drills the ball under the wall's feet as they jump.

2–0 (55): Given makes a bad error, smashing a left-footed clearance straight at Cacapa. The ball bounces off Cacapa to Giggs, he sidefoots the ball across goal and Tévez sweeps in. After a short tussle with his shorts, out comes Florencia's dummy again. Hope it's had a wash.

3–0 (70): The goal of the match. A rat-a-tat of one-touch passing, started by the superb Carrick and also featuring notable contributions from Rooney and Tévez, ends with Ronaldo killing the ball with the end of his toe and shooting home.

4–0 (85): Rooney floats a faultless, Eric-style ball over the Newcastle defence. Ferdinand gets the run on the dozing Enrique and volleys classily past Given. A (very) small piece of history here. Rio's goal – combined with Anton's earlier winner for West Ham against Fulham – makes the Ferdinands the first pair of brothers to in Premiership history to score on the same day. The Nevilles have only scored in the same year a couple of times.

5–0 (88): Ronaldo picks up a loose header, sends the bamboozled Cacapa sliding towards the Lowry Centre, and smashes in a low left-footer which deflects off Enrique and fizzes over Given. After all those braces, he's finally got his first United hat-trick.

6–0 (90): Nani flicks on O'Shea's long-range cross to Tévez and his smart volley strikes the bar and just crosses the line. Smudger, who endured a nightmare return to Old Trafford alongside Nicky Butt (remember Wes, the only way from United is down), picks up the season's most pointless red card for arguing that it didn't cross the line.

View from the broadsheets

⚽ 'As humiliations go, Sir Alex Ferguson's men have dealt out worse beatings in their time but perhaps never one with such brutal, methodical ruthlessness and a more callous sense of timing. Old Trafford is a formidable place for the most intrepid travellers, never mind a side of Newcastle United's callow nerve, and the upshot, once again, is that the team in black and white is living out football's equivalent of being tarred and feathered and left by the roadside.' – *The Guardian*

133

◎ 'To cap a thoroughly chastening experience for Newcastle, Alan Smith was so aggrieved at the Tévez goal that he got a red card for abusing the referee, Rob Styles. Since returning from a broken leg, Smith has been a Championship striker masquerading as a Premier League midfielder but he has evidently not lost the brat tendencies that have pockmarked his career under the tedious guise of being "fully committed".' – *The Guardian* ends by slagging off Smudger. Harsh and fair? Whatever you think, getting £6 million for a one-paced journeyman must qualify as one of the best bits of business of last summer.

Omen of the week
'The last time United beat Newcastle to go top, in October 2006, they could not be shifted.' – *The Times*

Best since Best
This was the fourth time United had put six or more past Newcastle at Old Trafford. Here are the others:

United 6 Newcastle 1 – 12 Jan 1957
Wood – Foulkes, Jones, Byrne – Colman, Edwards – Berry, Whelan (2), Taylor, Viollet (2), Pegg (2)

United 6 Newcastle 0 – 4 May 1968
Stepney – Brennan, Foulkes, Sadler (1), Dunne – Best (3), Crerand, Charlton, Aston – Kidd (2), Gowling

United 7 Newcastle 2 (League Cup) – 27 Oct 1976
Stepney – Nicholl (1), B.Greenhoff, Houston (1), Albiston – Coppell (1), Daly, McIlroy, Hill (3) – Macari, Pearson (1) (sub: McGrath)

Newcastle – the verbals
◎ 'Can we make this as pain-free as possible?' – Newcastle caretaker Nigel Pearson's first words to the press afterwards.
◎ 'I asked all the players and the staff to sign the ball for me because it is a special day.' – Ronaldo's chuffed.
◎ 'Sometimes, Cristiano puts in a performance and you think "he can't get any better than that". But he does. At times, he is simply unplayable and Saturday was one of those occasions. – Is Danny Simpson the next Paddy Evra?
◎ 'It was all happening so quickly, I didn't even know what the score was at one point.' – I reckon so...

Match facts

United: Van der Sar, O'Shea, Ferdinand, Vidic, Evra (Simpson 67), Ronaldo, Carrick, Anderson (Fletcher 72), Giggs (Nani 72), Tévez, Rooney*

Newcastle: Given, Carr, Cacapa, Taylor, Enrique, Milner (Viduka 64), Butt, N'Zogbia, Smith* 90, Duff†, Owen (Rozehnal 82) [Pearson]

FAPL 17.15 (Set) Att: 75,965. Ref: R. Styles. Half-time: 0–0

*Yellow card † Red card

Other scores

Arsenal 1 (Adebayor pen) Birmingham 1 (O'Connor); Chelsea 2 (Belletti, Wright-Phillips) Spurs 0; Boro 1 (Boateng) Liverpool 1 (Torres)

League table

1. United 51 (22) 2. Arsenal 51 (22) 3. Chelsea 47 (22) 4. Liverpool 39 (21)…11. Newcastle 26 (22)

Newcastle to Reading

'It's a Manchester United romp – and they are all getting in on the act.'

News

Reading's insane plan to use drug sniffer dogs to screen United fans before the game at the Madejski is dropped after a wave of supporter complaints. The Brazilian Nevilles, full-back twins Fabio and Rafael Silva, complete their move to Manchester from Fluminese. After a string of high-profile transfer flops, Chelsea revive their old tactic of signing everyone United are linked with. Days after paying over the odds for Anelka, they splash out £9.7 million on Lokomotiv Moscow's Serbian defender Branislav Ivanovic. Amusingly, he promptly sinks without trace.

Finally, Liverpool's owners Hicks and Gillett try to make the Glazers look good by admitting they'd approached Jurgen Klinsmann behind Benitez's back. Nice try, but it will take a lot more than that before they sink as low as Uncle Malc.

Lies, lies and damn lies

Interesting Glazer gossip from *The Guardian*:

'The government was told that Malcolm Glazer's sons were promising not to raise ticket prices at Old Trafford when the family took over Manchester United in the summer of 2005. Ministers were briefed that the assurance had been given in a meeting by Joel, Avi and Bryan Glazer, and partly in consequence, the government was advised

135

not to intervene in the United deal or introduce a requirement that those taking over football clubs prove they are doing so "in the public interest".'

Straying power

The Daily Mail gleefully reports on the press cock-up of the week:

'Sven Goran Eriksson was rarely bothered by anything written about him when England coach but he is furious about a *Daily Star* picture story this week that suggested he was canoodling with a young lady in a Manchester restaurant after City's defeat at Everton with his hand "straying towards her bum". The 21-year-old in question was Eriksson's daughter, Lina.'

Head over heels

Newcastle prove just how out of touch they are with reality – and how badly they are addicted to sentimentality – by reappointing Kevin Keegan as manager. Yes, the same Keegan who flounced out the first time round, who said he wasn't up to the job as England manager and who admitted he hadn't bothered watching a game since he left City. He's also developed a strange habit of slapping the cheek of everyone he meets. Not sure that Fergie will fancy that…

Thumb on the pulse

'I don't think it will happen [returning to management]. I think my life has gone in a different direction. You never know, I mean I do get offers to go back into football, but I made a decision that I would come and do something different with my life. I mean I haven't watched a game of football, I mean live, since my last game at Manchester City and I can't even remember what game that was now.' – 'King' Kev talking to *Inside Sport*, November 2007.

I'd love it

'I know what the fans want. As long as they are realistic and patient, we can try to help them have dreams and possibly win something.' – Kev really hasn't been paying attention to the football world has he? What do you think? Mad by Christmas?

Quotes of the week

- ☺ 'You are bound to get a damn sight more cokeheads at a play than you are at the Madejski Stadium.'
  – IMUSA's Mark Longden riles against the insinuation that Reds are a load of junkies.
- ☺ 'People like John Terry and Rio Ferdinand are amazing. But the toughest of all has to be Nemanja Vidic. He just doesn't care for his health at all! He throws himself around to try and get the ball, and I really respect that.' – No wonder Berbatov was so keen to come to Old Trafford.

Nonsense rumour of the week

The Sun reports that Fergie has fallen out with the BBC – again – after commentator Jonathon Pearce used the line, 'It's a Manchester United romp – and they are all getting in on the act' during the Newcastle battering.

The paper quotes a 'club source' as saying 'The gaffer feels the BBC grabs every opportunity to have a laugh at United. Many at the club feel they have an agenda.' It was clearly all a fuss about nothing. Mind you, if Pearce had slipped in a 'Good 'evans' at the start…

PS: I still haven't forgiven Pearce for the 'Ready, Teddy, Go' line from his Channel Five days.

Reading 0 United 2   19/01/2008

Rooney 77, Ronaldo 90

An open letter to Steve Coppell*: Sorry Stevie, but I hope you go down soon. It's not that I dislike Reading. I don't care much about them either way, and your chairman's hair fascinates me. But you roll over against teams like Chelsea and Arsenal, you get thumped by teams like Portsmouth and Tottenham and you play like men possessed against United. Last year you drew with us home and away in the League and Cup and only lost the other two games by the odd goal in five. This year you've been the only team to stop us scoring at Old Trafford and you gave us one of our hardest games of the season here. You even made Fergie lose his temper at the end, though he said he was more relieved than angry. I loved you as a player. I loved the way you beat Liverpool in the FA Cup semis in 1990. I loved your work at City too, but don't spoil things now. Please.

Goal action

1–0 (77): What a relief. After a dozy, flat and disjointed 50 minutes, United belatedly flick on the switch and start pummelling the Reading defence. Finally they crack when Tévez floats an angled ball through from the left and Rooney gets his touch just right to flick it past Hahnemann.

2–0 (90): What a relief (again). After Harper just misses with a drive that Van der Sar had no hope of touching, Murty's blocked shot falls to Ronaldo midway in the United half. As the only player near him is Rooney, what happens next has an air of inevitability about it. Seven seconds later Ronaldo is sliding his 23rd goal of the season into the net – that's as many as his 'unrepeatable' tally from last year.

What was bad?

⚽ The first half: Reading were really positive. United were really casual, at both ends of the pitch. If Ferdinand hadn't shown good anticipation to head Kitson's long-range lob off the line, they'd have trooped off a deserved goal behind.

What was good?

⚽ United's second-half recovery, the cameo from Giggsy that helped inspire it, Fergie's angry – I mean celebratory – arm gesture to the Reading bench after Ronaldo's clincher, and the three points.

*written before my wish was granted (honest)!

What was odd?

⚽ Watching a pensioner – and Knight of the Realm no less – do an 'Up Yours'.

Reading – the verbals

⚽ 'It was relief. All I was doing was expressing my relief in what was one of our hardest matches of the season. Reading always make it tough for us, and our players had to run so much we clocked up more kilometres than in any other game this season.' – Fergie's explanation for his celebratory gesture doesn't quite square with the 24,000 people who'd just seen him squabbling with Reading coach Wally Downes.

⚽ 'Two frighten me, the rest don't. If they don't play, they are a different team.' – Coppell thinks we rely on Rooney and Ronaldo too much. And he might well have a point (Rooney hasn't lost a League game this season, while Ronaldo is scoring at a rate of a goal a game).

Match facts

Reading: Hahnemann, Murty, Ingimarsson, Cisse, Shorey, Doyle, Hunt, Harper, Convey* (Matejovsky 80), Lita (Long 83), Kitson [Coppell]

United: Van der Sar, Brown, Ferdinand*, Vidic, Evra, Ronaldo, Carrick, Hargreaves (Nani 70), Park (Giggs half-time), Rooney, Tévez (Fletcher 81)

FAPL 15.00 Madejski Stadium. Att: 24,135. Ref: S. Bennett. Half-time 0–0

Other scores

Birmingham 0 Chelsea 1 (Pizarro); Fulham 0 Arsenal 3 (Adebayor 2, Rosicky); Liverpool 2 (Benayoun, Crouch) Villa 2 (Harewood, og)

League table

1. United 54 (23) 2. Arsenal 54 (23) 3. Chelsea 50 (23) 4. Everton 42 (23)…14. Reading 22 (23)

Reading to Spurs
'I'm only on because you are so s**t!'

News I

United unveil a superb tribute to the Busby Babes across the glass exterior of the East Stand. There are just two problems with it. The poster gets the words of the United calypso wrong (forgivable). It's also got AIG's logo on the bottom (unforgivable). United's money-making kickabout in Saudi Arabia ends in a 3–2 defeat to Al Hilal. Tévez and Ronaldo score United's goals while Danny Welbeck misses a last-minute penalty. And the City

Supporters' Club's request for a minute's applause for the Babes – rather than a minute's silence – is rejected on the grounds that it's a staggeringly bad idea. I don't know what happens in Cheadle, lads, but it's just not right to applaud the tragic deaths of 23 people.

Stinkin' thinkin'

Typical. After doing the right thing with the sponsors-free kit for the derby, and after unveiling a stunning tribute to the Babes at Old Trafford, United undo all their good work by refusing to see just how tacky and wrong it is for the AIG logo to feature on the Munich tribute.

'It is entirely appropriate that a partner as closely involved with the club as AIG would want to remember that extraordinary team, cut down in its prime,' whimpered David Gill.

Funny that. Most of us thought it would be far more appropriate for a company with no connection to the club (apart from trying to exploit our fan base since 2006) to stay out of the limelight rather than attempt to profit from the grief of others.

Kings of the world

The Guardian's Daniel Taylor reckons that the fervour generated in Saudi for Al Jaber's testimonial reaffirmed United's status as the 'most fashionable football club on the planet':

'Real Madrid might want to argue the point. Barcelona will, too, and Peter Kenyon, a man who really should know better, will try to convince himself that Chelsea could inspire the kind of hero-worship that came the way of his former employers in Riyadh. But they would be kidding themselves. Would Avram Grant's players have the wow factor to draw an over-capacity crowd to the King Fahd Stadium five hours before kick-off? Would the prospect of seeing Madrid or Barcelona have brought the people of Riyadh to such a state of feverish excitement that the dual carriageway leading to the ground would be transformed into six lanes of Wacky Races?'

It might be best to take all this with a pinch of salt though. Taylor desperately needed to get back onside with Fergie after his behind-the-scenes book on United got him banned from press conferences.

News II

David Gill's house gets the LUHG graffiti treatment. Phil Bardsley joins Sunderland for £2 million. Ryan Shawcross moves to Stoke for the same amount.

And then there were two

Bardsley's exit means there are only two members of the 2003 Youth Cup-winning squad still left at Old Trafford. And I'll snort crack off a mermaid's tail if Tom Heaton or Chris Eagles* ever make it properly!

---

*Eagles was sold to Burnley in the 2008 close season.

The 2003 Youth Cup winners (current club in brackets where known):

Goalkeepers: Luke Steele (Barnsley on loan from West Brom), Tom Heaton (United)

Defenders: Lee Sims, Phil Bardsley, Paul McShane (Sunderland), Mark Howard, Lee Lawrence, Phil Picken (Chesterfield).

Midfielders: Chris Eagles (United), Kieran Richardson (Sunderland), David Poole (Stockport), David Jones (Derby), Ben Collett (retired).

Strikers: Eddie Johnson (Bradford), Sylvan Ebanks-Blake (Wolves), Ramon Calliste, Mads Timm (Odense)

News III

Manucho scores a cracking flying header in Angola's 1–1 African Nations draw with South Africa. Adebayor headbutts Bendtner during Arsenal's Carling Cup 5–1 semi-final humiliation at the hands of Spurs. Crazy as it sounds, Wenger doesn't see the incident. Just as predictably, the FA decide to take no action over it, leaving Adebayor free to go on a scoring spree that bags him six goals in his next 4 games.

Quotes of the week

- ☻ 'I'm only on because you are so s**t!' – What Adebayor reportedly said to Bendtner just before headbutting him on the nose.
- ☻ 'Kevin Keegan has approached me and they've offered me more money. I am definitely leaving Spurs. It's all about the money. I don't care about the [Carling Cup] Final, I don't care about the Cup.' – Pascal Chimbonda makes a case for being the biggest c*** in football. Though Ashley Cole would raise the bar to new levels within days.
- ☻ 'Bouncing babes we deserve to get knighted.' – The United calypso, 2008 style.

United 3 Spurs 1 27/01/2008

Keane 24, Tévez 38, Ronaldo 69 (pen), 88

As the moments ticked away to Bayern's victory in the 1999 European Cup Final – and Bestie headed for Las Ramblas – German TV commentator Marcel Reif succumbed to a surge of uncontrollable confidence. 'Yet again in the crucial game,' he purred, 'the English team has proven inferior to the German team. Maybe I shouldn't say it, but I promise never to say it ever again. Football, as Gary Lineker once said, is a simple game – 22 men chase a ball for 90 minutes, and at the end the Germans win.'

Happily, Sheringham and Solskjaer soon rammed Reif's words back down his throat, but I can sort of see why he was cocky enough to say them. I'm starting to feel the same way when Spurs come to Old Trafford. No matter how well Spurs play, something always seems to crop up that stops them winning. In 2005 it was the linesman who failed to spot that Pedro Mendes long-ranger had crossed the line and was halfway to Stretford. In 2006 and 2007 it was the series of good chances they missed in games that United sneaked 1–0, and here it was a combination of Jermaine Jenas and Michael Dawson. Jenas missed two big chances at 1–0 and 1–1 that would have left United vulnerable to being picked off on the break, and Dawson made two basic errors that gifted United their first two goals and earned him a red card. And the good news for United was that he hadn't finished yet...

Match action

Preamble (0): It's been eight days since United last played so they should be fresh, unlike Spurs who arrive with their midweek Carling Cup victory in their legs. Hold on a minute, though. United opted to rest up in the week by travelling for god knows how many hours to play in a testimonial for god knows who. Will chasing the Saudi moola cost them?

0–1 (24): Things don't look good early on as Spurs take a deserved lead. Lennon demolishes the usually invincible Evra with the oldest trick in the winger's book (the one where they feint to go inside before going outside instead), he fires in a low cross and, as Brown and Ferdinand freeze, Keane slides in to score. We could have done with Vidic there. Bloody camels*.

1–1 (38): As Spurs continue to threaten through Lennon, Jenas and the uber-classy Berbatov, you can almost hear the pressbox penning their Riyadh-related headlines –

'Sheikh-en and stirred', 'United get their just deserts', that sort of thing. But then United get an equaliser out of nothing. Dawson makes a mess of clearing a routine thump into the area, Giggs lays the ball off neatly to Tévez and his left-footer skims past Cerny.

2–1 (69): Though Jenas misses his second one-on-one of the afternoon just after the break, the initiative is clearly with United now. Their second goal is no more than their just deserts. Van der Sar smashes a clearance into the Spurs area, Dawson misjudges the flight, Rooney produces a sensational piece of control, Dawson topples over and, as he falls, nudges the ball away with his elbow. Peter Walton has no doubt and no choice. He shows a red card to Dawson and awards a penalty to United, which Ronaldo nervelessly sweeps in.

3–1 (88): Even with 10 men, Spurs continue to threaten, and Brown gets lucky when he turns Malbranque's cross against his own post. But another defensive howler finally kills them off, Ronaldo cuts in from the left and hits a low shot that Cerny allows to squirm under his body and into the net.

Views from the broadsheets
- ☺ 'Rarely, since Gary Lineker's 1989 goal last taught the north Londoners how it feels to win at Old Trafford, have Spurs players arrived here so energised, their fans' reminders of the Carling Cup demolition of Arsenal ringing in their ears, and then they were offered a handful of gilt-edged chances. But Jermaine Jenas spurned the best two and kept United going until the defence Ramos had put together came unstuck too, when Michael Dawson sealed his side's defeat by throwing a hand at the ball which had just looped over his head into Wayne Rooney's path.' – *The Independent* chalks it down as a missed opportunity for Spurs…
- ☺ 'Outstanding teams just cannot kick the habit of victory. Manchester United might almost have been trying to avoid a win in this FA Cup-tie against resurgent Tottenham Hotspur, but could not stop themselves from meandering into the fifth round.' – And *The Guardian* agrees.

Rumour of the day*
According to the pre-match whispers, Vidic was missing, not because of a virus (as the club claimed), but because he injured himself while trying to get off a Saudi camel.

Quote of the day
'My experience of Cup ties is…sometimes you're scrappy, sometimes you're brilliant but the bottom line is you're in the hat tomorrow at 1.30.' – Fergie's just happy to be through.

Match facts

United: Van der Sar, O'Shea, Ferdinand, Brown, Evra* (Simpson 90), Ronaldo, Carrick (Scholes 64), Hargreaves, Giggs, Rooney, Tévez (Anderson 81).

Tottenham: Cerny, Tainio (Defoe 81), Dawson† 69, Huddlestone, Lee (Gunter 59), Lennon (Boateng 72), O'Hara, Jenas, Malbranque, Keane, Berbatov [Ramos]

FAC4 14.00 (BBC). Att: 75,369. Ref: P. Walton. Half-time: 1–1

* Yellow card † Red card

Other scores

FA Cup fourth round: SHEFFIELD UNITED 2 (Balloons, Stead) CITY 1 (Sturridge); Arsenal 3 (Adebayor 2, Butt og) Newcastle 0; Liverpool 5 (who cares?) Havant & Waterlooville 2 (Pacquette, Potter); Wigan 1 (Sibierski) Chelsea 2 (Anelka, Wright-Phillips)

Spurs to Portsmouth

'Everyone thinks the draw is fixed...I'm beginning to wonder!'

News

United are drawn against Arsenal in the FA Cup fifth round. Chelsea are paired with QPR while Liverpool get a home banker against Barnsley (or so we all thought!). Vandals throw paint bombs at the Munich tribute. Was it a misguided protest against the AIG logo? Or was it the work of City fans (the paint was light blue)? The FA finally backtrack on their disgraceful decision not to hold a minute's silence before England's game with Switzerland on 6 Feb. And the football world sits back and smiles at City, who get knocked out of the Cup by Sheffield United and a handful of stray balloons.

Then, like my dreams, they fade and die

Just in case you missed it – or couldn't see properly through the tears of laughter – here's what happened at Bramall Lane. Before the game, the City fans behind the goal threw a pile of balloons onto the pitch. Before Joe Hart had had the chance to clear his area, United loanee Lee Martin scampered down the left and sent in a low cross. The ball ricocheted off the balloons, distracted Michael Ball into a fluffed clearance and presented Sheffield forward Luton Shelton with a chance he couldn't miss. Ten minutes later Jon Stead grabbed a non-balloon-assisted second and the 31-year drought had officially become 32.

Luck (?) of the draw

The Arsenal draw means that United have now been drawn against Premiership opposition on 10 consecutive occasions. And that's not the only stat which shows how much harder we've had it than the rest:

Since 1998–99, 82 per cent of United's FA Cup games have been against Premiership teams. By comparison Chelsea have faced Premiership opposition 51 per cent of the time, Arsenal 62 per cent of the time and Liverpool just 58 per cent. In that time one in five of United's third round ties have been against Premiership teams (usually Aston Villa). Chelsea, meanwhile, have only played Premiership teams in the third round once in every 10 draws.

News II

It never rains but it pours. Thieves enter the City dressing-room during the Cup match and steal £2,000. United new boy Manucho scores twice more in the Cup of African Nations, hitting two in Angola's 3–1 upset win against Senegal. Ashley Cole sees off Pascal Chimbonda in the battle for the title of the most despicable man in football. And Micah Richards hits the toilets en route to becoming the latest England player to be caught up in a roasting scandal...

Letter of the week

'The balloons of Bramall Lane may be destined for a place in FA Cup folklore but Sven-Goran Eriksson could be forgiven for not seeing the funny side as Manchester City sent a strongly worded letter of complaint to the Football Association. Eriksson has consulted the rule book and believes there is a watertight case that Sheffield United's first goal should not have been allowed to stand after the ball ricocheted off the balloons in Joe Hart's goalmouth' – *The Guardian*. Just let it go chaps. It's probably just god's way of paying you back for all those 'hilarious' inflatables from the '80s.

Girls allowed

The nation's favourite son Ashley Cole lays on the charm after *The Sun* revealed he played away in 22-year-old hairdresser Aimee Walton's 'kiss, dodge the vomit and tell' story.

Quotes of the week

☺ 'I just can't believe it! Everyone thinks the draw is fixed so BBC can get the best game – I'm beginning to wonder!' – Fergie 'jokes' about the Arsenal draw.

United 2 Portsmouth 0 30/01/2008

Ronaldo 10, 13

Remember the words of the Ronaldo song when it first came out? He plays on the left, he plays on the right, that boy Ronaldo makes Beckham look, well, it rhymes with right. The Beckham reference was soon taken out and replaced with England because: a] time had started healing the wounds created by Beckham's departure, b] Beckham is a bona fide Red legend, c] swapping England for Beckham did a better job of winding up little Ingerlanders, and d] it just wasn't true – for one thing, Ronaldo couldn't hold a candle to Beckham when it came to free-kicks.

Well, that just doesn't ring true any more. Beckham's free-kicks could be, and often were, stunning. But, as he demonstrated to a bewildered David James here, Ronaldo has reinvented the art. I reckon I've only ever seen one better free-kick in my life. And the taker of that one, Roberto Carlos, spent the next decade trying to repeat the feat. Ronaldo looks like he's going to do something extraordinary every time he presses the ball into the turf and puffs out his cheeks…

Goal action

1–0 (10)): United start sensationally, open up Portsmouth at will and go in front courtesy of a mini-masterclass of first-time passing and another cool finish from Ronaldo. Carrick and Scholes play in Nani, he frees Ronaldo, and he guides the ball past the spreadeagled James. It's tempting to write that James had no chance of saving it. But he had far more chance of laying a glove on that Ronaldo shot than this one…

2–0 (13): Perfection. Ronaldo sizes up a free-kick 30 yards out, runs up and launches a bomb of a shot that swerves, dips, arrows, wobbles, thunders and flies (or whatever verb you care to use) over the wall and into a space about two inches from the corner of post and bar.

Views from the broadsheets

- 'Another two goals, another match-winning performance, another team brutally dispatched by the player with gelled hair, tangerine boots and magic in his feet. The eulogies are beginning to sound repetitive, but nobody at Manchester United will mind while Cristiano Ronaldo is bewitching Old Trafford and seeing off all contenders to be known as the most devastating player in the Premier League.' – *The Guardian* on the Ronaldo show.

✪ 'United had just delivered probably their most complete period of football of this season; 45 minutes in which it hardly seemed possible that only eight clear chances had accrued from a labyrinth of exchanged passes and precision balls through the centre. And at the heart of it all yet again was Cristiano Ronaldo, for whom comparisons with George Best are becoming less and less far-fetched.' – Like the rest of us, *The Independent* can't believe we only scored two.

High Fidelity

My top 10 favourite free-kicks. Well, if Hornby can get away with it…

✪ Roberto Carlos, Brazil v France, Le Tournoi 1997: It's the distance. The fact it bent the wrong way. And Barthez's bemused look when he realised it had gone in.

✪ Ronaldo v Portsmouth 2008: It's the pace. The dip. And the equally bemused look on James's face.

✪ Pallister v Blackburn 1993: Giggsy's was better. But this was just meant to be (with just moments remaining of the first title-winning season, Pally was the only outfielder not to have scored).

✪ Cantona v Arsenal 1993: Ince lays it off, Eric thumps it in and races off waving his strapped up wrist.

✪ Beckham v Greece 2001: It's funny. Becks curled in so many brilliant free-kicks for United that none really stand out – not like this one anyway.

✪ Koeman, Holland v England 1993: OK, I'm joking. But I love Taylor's tirade… 'Linesman! Linesman, that's a disgrace…Hells Bells!'

✪ Irwin v Liverpool 1993: Right into the stanchion. Grobbelaar can only catch the ball as it bounces out. If only we'd held on for the 3–0.

✪ Blackmore v Montpelier 1991: United are up against it away to Valderrama and co. And then Sunbed launches a low bullet from 98 yards…

✪ Jose Luis Chilavert, Velez Sarsfield v River Plate. It's outrageous, unsporting, brilliant and well worth a look on *youtube*. As a fouled teammate writhes around in agony – and the River Plate players stop to comfort him – goalscoring Paraguayan 'keeper Chilavert beats his opposite number from inside his own half.

✪ Ronaldo v Euro XI 2007. I know it was only a friendly. But this was almost as good as his Portsmouth one. Gains marks for more sideways wobble, but loses marks for not being as close to the corner.

The free-kick – the reaction

✪ 'I've seen the replay and it is difficult. Maybe it's the best, maybe, I don't know.' – What's this? Modesty from Ronaldo? Surely not.

✪ 'Ronnie's free-kick was unbelievable, the best goal I've seen in a game I've been playing in.' – You can't argue with Vidic – and not just because he'd break you up, little bone by little bone.

☻ 'There is no goalkeeper in the world who could have saved that. We've had some good free-kick takers here – Ryan Giggs, Eric Cantona, David Beckham – but Cristiano's record is phenomenal. That without doubt must be the best I've seen.' – Fergie on a genius.

Match facts

United: Van der Sar, Brown, Ferdinand, Vidic, Evra, Nani, Scholes (Anderson 62), Carrick, Park, Ronaldo (Hargreaves 73), Rooney (Tévez 73)
Portsmouth: James, Johnson, Campbell, Distin (Hreidarsson 46), Pamarot*, Lauren (Mvuemba 46), Davis, Diarra, Kranjcar, Baros (Hughes 78), Benjani [Redknapp]
FAPL 20.00* (Sky). Att: 75,415 Ref: M. Atkinson. Half-time: 2–0
*Yellow card

Other scores

Chelsea 1 (Ballack) Reading 0; Derby 1 (og) City 1 (Sturridge); West Ham (Noble pen) Liverpool 0

League table

1. United 57 (24) 2. Arsenal 57 (24) 3. Chelsea 53 (24) 4. Everton 43 (24)...10. Portsmouth 37 (24)

Portsmouth to Spurs
'There are other more ridiculous things we could have done'

News

Premier League chairman Richard Scudamore announces the barmiest plan of the year. Starting in January 2011, each Premier League club will play an extra game a season in one of five host cities across the world. The points earned from the games will count towards the final Premier League table. And every game will be preceded by a naked grandma wrestling match.

Now there's no need to be facetious...

Yes there is. Even if you go along with the idea of prostituting England's biggest clubs around the world, there are still all sort of reasons to treat this money-grabbing plan with contempt. How will they decide which teams play each other three times a year? Can we baggsy Derby? Which country is going to stump up the readies to watch Bolton play Reading, or Fulham take on Boro? The mind boggles.

A step too far

⚙ 'There are other more ridiculous things we could have done' – Scudamore tries to make us feel grateful the Premier League hasn't suggested dwarf rolling,

⚙ 'This game relies on having supporters in the ground and when the day comes that they completely think that match-going fans are of no value, then that's the day when the game will severely suffer' – Malcolm Clarke, co-chairman of the Football Supporters' Federation, warns of the consequences.

⚙ 'What disappoints me is David Gill phoned me and said "keep this quiet, we are going to discuss it" and then it's all over the papers this morning. They can't keep their mouth shut down there. I think if they are going to do these things, they should have been enquiring and having discussions with managers and players before they come out with all this stuff and make an issue of it' – Strangely, Fergie isn't annoyed at the 39th Step idea, just angry nobody asked him first.

Rumour of the week

'Manchester United are embroiled in an unseemly row over the Munich memorial service after trying to charge £5,000 for television footage of the event. BBC top brass in London were furious after being told they would have to pay for pictures from a service commemorating the plane crash 50 years ago, which killed eight of the Busby Babes and three club officials' – *The Daily Mail*

Overreaction of the week

'Devastated Cheryl Cole fears for her sexual health after lurid tales of her husband's alleged bed-hopping, sources say. The feisty singer was stunned by allegations that football star Ashley had bedded a string of beauties – without protection. Now she plans to see doctors for a head-to-toe health check and to have a sex test' – *The Daily Star*

I'm not sure that even Cashley could have passed on something that will turn Tweedy into a man.

Spurs 1 United 1 02/02/2008

Berbatov 21, Tévez 90+

I can be as Red-eyed as the next fan. In fact I've been known to make Terry Christian, who spends his Saturdays winding up ABUs brilliantly on Talksport's version of the god-awful 606, look objective. But even I wouldn't have argued if United had ended up with nothing from this one. Sure, the hapless Mark Clattenburg did us no favours with his stop-start approach and his apparent determination to take the names of every United player. Van der Sar also argued – dubiously – that Berbatov's opener should have been struck off for handball in the build-up. But for most of the game Spurs were sharper to the ball, they were better with the ball, they were stronger at the back, and they had the better chances.

Fortunately they also had a Red agent in their ranks. And that's why the match ended the way it did...with Spurs fans holding their heads, Tévez going berserk and bodies flying around, '70s-style, in the United end.

Goal action

1–0 (21): Spurs new boy Woodgate wins the ball and shuttles it on quickly via Keane to Jenas whose charge into the area is halted by Hargreaves. As Jenas claims a penalty, and Van der Sar claims a free-kick (Jenas's arm brushed the ball as he fell), Lennon picks up possession and plays in Berbatov for a simple finish.

1–1 (90): United didn't flow today. In fact they barely trickled. But, like all the best United teams, they just didn't give up. After stinking the place out for 65 minutes or so, Rooney, Ronaldo, Tévez and Nani finally start to have a go at the Spurs defence. And just when it looks like United are going to lose to Spurs for the first time in seven years, they get their reward. Nani curls over a corner from the right and the combination of Tévez and Agent Dawson deflects it in at the near post.

Interesting

Fergie reveals that Woodgate would have signed for United as a boy if United's Sunderland scout hadn't died playing 5-a-side.

View from the broadsheets

'It took an own-goal by Michael Dawson in the dregs of stoppage-time to prevent United from losing a fourth away match of their Premier League campaign. The champions were so jaded that Cristiano Ronaldo, as if bored with conventional awards, looked hellbent on collecting the booby prize for worst-performing star. He took it unchallenged.' – *The Guardian* is harsh on Ronaldo (didn't they see Giggsy and Scholes?) but fair elsewhere.

Spurs – the verbals

- ⚽ 'We deserved the point – just.' – Fergie's skating on thin ice here…
- ⚽ 'We don't stop trying and in the last 25 minutes we absolutely battered them.' – But he's on firmer ground here…
- ⚽ 'For Manchester United it's not right. There is something wrong when Manchester United get seven bookings.' – And he's absolutely spot on here. God knows how many cards Clattenburg would have shown if this had been a dirty game.

Worst headline of the day

'Dawson's creak lets United save face' – *The Observer* needs pun-ishing.

Match facts

Spurs: Cerny*, Chimbonda, Dawson, Woodgate*, Hutton, Lennon (Boateng 79), Jenas, Huddlestone*, Malbranque, Berbatov, Keane (O'Hara 90) [Ramos]
United: Van der Sar*, Brown*, Ferdinand, Vidic, Evra, Ronaldo*, Hargreaves (Carrick 46), Scholes (Anderson 60), Giggs (Nani* 60), Rooney*, Tévez*
FAPL 15.00 White Hart Lane. Att: 36,075. Ref: M. Clattenburg. Half-time: 0–1
*Yellow card

Other scores

City 1 (Fernandes) Arsenal 3 (Adebayor 2, Eduardo); Portsmouth 1 (Defoe) Chelsea 1 (Anelka); Liverpool 3 (Crouch, Torres, Gerrard pen) Sunderland 0

League table

1. Arsenal 60 (25) 2. United 58 (25) 3. Chelsea 54 (25) 4. Everton 44 (25)…11. Spurs 29 (25)

Munich Remembered
6 February 1958 – 6 February 2008

Babes

Geoff Bent
Full-back, aged 25, 12 apps, 0 goals

Roger Byrne (c)
Full-back, aged 28, 245 apps, 17 goals

Eddie Colman
Wing-half, aged 21, 85 apps, 1 goal

Duncan Edwards
Wing-half, aged 21, 151 apps, 20 goals

Mark Jones
Centre-half, aged 24, 103 apps, 1 goal

David Pegg
Left-winger, aged 22, 127 apps, 24 goals

Tommy Taylor
Centre-forward, aged 26, 166 apps, 112 goals

Liam 'Billy' Whelan
Inside forward, aged 22, 79 apps, 43 goals

United staff

Walter Crickmer
Bert Whalley
Tom Curry

Journalists

Alf Clarke, Don Davies, George Follows, Tom Jackson,
Archie Ledbrooke, Henry Rose, Eric Thompson, Frank Swift

Crew members and other passengers

Captain Kenneth Rayment, Tom Cable, Bela Miklos, Willie Satinoff

The Flowers of Manchester

One cold and bitter Thursday in Munich, Germany,
Eight great football stalwarts conceded victory.
Eight men will never play again, who met disaster there,
The flowers of English football, the flowers of Manchester.

The Busby Babes were flying home, returning from Belgrade,
This great United family all masters of their trade.
The pilot of the aircraft, the skipper Captain Thain,
Three times tried to take off and twice turned back again.

The third time down the runway disaster followed close,
There was slush upon that runway and the aircraft never rose.
It ploughed into the marshy ground, it broke, it overturned.
And eight of that team were killed when the blazing wreckage burned.

Roger Byrne and Tommy Taylor, who were capped for England's side,
And Ireland's Liam Whelan and England's Geoff Bent died.
Mark Jones and Eddie Coleman and David Pegg also,
They all lost their lives as it ploughed on through the snow.

Big Duncan he went too, with an injury to his brain,
And Ireland's brave Jack Blanchflower will never play again.
The great Matt Busby lay there, the father of this team,
Three long months passed by before he saw his team again.

The trainer, coach and secretary and three members of the crew,
Also eight sporting journalists who with United flew,
And one of them was Big Swifty who we will ne'er forget,
The finest English 'keeper that ever graced a net.

England's finest football team its record truly great,
Its proud success mocked by this cruel turn of fate.
Eight men will never play again who met disaster there,
The flowers of English football, the flowers of Manchester.

by The Spinners

United 1 City 2 10/02/2008

Vassell 24, Benjani 45, Carrick 90

The scene at Old Trafford before this match will live long in the memory. The thousands of red-and-white scarves held aloft, the lone piper, the sunshine, the wreaths, the perfectly observed silence…the 50th anniversary could not have been marked with any more style or respect.

What happened afterwards should be filed away in the section of your brain marked Maine Road '89 – and then dumped along with memories of David Oldfield, Clive Wilson, Ian Bishop and the rest. It was no surprise to see United struggle to deal with the emotion enveloping Old Trafford. I can't remember the last time we played well on a Munich anniversary – on the 40th anniversary we even managed to lose to Leicester. But it was a major shock to see us roll over as tamely as we did. City were outrageously fortunate to win the derby in August. After winning every important battle here – and playing some pretty decent stuff on the counter attack – they could count themselves unlucky to only win by one.

Goal action
I'll keep this brief.

0–1 (24): Van der Sar saves at Ireland's feet, Vassell scores at second attempt.

0–2 (45): The Denis Law moment. Benjani flicks in Petrov's cross.

1–2 (90): Carrick passes in a consolation.

Views from the broadsheets
- 'This was supposed to be the day in which we saw all that was best about Manchester United and, in the opening ceremony, it was exactly like that. A lone piper led out the two teams through a guard of honour formed by United's academy players and wreaths were laid in the centre of the pitch by Ferguson and Eriksson. The minute's silence was, in Eriksson's words, "absolutely perfect" but then it should never have been anything but. What followed was most definitely not in the script.' – *The Independent*
- 'Manchester United are so unaccustomed to losing on their own ground that the first thing to digest when it happens is the collective sense of shock. Manchester City had

not won here since 1974 and, when everything is taken into consideration, Sir Alex Ferguson and his players will feel only regret and aching disappointment as they reflect on the 150th Mancunian derby, on the club's own "Remembrance Day", and on their failure to produce a performance fitting for the occasion.' – *The Guardian*

☺ 'The weight of their club's history is a burden that every great Manchester United team must learn to bear and yesterday – of all days – it bore down on Sir Alex Ferguson's side like an anvil. The tribute to those they lost at Munich 50 years ago was moving, profound and fitting in all but one regrettable respect: the performance of the men in the retro 1958 red shirts.' – *The Independent*

What was good?

☺ The silence. Well done Blues.

☺ The applause for the City players as they left the pitch. Well done Reds.

☺ The sponsor-free, '50s-style kit (though it didn't do Tévez any favours – and it wouldn't look good stretched over beer bellies in the stands).

☺ The free scarves. A great idea. Looked brilliant. And would look even better being twirled in mass celebration later in the season.

What was bad?

☺ The helicopter noise. After all the fuss about the silence, what were Sky thinking sending a helicopter buzzing above the stadium?

☺ The idiots who set off rockets behind the South Stand.

☺ The result. City's first win at Old Trafford since Arthur Albiston's testimonial. And their first derby double since '74.

☺ The performance. Terrible, hesitant, confused. How much did we miss Rooney?

☺ A week ago United were level with Arsenal. Now we're five points behind.

Match facts

United: Van der Sar, Brown, Ferdinand, Vidic, O'Shea* (Hargreaves 73), Nani (Park 65), Scholes, Anderson (Carrick 73), Giggs, Ronaldo, Tévez

City: Hart, Onuoha, Richards, Dunne, Ball, Hamann (Sun Jihai 84), Vassell, Fernandes, Ireland, Petrov (Garrido 87), Benjani (Caceido 76) [Eriksson]

FAPL 13.30 (Sky). Att: 75,970. Ref: H. Webb. Half-time: 0–2

Other scores

Chelsea 0 Liverpool 0

League table

1. Arsenal 60 (25) 2. United 58 (26) 4. Chelsea 55 (26)4. Everton 47 (26)...7. City 44 (26)

City to Arsenal
'The ref blew his whistle…and a miracle came to pass.'

News

Sheffield United sack Robbo after barely six months in charge. The anti-Robbo media jump at the chance to remind everyone what a bad manager he is. But is he really that bad? He kept West Brom in the Premier League after they were miles adrift at Christmas. He also put Middlesbrough on the map, leading them into the Premiership and taking them to three Cup Finals inside two seasons – the first Finals in their history. Tell me. What has Terry Venables, the darling of the tabloid press, done in English club football that's better than that?

Basic human dignity

The press go over the top in their coverage of the City fans' silence at Old Trafford. *The Sun* leads the way with the headline:

'The referee blew his whistle…and a MIRACLE came to pass.'

That's right. As *football365.com* put it, '3,000 football people managed to maintain a basic level of human dignity for 60 seconds. A miracle indeed.'

Emily Bishop's kid, Oliver Holt, was at it in *The Mirror* too, yammering:

'Because the truth is that City and their fans helped to turn a fittingly solemn occasion into a magnificent tribute to the spirit of a lost age. Let's not stint in our praise of the City supporters for honouring the minute's silence to remember the 23 people killed in the Munich air crash. Let's not gloss it over just because nothing went wrong.'

Whatever next. Hoodies praised for not attacking pensioners? Footballers for only sleeping with girls two at a time? Richard Scudamore for his 39th Step?

Out of Africa

Egypt win the Africa Cup of Nations, beating Cameroon 1–0 in the Final. Four-goal Manucho is selected above Eto'o and Drogba in the team of the tournament. Eto'o wins the Golden Boot with five goals for Cameroon while Egypt midfield Hosny Abd Rabo is named the player of the tournament. Manucho is loaned to Panathinaikos for the rest of the season.

The ACN team of the tournament in full:

El-Hadary (Egypt), Geremi (Cameroon/Newcastle), Gomaa (Egypt), Muntari (Ghana/Portsmouth), Y. Toure (Ivory Coast/ Barcelona), A.Song (Cameroon/Arsenal), Rabo, Aboutreika, Zaky (all Egypt), Manucho (Angola/United)

No team talk required

William Gallas chooses an odd time to shoot off about United – the team, the party and the superstar:

'They are a strong team with lots of experienced players. But, sometimes, they think they're too good. Too arrogant, yes. It can make you complacent. We understand that problem. We know we have to score goals, be strong in defence and kill teams in the first half. Our squad can win things. And I know that it will be difficult for Manchester United to win.'

About the Xmas party:

'It would not happen at Arsenal. We have dinner parties with the wives and girlfriends. It's hard to understand why they did it.'

On Ronaldo:

'It was not easy against him, but it was not that difficult either.'

International Reds (from 6 February)

Rooney, Ferdinand, Brown and Hargreaves feature as England beat Switzerland 2–1 in Capello's first game in charge. Ronaldo and Nani finish on the losing side as Portugal go down 3–1 in Italy. Park scores South Korea's third goal in their 4–0 demolition of Turkmenistan. Anderson's Brazil beat O'Shea's Ireland 1–0 in Dublin. Van der Sar keeps a clean sheet as the Dutch thump three past Croatia. Vidic's Serbia draw 1–1 with Macedonia. Jonny Evans scores a crucial own-goal as Northern Ireland's go down 1–0 against Bulgaria.

Quotes of the week

- 'I had never played at Burnley before and I didn't even know where it was' – Andy Cole shows an amazing lack of geographical awareness after his move from Sunderland to Burnley. He did play for Blackburn after all.
- 'Nani never stops talking. I lived with him for two months when I first came to Manchester and he just never kept quiet! I wanted to sleep, he'd keep talking, and never seemed to stop!' – Anderson gives us another insight into Nani.
- 'I don't feel particularly comfortable among United fans even now. Most of them are fine, but there have been a few…situations. I don't think I'd go to Old Trafford to watch a game.' – Martin Keown explains why he won't be at the Arsenal Cup game. Clearly he's worried about being surrounded and set upon by a group of thugs led by a deranged ape. It's happened before you know.
- 'My favourite tie was the semi-final in 1999 at Villa Park against Arsenal. It had everything.' – As he prepares for his 100th FA Cup tie, Fergie nominates his favourite FA Cup memory. And, perhaps surprisingly, it's not the City Ground in 1990 (for what it's worth, I've got a soft spot for Denis Irwin's penalty-winning triple salko at Wembley in '94).

Fergie's Cup Quiz

1. Who scored United's first FA Cup goal under Fergie?
2. Who did they beat in that first game?
3. Which players have missed penalties in the FA Cup (not including penalty shootouts)?
4. Which Reds have been sent off in the FA Cup?
5. Which players were fouled for the two penalties in the 1994 Final?
6. What was special about the 1992 tie with Southampton?
7. How many games did Eric lose for United in the FA Cup?
8. What was Fergie's longest winning streak in the FA Cup?
9. Who should United have played in the 2000 FA Cup?
10. What was significant about Ian Rush's last Liverpool touch?
11. What was the first televised FA Cup game under Fergie?

Answers: 1. Whiteside 2. City 3. McClair, Bruce 4. Schmeichel, Keane x 2 5. Irwin, Kanchelskis 6. First FA Cup game to go to pens 7. 0 8. 1998–2001 9. Villa 10. It set up Eric for the Cup winner in '96 11. Ipswich Town 2–1 Jan 1988

158

United 4 Arsenal 0   17/02/2008

Rooney 14, Fletcher 18, 73, Nani 37

This had been a tough week for United fans. The derby was awful, just awful, and so was work on Monday. The League suddenly looked a tall order. Defeat here would pile the pressure on the game in Lyon. But the great thing about football is its ability to take you from the brink of suicide to the brink of an orgasm in an instant. Or in this case within a few minutes. First Barnsley dump Liverpool out of the Cup – and send Dickie Bird mental – with the last kick at Anfield. And then this happens at Old Trafford. The FA Cup is a shadow of the competition it once was, but there's no doubt that the old boy can still bang out some cracking tunes…

Arsenal-beating – a minute-by-minute guide:

0: As usual, Fergie and Wenger both take the opportunity to sprinkle their Cup teams with reserves. For United there's no Tévez, Ronaldo, Hargreaves or Giggs. For Arsenal there's no Clichy, Sagna, Flamini or Adebayor. Maybe it's because of the changes that the game takes a while to get going. Maybe it's because of the pitch, which is terrible. Whatever, there's nothing much to shout about early on.

8: The first sniff. Evra's cross is deflected to Anderson and his snap-volley (is that a word?) forces a decent-ish save from Lehmann low to his right.

PARK! CHANCE!
12: Gallas, under pressure from a typically pumped-up Fletcher, gives Rooney a sniff with a poor back pass, but Lehmann does well to slide out and clear. The ball gets recycled to Fletcher again and his cross picks out Park unmarked 15 yards out. It's a difficult chance on the volley, but it's not as difficult as Parky makes it look. He can't decide which foot to go for the ball with, ends up going with both and barely makes contact with either. Still, it's a clear sign that United are hitting their stride…

CORNER! ROONEY! GOAL!
14: Here's an even clearer one. Evra and Anderson turn into a left-footed blur on the left and force a corner. Vidic clears out the defenders at the near post, the ball loops up for Anderson and his header back into the six-yard box is flicked past Lehmann by Rooney. Amazingly, Motty doesn't give us any stats afterwards. I want to know how many headers Rooney's scored for us. It can't be many.

17: A superb cameo from Anderson who gets the ball in his own half, quicksteps around Gilberto, surges past three more Arsenal players and makes it as far as the area before trying one trick too many. Lawro raves 'he's going to be a wonderful football player' in that special Lawro voice of his. He then says he's not quite so convinced about Nani. That's fair comment. But the mini-Ronaldo's going to have a brilliant night too...

FLETCHER! GALLAS! GOAL!

18: What a start! Anderson rolls it to Nani on the left, he dummies Hoyte out of the game, brings the ball back onto his right foot and dinks in a cross that Fletcher wants more than Gallas. The ball flicks off Fletcher's head and then Gallas's and finds a gap at the near post. As Fletcher slides on his backside towards the corner flag, Old Trafford bellows 'Who are yer'. I'm not sure about that chant. Sounds cheap.

20: It's all United. Anderson feeds Park on the right, he cuts back onto his left foot and floats over a centre that Rooney – who's got defenders all around him but keeps on getting himself free – nods just over.

22: Anderson's started brilliantly. So has Nani. Rooney too. But Fletcher is perhaps outplaying them all. I can remember him doing brilliantly against Vieira in the Cup semi in 2004 – back in the days when many people thought he might really make it. He's playing just as well here. In the space of a minute he dumps Hleb on his backside, takes out Fabregas, wins the ball off Traore and forces a free-kick out of Toure that Nani chips straight at Lehmann.

24: Hleb tries to play a one-two with Bendtner on the edge of the box but gets it all wrong, the ball rolling miserably out of play. It's the closest Arsenal have come.

25: As *Take me Home* goes round the stadium, Arsenal create their first half-chance, Bendtner setting up Hleb for a volley that the flying Evra blocks.

31: Arsenal just can't handle Rooney – though it would help their chances if they got within a couple of yards of him. Evra volleys Lehmann's weak goal-kick over Toure, Rooney tries to flick the ball over Gallas à la Gazza in Euro '96 but doesn't quite get the connection right. Instead he has a swing at the ball with his left foot and drags it wide.

33: Fletcher's playing like he's been snorting powdered Irn Bru. Here he holds off the spindly Hleb, bursts past three Arsenal defenders and picks out Rooney's hairy chest. Rooney kills the ball but drags his volley wide. He could have had a hat-trick by now.

34: 'Arsenal are being outplayed here, one has to say that.' What's this? Motty giving an opinion? Eat your heart out Andy Gray.

36: After Evra is fouled, Van der Sar chats with Alan Wiley. The man is literally half his height. Is he the smallest ref ever? Or was that Paul Durkin? It's strange, I couldn't stand Durkin – who looked like a ginger relative of Postman Pat – at the time, but I sort of miss him now. I'm the same with David Elleray and that guy with the grey permed hair. I guess you only realise what you had when they're gone – and you're stuck with the likes of Bennett, Clattenburg and Rennie instead.

CARRICK! NANI! GOAL!
37: I didn't say that Carrick was playing well did I? He's not. He's playing superbly, unleashing a barrage of astute and devastating passes over and through the Arsenal defence. This time he takes out two white lines of players – nine Arsenal players in all – with a lofted ball from near halfway. Nani reacts quicker than Traore, kills the ball with his right foot and thumps it past Lehmann with his left. After the obligatory somersault, Vidic and Park rub his hair. Might be a mistake that. What with the amount of product he uses, they'll be gluing themselves to things all night.

38: 'That's why we're champions'... 'Who the f*** are Man United'...Old Trafford is enjoying this. Remember that Arsenal fan from the game we lost in 1998 – the dark-haired madman with the deranged face? I always like thinking about him at times like this. Bin Laden must be gutted too. I wonder if he really does support Arsenal – and if so, is he watching? And where? I guess he's not going to let on.

39: As United indulge themselves with some Ole keep-ball, Motty reveals it was 50/1 for them to be up 3–0 at half-time.

42: 'Are you watching Merseyside?' Old Trafford asks. They probably won't be. Everton lost to Oldham weeks ago. Liverpool lost to Barnsley minutes ago. Barnsley. Yes Barnsley. At home. Brilliant. As I said earlier, sometimes the FA Cup really is as good as it's supposed to be.

43: Brown pulls a Ronaldo move on Traore, Anderson batters Gilberto again, Fletcher bullies Hleb again (it's a skinny man thing, I think). All across the pitch United are doing more and wanting it more, much more. Arsenal really have been appalling. They're playing terrible football with no guts.

45+: The half ends with Viv showboating in the corner. That man-boy has got the strongest backside I've since Hughesie started rampaging through centre-halves in '84. 'Hunger and desire,' Hansen growls in the studio as a teenage United fan pulls faces behind him. 'One team are playing as if their lives depend on it. The other team playing with an air that it really doesn't matter who wins.'

45: It'll be interesting to see how Arsenal react to their first-half drubbing. Will they bring on Adebayor and Flamini and have a go? Will they settle for 3–0? Will they sulk? Will they get themselves pumped up? There's a definite clue in the way they loiter around the entrance of the tunnel and only reluctantly come back on the pitch. Pumped up? Most of them look terrified – like an overweight teenager heading for a nudist beach for the first time.

46: There are more clues as the match starts. United are still right on top. Arsenal are still treading water. United almost score with their first attack. Park heads Carrick's ball over the top, Rooney's movement kills Gallas, but his rasping volley hits Lehmann. 'Looks like the Arsenal team talk's worked then', Lawro observes wryly.

46: One to remember for later (a week or so later). Nani overruns the ball after a short corner on the right, pulls out of the challenge with Eduardo and is rewarded with a set of studs landing on his inside thigh. It's a terrible tackle, even if the commentators try to hide behind the 'just a forward's tackle' cliché (it shouldn't matter what position you play, if you nearly castrate someone you should walk). Eduardo survives with a yellow card. From the free-kick, Rooney – with the aid of a small deflection off Fletcher's chest – brings a smart save out of Lehmann.

EBOUE! RED!
48: It's not long before Arsenal do find themselves a man light though. This time it's Eboue with an awful studs-up lunge on Evra as he's jumping for a high ball. This time Lawro and Motty are unanimous. It's a definite red. Or as Motty puts it, 'it's a black-and-white case to show a red'.

49.55: Eboue finally leaves the field, 70 seconds after he should have done.

51: Wiley's cards are out again as Ferdinand, perhaps getting bored with having nothing to do, goes right through Bendtner on the touchline. This has definitely got the feel of a United-Arsenal game now.

57: Carrick's at it again, taking the Arsenal defence out with a long floated ball over the top. Park, running in from the right, should take the ball down and slide it past Lehmann. Instead he goes for a super-difficult lob on the volley and for the second time barely makes contact.

59: Ridiculous. Wiley books Rooney for delaying an Arsenal free-kick. Let's see, his team is 3–0 up with a one-man advantage. It's unlikely he's going to be wasting time is it Alan?

60: It's Gilberto's turn to go in Wiley's book. Park bullies the pathetic Hleb, spins away from Fabregas and the Brazilian chops him down at the ankles.

CARRICK! ROONEY! HANDBALL! PENALTY! WHAT? : 61: Carrick fires another missile of a pass onto Rooney's chest on the left side the area. He instantly flicks the dropping ball past Toure who instinctively flicks his arm out. It's a clear penalty – and red card? – but Wiley plays the 'advantage' and Rooney gets his finish all wrong. Arsenal really are lucky to be just three behind.

62: Rooney is giving a masterclass in how to play up front on your own. The only thing that's spoiling his evening is his finishing. This time he's sent clear on Lehmann by Anderson, but once again he can only find the German's legs.

63: Arsenal finally create a chance that sort of goes near the goal. Fabregas plays the ball into the area and Eduardo nods it onto the roof of the net.

66: Rooney's square pass gives Anderson the opportunity to charge past Gallas and go one-on-one with Lehmann. Unfortunately, he takes option B – a difficult poke shot on the wide – and sends it wide.

68: Brilliant stuff. Carrick shimmies through traffic and picks out Rooney on the edge of the area who pokes the ball first time to Anderson to curl a much better effort straight at Lehmann.

69: Wholesale changes as Senderos, Adebayor and Flamini come on for Fabregas, Hleb and Eduardo. Saha comes on for Rooney and Scholes for Anderson. As the two embrace Scholesy nods at Viv as if to say 'You'll do for me'. He will too. He only needs to find his range with his shooting and he'll be just about perfect.

NANI! CROSS! FLETCHER! GOAL!
73: Yes, you beauty (and no, I'm not being literal here). Fletcher scores with a header. And this time it's definitely all his own work. Nani slows Hoyte down on the left, then squares him up, then speeds up, then slows him down and then squares him up and finally dinks a left-footed cross to the back post. Lehmann is too late to stop Fletcher's header crashing over the line.

74: Another harsh yellow – this time for Fletcher, who barely touches Senderos.

74: Adebayor makes his only notable contribution, flinging himself to the floor in the worst attempt to con a penalty you'll ever see. 'Dear oh dear oh dear', Lawro says as Adebayor becomes the seventh player in half an hour to go in the book.

SHOWBOATING! NANI!
75: Van der Sar's rushed clearance kicks off the most memorable cameo of the night. Evra backheels the ball in midair to Nani. He takes it on his thigh with Hoyte all over his back. Then he heads it twice while running towards his own goal. Then he uses his thigh twice. Then it's the left foot and the right foot. He's now near the penalty area as he finally lets the ball hit the ground and spins past Hoyte. Hoyte tries to kick him once, then twice and then, after Flamini tackles the ball out of play, he takes a petulant swipe. The crowd are loving it. Arsenal aren't.

GALLAS! RED! NO!
76: Gallas succeeds where Hoyte fails, fouling Nani from behind and then, as the ball gets cleared, giving him a belt up the back of a leg. It's more petulance from the pizza throwers. And it should be a red card. But Wiley gives Arsenal a free-kick. Bizarre.

GILBERTO! RED! NO!
80: Arsenal are still not doing anything when they have the ball. But they're reverting back to their petulant, sly old ways when they don't. Gilberto blatantly takes out Saha from behind as he charges towards the area and then does the old trick of limping away from the scene of the crime. He should be limping all the way to the showers. In fact, if Wiley hadn't been so lenient they'd be five goals and four men down by now.

87: As *Cheer up Alan Shearer* gets an airing another terrible tackle comes in on Nani, this time from the out-of-his-depth Traore. I thought Wenger said it's always Arsenal who get the kickings...

88: Carrick splits the defence yet again. Saha should score, but his toe-poke is smothered by Lehmann. As good as Carrick, Fletcher, Nani, Rooney, Evra, Anderson and the rest have been, I reckon Lehmann might just be Man of the Match. I can't remember the last time a 'keeper made so many saves at Old Trafford.

92: Evra squares the ball and Saha lashes in a first-time curler that beats Lehmann but also the upright. And that's it. A brilliant win. A terrible defeat. And one big question. How would this demolition affect Arsenal's season? There was only ever going to be one answer to that, as we'd soon see...

View from the broadsheets

✪ 'Napoleon can hardly have retreated from Moscow with less dignity than Arsenal returned to London from Manchester. This drubbing exposed not only the team's inadequacy on the day in the face of a rampant United side who sensed miserable resistance almost from the kick-off, but also Arsène Wenger's tepid commitment to the FA Cup, whatever his ready-made complaints of depleted resources before and after.'
  – *The Observer*

Pun of the day

'He showed what a good player he really is. Sometimes you go with horses for courses and this game was tailor-made for Darren. He always does well against Arsenal. It was Darren's day.' – Fergie on the man formerly known as the Scottish player.

Excuse of the day

'The groundsman had as bad a day as us. You will see us in a different shape when we come back and play on a different pitch. The pitch is a disgrace. You have players worth £20–25million and you cannot play a pass without it bouncing' – Wenger blames the pitch. Now it didn't seem to affect United much did it?

Quote of the day

'He was sharp, he was mobile, he was quick, he was aggressive, he was even good in the air. I think he was just amazing.' – Wenger's on firmer ground here (no pun intended), raving about Rooney's performance as a lone striker.

Match facts

United: Van der Sar, Brown, Ferdinand*, Vidic, Evra, Fletcher*, Carrick, Anderson (Scholes 72), Park, Rooney* (Saha 71), Nani
Arsenal: Lehmann, Hoyte, Gallas, Toure, Traore, Eboue 49†, Fabregas (Flamini 70), Silva*, Hleb (Adebayor 70*), Eduardo*, Bendtner
FAC5 17.15 Old Trafford. Att: 75,550. Ref: A. Wiley. Half-time: 3–0
*Yellow card. † Red card

Other scores

FA Cup fifth round:
Liverpool 1 (Kuyt) Barnsley 2 (Foster, Howard); Chelsea 3 (Lampard 2, Kalou) Huddersfield 1 (Collins)

Arsenal to Lyon

'We went for a walk before the game and a bird dumped right on my head.'

Warm your balls

What are the chances? United get another Premiership team, Portsmouth, in the quarter-finals of the Cup. Chelsea, the conquerors of the mighty QPR, Wigan and Huddersfield, get another bag of crap. Liverpool get, er, to watch the games on telly. Lovely.

On a loop

'They are a strong team with lots of experienced players. But, sometimes, they think they're too good. Too arrogant, yes…Our squad can win things. And I know that it will be difficult for Manchester United to win.' William Gallas's pre-match outburst sounds even better second time round.

And as for you

'Clearly this is a Cup Final for them, so we must be careful and give them a lot of respect. If we score first everything will be okay.' – Looking back, Rafa Benitez might have kept this nugget inside him too.

Out of their depth

Just a few weeks after sending out a signal that it's OK to headbutt a teammate – as long as you play for Arsenal – the FA get it hopelessly wrong again, letting Gallas off scott free for kicking Nani. Clearly, then, if you show some skill in a game, maybe (horror of horrors) juggle the ball for a couple of seconds, then it's quite OK for petulant cry babies to give you a kicking. I'd like to see the FA's reaction if Rooney or Ronaldo ever put that principle into practice.

Quotes of the week

- 'The referee was not satisfied that it [footage of the Gallas incident] showed evidence of violent conduct and no action will be taken.' – The FA explains why Gallas won't be punished. Apparently, Alan Wiley looked at the tape of Gallas's kick and concluded that there wasn't one. Christ, with eyesight like that, it's a wonder he can even find his Y-fronts in a morning.
- 'What I will say is that there's one law for Arsenal and another for everyone else. Or a different rule.' – Justifiably, Fergie is left fuming.
- 'We went for a walk before the game and a bird dumped right on my head. They say that can be a lucky omen – and it was!' – Barnsley manager Simon Davey reveals the secret of the Tykes' shock Anfield success.

Journalist of the week

The Times's excellent Martin Samuel on Arsenal's surrender and Nani's showboating:

'Lack of respect? Falling over in the penalty area when nobody has tripped you: that is a lack of respect. Playing half a team in an FA Cup tie at Old Trafford: that is a lack of respect. But, in the middle of a match, running with the ball while juggling it masterfully between feet, knees and head? If you are good enough, then why not?

Nani did nothing wrong in his little moment of showboating on Saturday and paying fans know it. They want to be entertained, not to have Arsène Wenger put his best players on the bench, or to see Emmanuel Adebayor fall to the ground in a wretched attempt to win a penalty by cheating.

Arsenal surrendered the moral high ground long before they tried to hack down Manchester United's winger as he performed his little seal act. They are lucky Nani didn't blow raspberries and stop to make bunny ears as he dribbled around them, really. It was what their performance deserved.

The game is about skill. It is, in its purest form, about trying to do something that places one player beyond the ability of his opponent. That is why it is so terribly depressing to hear a chorus of disapproval greet Nani's cameo. It was the highlight of a second half that had been rendered redundant by Arsenal's inability to compete, yet even Sir Alex Ferguson said he would have a word with his player about treating opponents with dignity.

Nani gave Arsenal the respect they deserved. He demonstrated what a good player can do against a team who play without heart. And he showed that, in the heat of battle, he has the wit to keep the ball and shield it in mid-air, while dribbling, a display of dexterity as impressive as any seen this season.'

Respect.

Lyon 1 United 1 20/02/2008

Benzema 54, Tévez 87

Plus ça change, plus c'est la meme chose, as the locals might say. United never seem to turn it on in France. Or at least they haven't since Montpelier in '91. But they do have a nice knack of getting themselves out of trouble right at the death. This game played like a rerun of a French trip from the Ole and Ruud days. Lyon's disciplined tactics and eagerness to close down space bogged United down. Benzema's sensational goal out of nothing left us in a precarious position, but Tévez's deserved late equaliser changed the whole complexion of the tie. If Lyon were to progress they'd have to do something that only two French sides have ever managed at Old Trafford. And that's score.

Goal action

1–0 (54): Non! In France Karim Benzema has already been dubbed Le Phenomene and L'Extraterrestre, and it's moments like this that explains why. Toulalan plays in ET, he takes the ball with his right foot and instantly thrashes it across Van der Sar with his left. 'A fantastic goal,' Fergie said.

1–1 (87): Yes! Carrick's goalbound shot is blocked, the ball gets recycled to Nani on the right, he launches the ball into a chaotic goalmouth, Squillaci fails to clear and Tévez slams it into the roof of the net.

What was good?

🅥 We didn't lose. We got a vital away goal. And we didn't get tear-gassed.

What was bad?

🅥 Once again in Europe, we didn't impose ourselves on the game – in fact we didn't really try.

🅥 'L'Etoile Benzema' will be waiting for us at Old Trafford.

🅥 And it wasn't just *The Telegraph* that was left with nagging doubts about the futures of Giggs and Scholes (see below).

View from the broadsheets

'THE board was held up into the night air and the numbers conveyed a deeper significance than just the names of the substitutes, Ryan Giggs and Paul Scholes, the men who had carried Manchester United through so many campaigns, walked off to be replaced by the new generation of Carlos Tévez and Nani.

'In the event, both men played a role in the move that finished with Tévez volleying the ball into the roof of the Lyon net three minutes from the end of a match that United ought to have lost. In games past, it was Scholes and Giggs who provided these late goals.

'They may simply just have had a bad game but last night it felt like something more, something sadder. That it came in Giggs' 100th game in the Champions League made it rather more poignant although United should be deeply grateful that they can still retrieve this tie at Old Trafford.' – *The Telegraph* might have overstated the case. After all Scholesy had only just come back from a knee operation. And now that he's lost his searing pace Giggsy is far more effective playing centrally than on the wing. But watching them here it was hard not to fight the feeling that the two United legends were finally starting to lose their battle against time.

Lyon – the verbals

- 'It was a crucial goal to take back to Old Trafford. I felt we controlled the game for most of it.' – Rooney's confident.
- 'This has given us a good opportunity to qualify. I don't think Lyon had that many clear chances. Our goalkeeper has not had a save to make, and I didn't feel that threatened.' – Fergie's calm.
- 'As things stand, we're out.' – Alain Perrin's depressed.
- 'We were disappointed not to win after taking the lead. But we knew that, along with Inter Milan, Manchester United were the best team in Europe and have many players who can do you damage. Ronaldo, Rooney, Tévez – what an attacking line-up! Against a team like United, you have to play perfectly. We nearly did it – but not quite.' – Juninho, the Lyon version.
- 'Carlos reminds me of Eric Cantona in the way that he has a knack of rising to the occasion with a goal just when it's needed' – Fergie again.

Allo Allo

United's results against French teams at Old Trafford (and Home Park*):
1964–65 United 0 Strasbourg 0; 1977–78 United 2 St Etienne 0*; 1990–91 United 1 Montpelier 1; 1999–2000 United 2 Marseille 1, United 2 Bordeaux 0; 2001–02 United 1 Lille 0, United 5 Nantes 1; 2004–05 United 2 Lyon 1; 2005–06 United 0 Lille 0; 2006–07 United 1 Lille 0

Home: P 10   W 7   D 3   L 0   F 16   A 4

United's record in France:

1964–65 Strasbourg 0 United 5; 1977–78 St Etienne 1 United 1; 1990–01 Montpelier 0 United 2; 1999–2000 Marseille 1 United 0, Bordeaux 1 United 2; 2001–02 Lille 1 United 1, Nantes 1 United 1; 2004–05 Lyon 2 United 2; 2005–06 Lille 1 United 0; 2006–07 Lille 0 United 1; 2007–08 Lyon 1 United 1

Away: P 11   W 4   D 5   L 2   F 16   A 9

Match facts

Lyon: Coupet, Reveillere*, Squillaci, Boumsong*, Grosso, Clerc (Ben Arfa 78), Juninho (Bodmer 73), Toulalan*, Kallstrom, Govou, Benzema (Fred 83) [Perrin]
United: Van der Sar, Brown, Ferdinand, Vidic, Evra, Ronaldo, Scholes (Tévez 65), Hargreaves* (Carrick 78), Anderson, Giggs (Nani 65), Rooney
CL1/8 19.45(Sky). Att: 39,230. Ref: L.M. Cantalejo (Sp). Half-time: 0–0
*Yellow card

Other scores

Roma 2 Real Madrid 1; Olympiacos 0 Chelsea 0; Liverpool 2 Inter 0; Celtic 2 Barcelona 3; Fenerbahce 3 Sevilla 2; Arsenal 0 Milan 0; Schalke 1 Porto 0

Lyon to Newcastle

'Let's put Liverpool's achievement in context: Inter are crap'

Song of the week

Anderson!-son! -son!
He's better than Kleberson,
Anderson!-son! -son!
Our midfield mag-ic-i-an
To the left, to the right,
To the samba beat tonight,
With the brass he is class,
And he shits on Fab-re-gassss!
(To the tune of Black Lace's *Agadoo*)
I struggle to fit in the Kleberson bit. What do you think?

Surprise of the week

I never thought I'd hear Manchester's finest singing along to *Agadoo*.

Aiming low

Amusing quote from Peter Kenyon after the 'world's greatest football empire TM' unveils losses of 'just' £74.8 million for last season:

'Our long-term target of operating profit break even by 2009–10 remains ambitious, but we are determined to meet it or get as close as we can.

'In the meantime, we have made good on our pledges of last year, hitting all of our aims.'

Anyone missing him at Old Trafford do you think?

A game too far

⚽ 'You can't stand still, and if we don't do this then somebody else is going to do it, whether it be football or another sport. Therefore it's trying to ride the crest of that wave at the same as protecting what is good and great about what we do. Every time there is an evolutionary step, the reaction of the fans is not always great, but I would ask them to take a step back and look at the positives.' – As the idea gets widely trashed, Richard Scudamore asks us to think of all the positives to the 39th game. No I can't think of any either...

⚽ 'This does not take into consideration the fans of the clubs and it gives the impression that they just want to go on tour to make some money. This will never happen, at least as long as I am the president of FIFA.' – For once, FIFA president Sepp Blatter gets something right.

Damn him

'A move to United wouldn't be right for me at this time. I have said I wouldn't leave Lyon until we've won the Champions League, and I have no intention of trying to go too quickly.' – Karim Benzema plays down the Lyon to United talk.

Commentator of the week

'Let's put Liverpool's achievement in context: Inter are crap' – RTE's Eamon Dunphy after Liverpool get a massively flattering 2–0 win over 10-man Inter Milan.

Misleading headline of the week

A top spot from *football365*: 'Fergie To Front Calvin Klein Campaign' – Digital Spy nearly give us a heart attack.

Rumour of the week

'Paul Gascoigne stunned hotel staff before being sent to a psychiatric unit by answering his door in the buff – with "MAD" scrawled on his forehead. The fallen soccer hero's only companions while he remained holed up in his room on a two-month drugs and booze binge were battery-operated PARROTS. Ex-England ace Gazza, 40, would talk to one of them as if it were real, a source revealed. He also wandered around the hotel with them under his arm, getting them to squawk "f*** off" to fellow guests' – *The Sun* reports on the sad story of Gazza, who was sectioned after a series of bizarre incidents during his stay at Gateshead's Malmaison Hotel.

Newcastle 1 United 5   23/02/2008

Rooney 25, 80, Ronaldo 45, 56, Faye 79, Saha 90

In every title race there are days you just know are going to change the course of the season. No one ever thought this was going to be one of them. As Arsenal kicked-off in their lunchtime game at struggling Birmingham they were odds on to stretch their lead at the top to eight points. Three minutes into it, when Birmingham's Martin Taylor was sent off for his infamous lunge on Eduardo, it seemed an absolute certainty. But then something very strange happened. First McFadden curled in a free-kick to give Birmingham a half-time lead. Then, after Walcott had turned the game round with two quick goals, madness took hold of the French half of the Arsenal back four. First, Clichy had a Mickey Silvestre moment in his area and conceded a needless penalty, which McFadden converted. And as the spot-kick was hitting the net, William Gallas showcased his captaincy prowess by storming down to the other end of the pitch and throwing his toys out of the pram.

So, in the course of one lunchtime, Arsenal had lost two points, their heads and one of their key strikers. And Gallas had lost the respect of the press, the public and his teammates. And once United had gone through Newcastle like a bad curry, they weren't just back in the title race, they had the momentum back with them too.

Goal action

Preamble (0): Despite the 6–0 battering at Old Trafford, and Newcastle's relegation form, there was still a worry that United might come unstuck at St James', that Keegan might come up with a fairytale first victory, that Smudger might choose the worst possible time to finally score his first Newcastle goal. But then the game started, and it immediately became clear that that Newcastle's mismatched defence wouldn't be able to hold Beardsmore and Milne, never mind the two Rs...

1–0 (25): United were guilty of over-elaborating early on, but as soon as they get back to basics they make the breakthrough. Ronaldo spins past Beye near the corner flag, his dipping centre takes Given out of the game and Rooney volleys in, unmarked, at the far post.

2–0 (45): What with the problems facing Gazza, Keegan and Tweedy, these were tough times for the Geordie nation. But one Geordie, Michael Carrick, was having a ball, one minute relieving Barton and Butt of possession, the next threading beautifully judged passes to the front four. On the stroke of half-time he produces the ball of the night, releasing Ronaldo down a narrow corridor between Taylor and Beye. After judging his first touch perfectly Ronaldo never looks like missing. And he doesn't.

3–0 (56): The first two goals were a mix of United excellence and flawed defending. Number three was all Newcastle's work. First Faye picks out Fletcher with his attempted clearance, then Taylor collapses inexplicably to the floor to allow Ronaldo a free run on goal. A neat sidestep later and he's got his fifth against Newcastle in two games.

3–1 (79): After Ronaldo is denied another Newcastle hat-trick by Fergie (who dragged him off for a rest), the game meanders for a few minutes. And it probably would have carried on meandering right to the end if Faye hadn't tweaked the lion's tail by thumping in a corner.

4–1 (80): United's reply is as stunning as it is quick. Smith clears a corner straight to Rooney, who's lurking on the edge of the box. He gets the ball out of his feet and then bends a gorgeous shot into the right corner.

5–1 (90): And there's still time for Saha to remind us what an enormous asset he could be to United, if only he could stay fit. First he surges past three Newcastle players in midfield, then he kills Rooney's return ball and, with defenders all around him, instantly passes it right-footed into the net.

Views from the broadsheets

⊙ 'Some day Sir Alex Ferguson will get the credit he deserves. Perhaps it will be when he is gone from Manchester United. A result as comprehensive as this inevitably provoked another outbreak of sneering at Newcastle United and Kevin Keegan, but that should not be allowed to obscure the controlled swirl of the champions' attacking on Saturday night and Ferguson's primary role in assembling both the personnel involved and instilling in them a philosophy that embraces risk and beauty with the overlooked genius of common-sense defending.' – *The Independent*

⊙ 'One of the best days of Sir Alex Ferguson's season, one of the worst of Kevin Keegan's managerial career. That 5–0 Newcastle video from 1996 can go back on to the shelf where it belongs as Manchester United's 5–1 victory last night was of such emphasis and ease that it obliterated memory. All that could be seen was the here and now and while for the champions it is beguiling and full of anticipation following Arsenal's dropped points at Birmingham, for Newcastle it is miserable and the worst may yet be to come.' – *The Independent on Sunday*

☺ 'In the build-up Kevin Keegan had, unwisely, been persuaded to reminisce about his famous 5–0 victory 11 seasons ago but that result stands as a gross exception when it comes to meetings between these sides. In history, no team has put the ball more often in Newcastle's net nor won against them more times than Manchester United. And, in the present day, certain things seem guaranteed. When the black and white shirts are before them, Wayne Rooney will play a blinder and Ronaldo will fill his golden boots.' – *The Sunday Times*

☺ 'The only good news for Newcastle was that Manchester United did not hit six, as they did at Old Trafford last month. The bad news was that they could easily have had eight or nine.' – *The Observer*

☺ 'Arsène Wenger should be grateful United do not face Newcastle every week.' – *The Guardian*

☺ 'Pre-kick-off entertainment was a ball-juggling show by two "football freestylers", but it was Rooney who staged the real exhibition. He scored twice and played three positions, striker, midfielder, winger, each of them consummately. It is not always the case, but sometimes there are games when you understand why comparisons made early in his career between Rooney and the multi-faceted Duncan Edwards may prove prophetic. Ronaldo was an effortless virtuoso. Without nearing full intensity, the Portuguese piled two lovely goals upon the hat-trick he scored against Newcastle at Old Trafford.' – *The Sunday Times*

Stats of the day

United have put 10 or more goals past the same side in a season four times in the Fergie era. They've done it twice against Newcastle in the last six seasons:

Ipswich 1994–95: 11 (2–3, 9–0)

Nottingham Forest 1998–99: 11 (3–0, 8–1)

Newcastle 2002–03: (5–3, 6–2)

Newcastle 2007–08: (6–0, 5–1)

United's 5–1 win is their third biggest at St James' ever, after:

1907–08: Newcastle 1 United 6 (Wall 2, J. Turnbull, S. Turnbull, Roberts, Meredith)

2002–03: Newcastle 2 United 6 (Scholes 3, Solskjaer, Giggs, Ruud pen)

But United haven't scored more goals against Newcastle than any other club, as many of the papers reported. Here's the top six, with the total games in brackets:

Arsenal 305 (202)

Aston Villa 303 (168)

Newcastle 291 (148)

Everton 259 (175)

Chelsea 242 (149)

Liverpool 240 (174)

Newcastle – the verbals

- '5–1 is not really a fair reflection – we were 2–0 down at half-time without having really done anything wrong. But it's bad mistakes and in the end they punished us. Sadly for us it could have been worse.' – King Kev can't seem to make up his mind if 5–1 score wasn't a fair reflection because Newcastle deserved better, or worse.
- 'We can say that this week was our week.' – Carlos Queiroz is a satisfied man.
- 'They're full of football.' – Keegan's excellent tribute to United.
- 'I'm 110 per cent committed to this club, and you can't get more committed than that.' – Kev with another Keeganism.

Match facts

Newcastle: Given (Harper half-time), Beye, Taylor, Faye*, N'Zogbia*, Milner (Geremi 84), Butt*, Barton (Carroll 61), Duff, Smith, Owen* [Keegan]

United: Van der Sar, Brown, Vidic (Scholes 74), Ferdinand, Evra (O'Shea 46), Ronaldo (Saha 67), Carrick, Fletcher, Nani, Rooney, Tévez

FAPL 17.15* (Set) St James' Park. Att: 52,291. Ref: C. Foy. Half-time: 2–0

*Yellow card

Other scores

Birmingham 2 (McFadden 2(1 pen)) Arsenal 2 (Walcott 2); Liverpool 3 (Torres 3) Middlesbrough 2 (Tuncay, Downing)

League table

1. Arsenal 64 (27) 2. United 61 (27) 3. Chelsea 55 (26) 4. Liverpool 47 (26)…13. Newcastle 28 (27)

Newcastle to Fulham
'S*** happens.'

I'm having my tea

There's no question which story dominated the football world this week. It was Eduardo's horrific ankle injury. Sky TV chose not to show footage at the time but then Sky Sports News spent a week showing the footage of Eduardo's left foot all but hanging off, Alan Smith screaming at Anfield and David Busst making Peter Schmeichel sick at Old Trafford. Cheers for that guys…

You only need to kill one person one time

'The tackle was horrendous, and this guy should never play football again. That kind of tackle was waiting to happen to one of our players. I've seen some bad ones, but they're not always punished with broken legs. You only need to kill one person one time [for these things to be taken seriously]. You cannot accept that on a football pitch. You could see that they went out with a "stop Arsenal, kick Arsenal" approach.' – Wenger rages after Eduardo's injury. But while his anger is understandable, he misses the point completely by launching into another 'everyone's out to get Arsenal' rant. Clearly he'd forgotten what his own players – including Eduardo – had done to Nani at Old Trafford the week before.

News II

Jamie Carragher is arrested and cautioned after assaulting a man on his way to training. *The Mirror* reports that Gary Neville and Neville Neville have a city centre bust-up with a crowd of people over a parking spot. (They're hardcore those Neville boys.) Doctor Death returns to Thailand for the first time as City owner and is taken straight to court to face charges of abuse of power during his time as PM.

Spot of the week

From *The Times*:

'Chelsea managed to airbrush José Mourinho from Carling Cup history – the Chelsea manager who won the Carling Cup, er, twice. The club took exception to six paragraphs praising the deposed Mourinho in a programme article written by a distinguished Fleet Street correspondent and insisted they were cut. The correspondent was then so incensed he demanded his name be removed from the programme.'

Quotes of the week

- ☺ 'I've done nothing wrong, why worry?' – Thaksin Shinawatra pleads his innocence before his court case. Amnesty International, the families of thousands of dead Thais etc, etc might beg to differ.
- ☺ 'S**t happens' – Top stuff from Eduardo, who refuses to join the widespread vilification of Martin Taylor. If the injury hadn't been so dramatic no one would have raised an eyebrow. In fact, Taylor's clumsy, but no way malicious, challenge wouldn't even have earned him a red card in most matches.

Fulham 0 United 3 01/03/2008

Hargreaves 15, Park 44, Davies 72 og

Last March's trip to Craven Cottage produced a bum-squeaker of a match, that beautifully dramatic late winner from Ronaldo and an orgiastic celebration in the United dugout. This March's trip produced one of those lazy strolls that Fergie must dream of before a big European night. As the ever-quotable Paddy Evra said, 'It's amazing to think we could win 3–0 so easily.'

Goal action

1–0 (15): After winning a tug-of-war with Nani over the ball, Hargreaves opens his United account with a delicate, curling free-kick from the edge of the D.

2–0 (44): Game over. Scholes, who was excellent all afternoon, stands up a cross to the edge of the six-yard box and Parky of all people leaps to head the ball into the net. Here's something I shouldn't be bothering you about, but will. Have you ever seen the top of Parky's ears? Is there something we should know?

3–0 (72): O'Shea hits the by-line, cuts the ball back and Davies inadvertently toe-pokes the ball between Niemi's legs.

View from the broadsheets

⚽ 'Rarely can a Premier League match have felt more of a sideshow than this three-goal dismemberment of Fulham, which was eclipsed in Saturday's sunshine by tomorrow's Champions League date with Lyon. No quarter was given, and no risks taken, as Sir Alex Ferguson used his second string to swat Fulham's challenge as if it were an irksome distraction from the main event.' – *The Telegraph* says all that needs to be said.

Fulham – the verbals

⚽ 'It's quite remarkable. All our players bring something different to the table. We can play in different formations with different players and I thought we were fabulous.' – Hargreaves.

⚽ 'This season the manager has picked the right team almost every time, and it was a good performance from everyone, I thought everyone played well. We looked comfortable all over the pitch, we created chances and I thought we could have scored more goals.' – Hargreaves again.

☺ 'He didn't seem too pleased. He protected the ball at first. He didn't want me to have it. I just took it because I felt I could score. He said that if I hadn't scored, then he would have been a bit upset with me, so I'm glad it went in.' – And again, commenting on his pre-goal tussle with Nani.

'No S**t Sherlock' quote of the day
'The situation at the club is weak at the moment.' – Roy Hodgson, after guiding Fulham to one win in 10 matches.

Match facts
Fulham: Niemi, Stalteri, Hangeland, Hughes, Konchesky, Volz (Kamara 90), Johnson (Nevland 90), Bullard, Murphy (Smertin 64), Davies, McBride [Hodgson]
United: Van der Sar, Evra, Ferdinand, Brown, O'Shea, Nani (Anderson 75), Scholes, Hargreaves, Park, Tévez (Ronaldo 69), Saha (Rooney 69)
FAPL 15.00 Craven Cottage. Att: 25,314. Ref: M. Dean. Half-time: 0–2

Other scores
Arsenal 1 (Bendtner) Villa 1 (og); Bolton 1 (Cohen) Liverpool 3 (og, Babel, Aurelio); West Ham 0 Chelsea 4 (Lampard pen, A.Cole, J.Cole, Ballack)

League tables
1. Arsenal 65 (28) 2. United 64 (28) 3: Chelsea 58 (27) 4. Everton 53 (28)…19. Fulham 19 (28)

Fulham to Lyon
'Every win is important when you are fighting for fourth place.'

News
Nothing much to report from Old Trafford as United prepare for the Lyon return. But over at Eastlands they'd just finished celebrating a rather special anniversary. As of 28 February it was 32 years since City last won a trophy…

The 32-year drought in numbers
(United stats in brackets, where appropriate)
0 – number of (proper) trophies City have won since '76 (21)

1 – number of World Players of the Year (0)

1 – number of Simod Cup Final appearances (0)

3 – number of Blues that Ricky Villa beat en route to that Cup Final goal

4 – number of times City have been relegated since '76 (0)

5 – number of managers City had in 1996–97 (1)

9 – number of goals scored at Wembley since '76 (39)

9 – number of derby wins (23)

14 – number of goals City scored at home in the 2006–07 season, the lowest ever total in the top flight (46)

16 – number of minutes they kept the ball in the corner in 1996 (rough estimate)

19 – number of managers City have had since '76 (4)

32 – number of days Stevie Coppell lasted in '96

69 – number of unsuccessful consecutive Cup campaigns (14)

Quotes of the week

☺ 'I think they were lucky bastards.' – Martin O'Neill after Arsenal's undeserved 95th-minute equaliser against his Villa side.

☺ 'It was the 95th minute of their usual seven minutes of injury time' – Fergie sticks his tongue firmly in his cheek as he winds up Wenger too.

☺ 'Every win is important when you are fighting for fourth place.' – Rafa Benitez. I thought this was meant to be the year you won the League old chap.

Alf won't like it

'West Ham may soon have a fan in the West Wing – White House contender Barack Obama. US Presidential hopeful Mr Obama, 46, has been following the Hammers ever since a visit to Britain five years ago. And he keeps in touch with the fortunes of his team through his relatives in England – who are all Hammers fanatics' – *The Sun*

Shut up mum

'I don't like English teams but I know I have to like them because he [Ronaldo] is at Manchester. Before I die, I would like him to play for Real Madrid. I would really like that and then I could die, it wouldn't matter.' – Ronaldo's mum, Dolores Aveiro.

United 1 Lyon 0 04/03/2008

Ronaldo 41

I don't know about you, but I hated this game. Every time Benzema got the ball within 40 yards of goal, memories of Trezeguet's wonder-bullet for Monaco in '98 flashed through my head. And when United fell further and further back in the second half, and every other pass seemed to be aimed at Van der Sar, it felt like we were practically begging them to score.

It was only when I read what the papers and Lyon players had to say afterwards that I realised just how comfortable United's progress had been. Benzema – a superstar in the making if ever there was one – was eventually suffocated by the pack of minders Fergie had sent out to contain him. The Lyon team as a whole only seemed to have one attacking plan, and that was to give it to 'ET' and pray. And Ferdinand and Vidic proved once again that there's no better centre-back pairing in the competition.

As French international forward Sidney Govou admitted with admirable candour afterwards, 'We knew we had to score at Old Trafford, but we weren't able to against a talented and experienced opposition. You have to say that, sometimes, we were powerless against them.'

Goal!
1–0 (41): It goes without saying that this was no classic Old Trafford European occasion. Ninety minutes provided plenty of armpit-soaking tension, one shot from Lyon substitute Kader Keita that clipped the post and just this one genuine chance. Brown crosses low and hard from the right, Anderson – who tends to look like the next Brazilian superstar outside the box but the next Terry Gibson inside it – miscues his shot, the spin on the ball confuses Clerc and Ronaldo reacts first to hook a left-footer past Coupet.

View from the broadsheets
⚽ 'Manchester United are in the quarter-finals courtesy of Cristiano Ronaldo's 30th goal of the season but, if they have genuine aspirations of winning the European Cup again, there might have to be a discernible improvement in the next phase of the competition. "We made life difficult for ourselves," Sir Alex Ferguson acknowledged after watching his team struggle to turn superiority into goals.

'Ferguson was not too harsh on his players because, on the whole, it was an evening of rich satisfaction, with United equalling a Champions League record, set by Juventus in 1997, with a 10th successive win on their own ground. Yet the manager had a valid point. Old Trafford is a seductive place under floodlights and these occasions tend to bring out the best in his men but this was a peculiar performance featuring some exhilarating attacking football but also pockets of action when the players in red – Ronaldo included – looked strangely out of sorts.' – *The Guardian*

Lyon – the verbals

☺ 'The performance was not the best, but sometimes you play bad and get the result.' – Fergie on doing just enough.

☺ 'I think the goal scored by Tévez in the home leg weighed heavy on us.' – Lyon's Fabio Grosso calls it right. The real winning goal tonight wasn't scored by Ronaldo but Tévez.

Post of the day

'There seems to be a lot of stuff in the press about the two young Lyon players (Benzema and Ben Arfa) not getting on with each other. I can tell you that means nothing: I live here in France and nobody gets on with anyone.' – T.Adams @ guardian.co.uk

Match facts

United: Van der Sar, Brown, Ferdinand, Vidic, Evra*, Fletcher*, Carrick, Anderson (Tévez 70), Ronaldo (Hargreaves 90), Rooney, Nani*

Lyon: Coupet, Clerc, Squillaci*, Cris, Grosso*, Ben Arfa, Juninho, Toulalan, Kallstrom (Fred 79), Govou (Keita 67), Benzema [Perrin]

CL1/8 19.45 (ITV). Att: 75,521. Ref: R. Rosetti (It). Half-time: 1–0

*Yellow card

Other scores

Milan 0 Arsenal 2 (0–2); Barcelona 1 Celtic 0 (4–2); Sevilla 3 Fenerbahce 2 (5–5, Fenerbahce win on pens); Inter 0 Liverpool 1 (0–3); Chelsea 3 Olympiacos (3–0); Roma 2 Real Madrid 1 (4–2); Porto 1 Schalke 0 (1–1, Schalke win on pens)

Lyon to Portsmouth

'Arsenal is a unique team. Their coach hasn't won anything for years and is still an idol.'

Insert your own Martin Edwards joke here

Darren Fletcher picks up a bizarre head injury after being knocked out by a toilet door after the Lyon win. A United source tells *The Daily Record*:

'It happened half an hour after the end of the match. I don't know if fittings had come loose or what – but when Darren went to open the door, it came away and clobbered him. It looked very, very nasty. I saw blood pouring out and the medical staff had to treat him there and then. I know he got stitches.'

Bizarre stuff indeed. But it wasn't the strangest injury a footballer sustained this week. Not by a long shot...

Assume the position

The Sunday Mirror reports on the injury of the week:

'Dutch striker Eldridge Rojer is fighting to save his career – and overcome his deep embarrassment. The Excelsior star suffered from torn cruciate knee ligaments – making love to his girlfriend in the shower at their home. Ambulance crew found the the player in the embarrassing position. His girlfriend had called the emergency number. She feared he'd broken his knee.'

The best of enemies

- ☺ 'I hope to play them next season in the Champions League. If I play them in the Champions League, I want to go there and kill them – that's my message.' – Jose Mourinho hits the headlines again by firing this warning shot at Chelsea.
- ☺ 'Why should you always have to kill other people to exist yourself? If you do that, then somewhere, you feel you are not good enough. If you have to come out all the time to destroy people, what is life about? Winning and destroying people can never be everything.' – For some reason, Arsene Wenger takes it on himself to answer back...
- ☺ 'Arsenal is a unique team. Their coach hasn't won anything for years and is still an idol. There is no pressure at Arsenal. But do not say he is growing young players into talents. What he does is take young players who are jewels and polishes them. It's different. He has time to work in a serene atmosphere and get result.'...and gets a mouthful in return. Mourinho hasn't lost it then.

Making your mind up

- ☺ 'If you ask Chelsea or Arsenal what they would like to win most of all, I am sure they would say the Champions League. How many teams have won the Champions League? That is a massive trophy and it is more difficult to win than any other trophy' – Rafa Benitez plays the only card he can, 30 January.
- ☺ 'For us the Champions League is a bit easier because we can be concentrated in two games. In the Premier League the top three English clubs are tough and it is hard every game. The difference is the Premier League is for nine months' – But then defeats his own argument, 11 March.

United 0 Portsmouth 1   08/03/2008

Muntari 78 pen

This always had the makings of a historic season. I just never expected it to be so historic for other clubs. First Bolton beat us in Bolton for the first time since the '70s, then City beat us at Old Trafford for the first time since that day in '74, and now Portsmouth beat us at home for the first time since 1957. And for the life of me I don't know how they got away with it. United poured forward at the start. They poured forward at the middle. And at the end. They fired in 27 efforts at goal to Portsmouth's three. They had a stonewall penalty appeal turned down. They hit the post and had three efforts cleared off the line. It's a funny old game, they say. Well, there was nothing funny about this. Nothing at all.

Spot the difference

35 secs: Ronaldo is taken out by a blatant barge from Diarra near the dugouts. Martin Atkinson has no hesitation in giving the free-kick.

6 mins: Rooney fires a crossfield ball to Ronaldo, he takes it on the sprint, races into the area and is taken out by a blatant barge from Distin. Atkinson has no hesitation in awarding a goal-kick.

It was a ridiculous decision, outrageous really. And if Atkinson hadn't made it, there would almost certainly have been no way back for Portsmouth, who had capitulated on each of their last four visits to Old Trafford after conceding early. That said, the non-penalty should never have proved as important as it did. United made enough chances here to have won four or five games. Rooney messed up a one-on-one and Tévez hit the loose ball straight at Johnson on the line. Tévez blocked Vidic's goalbound header. Carrick rounded James but didn't get his connection right allowing Distin to tackle him on the line. Evra went one on one with James but didn't shoot. James tipped Evra's sweet half-volley onto the post. Ronaldo headed over and shot wide. Vidic got in another header that was just hacked clear. And then this happened…

78 mins (0–1): Nani curls a free-kick into James's hands. His quick punt upfield catches out the two covering Reds, Anderson and Rooney, who first allow Baros to win a header and then leave him unmarked to collect Krancjar's square ball. Kuszczak takes Baros down, gets sent off and Ferdinand, who's drowned by the Pole's goalkeeping shirt, is given no chance by Muntari's spot-kick.

What was good?

☺ At least everyone else had as bad a weekend as we did. Chelsea embarrassed themselves at Barnsley. Even better, Arsenal's slump continued as they were held 0–0 on Wigan's cabbage patch. Two Premiership matches ago, United were five points adrift of Arsenal. Now United only needed to win their game in hand to reclaim top spot.

What was bad?

☺ Chelsea lost. So did Boro. And West Brom, Barnsley and Cardiff all made it to the Cup semis. Why was that bad? Because it effectively meant we could have won the Cup with our reserves. In other words, Martin Atkinson almost certainly cost United a second Treble.

Portsmouth – the verbals

☺ 'It's absolutely ridiculous. I cannot explain it. Managers get sacked because of things like that, and he's going to referee a game next week. They had great confidence to hang on knowing the referee was on their side.' – Fergie rages against the referee.

☺ 'They say sometimes that this is the best League in the world, but sometimes they don't protect the skilled players. It's a joke. I may have to change my game. After what happened to that Arsenal player [Eduardo] I'm scared to use my skills.' – Ronaldo's getting fed up with the abuse.

☺ 'We came here four weeks ago and got beat 2–0. They could have had 10. Today we had a game plan and stuck with it, and we grafted. But you always have to ride your luck here.' – Harry Redknapp, fresh from becoming the first manager to beat United in the FA Cup with three different clubs.

☺ 'I was hoping Sulley [Muntari] would just hit the target as I've seen Rio in goal when he was a kid at West Ham. I'll be honest with you, he wasn't very good.' – Redknapp again.

Match facts

United: Van der Sar (Kuszczak† half-time, off 76), Brown, Ferdinand, Vidic, Evra, Ronaldo, Scholes, Hargreaves (Carrick 68), Nani, Rooney*, Tévez (Anderson 68)
Portsmouth: James, Johnson, Campbell, Distin, Hreidarsson, Utaka (Lauren 74), Diarra*, Diop*, Kranjcar (Hughes 81), Muntari, Kanu (Baros 54) [Redknapp]
FAC6 12.45 (Sky). Att: 75,463. Ref: M. Atkinson. Half-time: 0–0
*Yellow card † Red card

Other scores

FA Cup quarters: Barnsley 1 (Odejayi) Chelsea 0; Boro 0 Cardiff 2 (Whittingham, Johnson); Bristol Rovers 1 West Brom 5

Premier League: Wigan 0 Arsenal 0; Liverpool 3 (Pennant, Torres, Gerrard) Newcastle 0

League table

1. Arsenal 66 (29) 2. United 64 (28) 3. Chelsea 58 (27) 4. Liverpool 56 (29)

Portsmouth to Derby
'Clattenburg – oh, Jesus, God.'

Good news

☻ The Champions League draw means we won't have to face an English side in the Champions League quarters or semis.

Bad news

☻ If we're going to get to Moscow we're going to have to get past Roma – again – and probably Barcelona. And if we do get there there's a 75 per cent chance we'll have to share the Luzhniki with Scousers, Rentboys or Gooners.

Here's the draw in full:

Quarters: Arsenal v Liverpool, Roma v United, Schalke v Barcelona, Fenerbahce v Chelsea (how do they do it?)

Semis: Arsenal/Liverpool v Fenerbahce/Chelsea, Schalke/Barcelona v Roma/United

Getting it off your chest

United's top two clearly believe that if you're going to get yourself charged by the FA*, you might as well make it count:

☻ 'Keith Hackett's got a lot to answer for in this country. I don't think he's doing his job properly. He's got his favourites, as everyone knows. You look at the refs we get away from home – Steve Bennett, Mark Clattenburg, Phil Dowd, all these people – we never get them at home, always away, and I think that tells you everything about him. Clattenburg – oh, Jesus, God.' – After accusing Martin Atkinson of playing for Portsmouth, Fergie turns his anger on referee chief Keith Hackett (a man so old he's refereed City in a Cup Final).

☺ 'I feel sorry that the game has moved to the situation where referees deserve red cards. This referee deserves somebody to come to the side of the pitch after five minutes, give him a red card and pull him out of the game. That is my opinion of this robber.' – Carlos Queiroz is on a roll too…

☺ 'This referee supports players who, in the first 10 to 15 minutes, do nothing but fouls. What does Diarra expect when he elbows our player [Ronaldo] and puts him over the line? That he becomes a saint? That's why the Taylors of this game can survive and some of the best players are out of the game.' – Though he later apologises for the dig at Martin Taylor.

Spot the difference

☺ 'To say Portsmouth rode their luck would be understating the case by the length of the Manchester Ship Canal. United were denied a clear penalty in the first half…' – Paul Wilson's Portsmouth match report in *The Observer.*

☺ 'Distin was involved in two of them [the match's major incidents], with a superb interception to deny Carrick and a perfectly timed shoulder charge to stop Ronaldo'. – Paul Wilson's Portsmouth match report in *The Observer.*

Story of the week

'Cartoon legend Homer Simpson is teaming up with Cristiano Ronaldo at Manchester United in an hilarious new episode of the cult TV show. Overweight Homer will take time out from a family holiday in England to work out with the likes of genius Ronaldo, Wayne Rooney and Rio Ferdinand in a bid to get fit. The special episode featuring Homer and his catchphrase "D'oh!" is likely to be aired on Channel 4 later this year.' – *The Daily Mail*

*Amusingly, Fergie and Queiroz both got away for their Portsmouth rant after an FA disciplinary commission found that the improper conduct charges against them were 'not proven'. Even more amusingly, the FA then tried to appeal against their own decision. YCNMIU.

Derby 0 United 1   15/03/2008

Ronaldo 76

If Derby hadn't played at Chelsea in midweek this would probably have been as easy a win as everyone expected it to be. But when you get thumped 6–1, as Derby did at Stamford Bridge, things can go one of two ways: you can turn up for the next game and roll over, or you can roll up your sleeves and do everything you can to salvage your reputation. Annoyingly, Derby took the second option, producing what the locals considered to be the performance of the season. They didn't deserve to win – United, and Ronaldo in particular, fashioned too many chances for that – but they were always in the game, and if Ben Foster hadn't lived up to his impressive billing at the close of the first half, they may well have finished up with a point. God knows how many kickings dogs across Manchester would have been on the end of if it had come to that…

Goal!

1–0 (76): I don't know about you, but I haven't got many great memories of Roy Carroll. In fact I can only remember a few things about them, and they're all bad (let's see…there's the Pedro Mendes 'goal', the horrible gaffe against Milan, the alleged fight with Giggsy at the Christmas do, the disturbing facial similarities to Jim Leighton and the gambling). But he's not a bad 'keeper, and he was very good here, pulling off a string of fine saves before finally being beaten by Ronaldo's umpteenth shot. Rooney breaks free on the left, clips in a cracking cross with the outside of his right foot and Ronaldo, showing great technique on the charge, places a difficult bouncing ball into the corner.

What was good?

- Ben Foster's debut – I could never quite get my head around the Ben Foster deal. How could he be United class if he wasn't even Stoke's second-choice 'keeper when we bought him? Why had we spent £1 million on a guy with only 17 League appearances – all with Wrexham – to his name? Did he only get rave reviews at Watford because his defenders gave him so many chances to look good?

   Then came the cruciate injury – his second one – and a pile more question marks. Could he live up to the unique pressure of playing for United? Was he just the next over-hyped young English 'keeper? Could his body take the strain? Was he going to be the next Chris Kirkland or Gary Walsh? It's still far too early to know, of course, but

Foster couldn't have done a better job of living up to the hype in here. Without his two saves at the end of the first half, particularly the lunge to keep out Miller's sharp low drive, this could have been the season's third-worst afternoon (after the derbies of course).

✪ The *Viva Ronaldo* song, which elevates Ronaldo to an elite group of Reds – including Eric, Ole and Keane – who have had two great songs sung in their honour.

✪ Arsenal drew again, this time at home to Boro. Is the arse falling out of the 'greatest football team in history'?

✪ Paul Jewell kept his clothes on (don't worry, that will make sense later on).

Views from the broadsheets

✪ 'On paper it looked like a total mismatch. Manchester United, one of the most feared clubs in Europe, against Derby County, heading for a place in the history books as statistically the worst team to have played in the Premier League and who were coming into this match off the back of a 6–1 defeat at Chelsea.

✪ 'In reality, United's joy at keeping their Championship hopes very much alive was laced with a large dose of relief. It needed a 31st goal of the season from Cristiano Ronaldo in the 76th minute to breach a resilient Derby team in which former United 'keeper Roy Carroll was brilliant and Robbie Savage inspirational.' – *The Observer*

✪ 'Wanted: easy warm-up match for debutant goalkeeper only a fortnight back from eight months out injured. Applicants must show willingness to roll over and offer no threat on goal. Recent victims of a thrashing considered a bonus. Derby County? They will do nicely. Yet, while the scoreline indicates that Cristiano Ronaldo was Manchester United's match-winner, Ben Foster, the young England goalkeeper who had been obliged to wait three years for this day, deserved a share of the plaudits as his team regained leadership of the Barclays Premier League.' – *The Times*

Worst headline of the week

'Derby manage rousing Carroll but Ronaldo stays on song.' – This one from *The Observer* would have been bad enough at Christmas. But in March?

Pride Park – the verbals

✪ 'What you have to admire is the boy's courage. He has carried us this season.' – Fergie on 31-goal Ronaldo.

✪ 'Ben gave an excellent performance on his debut for us, and he showed what England will enjoy for the next 10 years because I think he will be England's goalkeeper for the next decade or more.' – Fergie on Foster.

☻ 'I finally feel like a United player now! I've been here nearly three years, and it's good to finally get on the pitch for the first team in a competitive game.' – Foster on Foster.

☻ 'If he was good looking, he would probably have everything! But he's a brilliant footballer, surrounded by brilliant footballers.' – Jewell on Ronaldo.

Match facts

Derby: Carroll, Edworthy (Todd 55), Leacock, Moore*, McEveley*, Sterjovski (Robert 83), Savage*, Jones*, Lewis, Miller, Earnshaw (Villa 77) [Jewell]

United: Foster, O'Shea, Brown, Vidic, Evra, Park (Saha 62), Scholes (Carrick* 62), Anderson (Fletcher 74), Giggs, Ronaldo, Rooney

FAPL 15.00 Pride Park. Att: 33,072. Ref: P. Dowd. Half-time: 0–0

*Yellow card

Other scores

Arsenal 1 (Toure) Boro 1 (Aliadiere); Sunderland 0 Chelsea 1 (Terry); Liverpool 2 (Mascherano, Torres) Reading 1 (Matejovsky)

League table

1. United 67 (29) 2. Arsenal 67 (30) 3. Chelsea 64 (29) 4. Liverpool 59 (30)…20. Derby 10 (30)

Derby to Bolton

'When I play at Old Trafford I feel I have more power, more energy in my legs, more character.'

News

The police drop the rape charges against Jonny Evans on the grounds of insufficient evidence. After subjecting the 20-year-old to the worst four months of his life, the girl who accused him of raping her at United's Christmas bash is allowed to retain her anonymity. Not right is it?

Footballers, eh?

Norwich midfielder Matty Pattison is arrested for drink-driving. Nothing new there you might think. But, as *The Mirror* reveals, the former Newcastle man manages to give an old story a clever new twist.

'*Mirror Sport* understands Pattison visited a nightclub on Saturday night after the Championship side's 2–0 defeat at Sheffield United.

'And on Sunday, apparently still drunk, Pattison allegedly woke up and jumped into his car believing he was late for training.

'There was no training scheduled for that day. But wearing just his pants, a T-shirt and no shoes.' – He'll be talking to parrots next…

Worst excuse of the week
'It's true that Hleb saw [agent] Vigorelli and they went out from the Melia Felix but it's not true that they went to talk to Inter Milan. They went for an ice-cream.' – Italian super-agent Vincenzo Morabito 'explains' why Alexander Hleb left the Arsenal team hotel the night before their Champions League game against Milan.

Non-football headline of the week
'Pornocchio' – *The Sun* gets stuck into Heather Mills after she was branded 'underhand' and 'distasteful' by the judge in her divorce case.

Good luck with that one
'Foul-mouthed Premier League players could be silenced by a new zero-tolerance policy on bad language. More than 350 local teams in seven counties will take part in the experiment next season. Players who swear will get a red card and team officials who use foul language will be sent to the stand or out of the ground.' – *The Daily Mirror*

Quote of the week
'When I play at Old Trafford I feel I have more power, more energy in my legs, more character. It's strange, but teams can be scared when they come to here. It can be hard for them to cope. It's called the Theatre of Dreams – but that's only for United, not for any other team!' – Another classic from Patrice Evra.

United 2 Bolton 0 19/03/2008

Ronaldo 9, 19

There's a scene in the movie *Gladiator* where Ollie Reed takes his motley crew of gladiators to fight in a flea-ridden provincial town. As the gate into the arena opens, Russell Crowe's character strides out on his own. He looks around him, checks out the gladiators waiting for him with their assorted tridents, spears and swords and then proceeds to butcher them all in about 30 seconds. After decapitating the final guy – who must have regretted the bull's head costume he wore that day – he puffs out his chest Eric-style, hurls his sword at the toga-wearers in the box and then sarcastically bellows 'Are you not entertained?'.

No one dares answer him, particularly the people in the box, who are too busy hiding the fact their togas aren't as white as they should be. But when Crowe gets back inside, Ollie Reed goes mental, lecturing him on the need to give the crowd drama as well as blood. And that's what got me thinking about *Gladiator* in the first place. Many more games like this and Fergie might think about having a similar chat with Ronaldo. Brilliance is never tedious, especially when it comes in so many guises, but it might be better if Ronaldo didn't kill off flea-ridden provincial teams like Bolton quite so early. Looking back, we could all have spent the last hour of this mismatch in the Bishop's Blaize.

Goal action
1–0 (9): Matt Taylor half clears Ronaldo's header from Nani's corner, the ball falls to Ronaldo again and he bounces his shot off the ground and over Al Habsi's dive. The goal takes Ronaldo level with Bestie's record tally – for a United winger – of 32 goals in a season.

2–0 (19): Ten minutes later Bestie's record is gone as Ronaldo scores another astonishingly brilliant free-kick – a bomb from miles out that swerves, booms, curves and dips into the bottom right-hand corner. That's Ronaldo's fifth free-kick of the season, and they've all been brilliant.

What was good?
- Ronaldo's record-breaking 33 – Most Reds were convinced they'd never see a winger outscore Bestie. But Ronaldo hasn't just beaten his 32-goal record, he's demolished it. It took Bestie 53 games to score his 32 goals in '68. Forty years on, it's taken Ronaldo just 37 to score 33.

What was bad?

☺ If you're being nit-picky, you'd complain about United's finishing in the second half, but in reality the night went exactly to plan. United got the easy win they wanted, Fergie rested a whole host of players for the weekend's big game against Liverpool, and Robbie Keane scored late on to deny Chelsea two crucial points at White Hart Lane.

One for the trenches

It had to happen eventually. Afterwards it emerges that Bolton defender Meite was so traumatised by facing Ronaldo that he refused to come out for the second half:

'Meïté's future appears certain to lie away from the Barclays Premier League club after he removed his football boots during the interval in the wake of criticism by Megson for his part in the two goals conceded to Cristiano Ronaldo. He is understood to have claimed that he could not appear for the second half because of an injury, despite club physiotherapists assuring Megson that the central-defender was fit to continue.' – *The Times*

Understatement of the night

'He just decided he didn't want to play on against Manchester United in the second half. The players weren't happy with it, the squad wasn't happy with it.' – Megson on Meite.

Views from the broadsheets

☺ 'With a full sense of Old Trafford theatre, the night again belonged to Cristiano Ronaldo, who, having been handed the captaincy for the first time, broke George Best's record for a United winger of 32 goals in a season with two first-half strikes inside 19 minutes. They included another of those unfathomable dipping free-kicks, bearing out Sir Alex Ferguson's contention that Ronaldo now surpasses David Beckham with a dead ball at his feet.' – *The Independent*

Quote of the night

'There's no one who can do better in the game today.' – Fergie on his skipper.

Winging it

United's top five goalscoring wingers (in terms of goals in a season) since 1968:

1. Hill 22 (1976–77)
2. Strachan 19 (1984–85)
3. Giggs 17 (1993–94)
4. Beckham 16 (2001–02)
5. Kanchelskis 15 (1994–95)

Match facts

United: Kuszczak, Hargreaves, Pique, Vidic (Brown 58), O'Shea, Ronaldo, Fletcher, Anderson (Scholes 70), Nani, Saha (Rooney 70), Tévez

Bolton: Al Habsi, Steinsson*, Meite (Hunt 46), A. O'Brien*, Gardner, Diouf, McCann, Guthrie (Giannakopoulos 82), J.O'Brien, Taylor, Davies [Megson]

FAPL 20.00 (Sky). Att: 75,476. Ref: A. Wiley. Half-time 2–0

*Yellow card

Other scores

Spurs 4 (Woodgate, Berbatov, Huddlestone, Keane) Chelsea 4 (Drogba, Essien, J. Cole 2)

League table

1. United 70 (30) 2. Arsenal 67 (30) 3. Chelsea 65 (30)

Bolton to Liverpool

'If you are talking about the title, the United players will be sleeping like babies.'

News

He's back! United announce that Robbo is to rejoin the club as a global ambassador. Danny Simpson joins Ipswich on loan. Lyon are fined £2,520 after Ronaldo was targeted with a laser pen during the first leg in France. Ever get the feeling that UEFA are behind the times with the size of their fines? And The News Of The World publishes stills of the most disgusting sex tape starring, er, chubby Scouser Paul Jewell. On Easter Sunday of all days. Crikey.

.

Famous last words

- ☺ 'Compared to the last few seasons we have more confidence that we can beat United now. We have scored 99 goals this season, and we are in a good moment.' – Benitez.
- ☺ 'Now we are entering the decisive moments of the season. To be champions is difficult but not impossible. We are developing a sensational run, and we have not given up on anything.'– Xabi Alonso.
- ☺ 'Javier [Mascherano] has a fantastic mentality. He's a top player who can be a key figure for us over the next few years.' – Benitez again.

Quotes of the week

- ☺ 'Since signing for the club in 1981, it has always been special to me. I enjoyed the happiest and most memorable times of my career at Old Trafford, and it will be great to play a role in making the club even more successful.' – Ambassador Robson speaks.

☻ 'Get your money on United, it's their title without a shadow of a doubt.' – Keano's confident...

☻ 'If you are talking about the title, the United players will be sleeping like babies.' – Really confident.

News II

David Moyes is awarded £150,000 in damages after winning his libel case against the publishers of Rooney's autobiography *My Story So Far*. The book had claimed that Rooney told Moyes he wanted to leave Everton after it emerged he had visited prostitutes, and that Moyes had passed details of the conversation onto the *Liverpool Echo*. Meanwhile, at White Hart Lane, Ashley Cole plumbs new depths with a ridiculous display of dissent after Mike Riley had the temerity to book him for almost breaking Alan Hutton's leg, though I guess Riley got off lightly. After gobbing off and turning his back on him, Cole could have tried to sleep with him and puked in his car.

Double standards

☻ 'I think the haranguing of referees we have seen is absolutely ridiculous.' – Fergie is disgusted by Cole & co., 20 April.

☻ 'I told him [Mark Clattenburg] how bad he was, and he didn't like it. Some referees don't like the truth. I thought we should have got more protection, and it was becoming a shambles.' – Fergie at Bolton, 24 November.

So true in all walks of life

From *football365*:

'I always ask players for commitment. Yeah, money is important in life – but I've honesty and pride' – Paul Jewell, 22 February. Well, I think we can safely say the pride bit has gone down the toilet, eh Paul?

United 3 Liverpool 0

23/03/2007

Brown 34, Ronaldo 79, Nani 81

There were better performances this season. There were more important results too. After all, you don't get any prizes for beating the also-rans. But there wasn't a more enjoyable afternoon at Old Trafford than this one. Liverpool arrived with seven straight wins behind them and lots of big talk that they were going to muscle their way back into the title race. They left with their backsides ringing from another United hiding – the seventh in eight games under Benitez – and a candidate for the season's most idiotic footballer. Liverpool tried their best to hide behind Mascherano's buffoonery afterwards. But don't be fooled la's. As the man from *The Guardian* said, your boys 'were dismantled from A to Z'…

Scouse-busting – a minute-by-minute guide

1: Weird. Manchester was full of snow this morning. Now there's brilliant sunshine. And it's bouncing off Reina's head as he makes a complete mess of a simple clearance. It's the first hint of the fun to come…

2: A ball boy sheepishly rescues a stray ball from United's net. At least Liverpool can claim they had the ball in the net first. The last time they could say that in a League match was back in the Houiller days.

CHANCE! PENALTY! RED CARD! NO! (5): After a cagey, no punches-thrown start, Anderson picks up possession in centre field and slides a pass towards Rooney that Carragher should deal with but doesn't. Rooney smells the opener, but Carragher's desperate lunge makes him stumble and gives Reina the chance to smother his shot. If Rooney had gone down it would have been a red card and a penalty. Instead he's penalised for being honest and trying to stay on his feet. It doesn't exactly send out the right message does it?

CHANCE! ROONEY! (8): United have already spotted two major weaknesses at the centre of the Liverpool defence (they're called Carragher and Skrtel). And they waste no time trying to exploit them. Scholes lofts a quick free-kick over Skrtel, Rooney just fails to kill a difficult ball arriving over his shoulder and Reina pounces.

YELLOW! MASCHERANO! (10): United's passing is killing Liverpool in midfield – and annoying the hell out of Mascherano. When Carrick and Scholes pull off another double one-two on halfway he snaps, flying in with his studs up on Scholes. It's a definite yellow. In fact many players have been sent off for less this year. But that doesn't stop the ratty Argentine mouthing off when Steve Bennett takes his name. Hasn't he followed the football news? Doesn't he know he's picked completely the wrong weekend to stick it to referees?

11: On Sky Martin Tyler reminds us that Bennett was the fourth official when Ashley Cole embarrassed himself in midweek. That's one more reason for the players to keep their mouths shut today…

15: …but Mascherano isn't listening. When Anderson dumps Gerrard on his backside he makes sure he's first in Bennett's face, sniping and gobbing off. 'One would have hoped that the reaction to Ashley Cole's misbehaviour might just get through to the players.' Tyler observes in his best 'kids today' tone.

17: The Sky cameras pan to the crowd where David Moyes is sitting behind a man with long grey wavy hair and a ginger goatee. He can only be a Liverpool fan.

18: The cameras now focus on Ole and Gary Neville in the stands. Gary's goatee's looking good. Only kidding. It really isn't a good look for someone who's supposed to hate Scousers. Mind you, his isn't the most ridiculous facial hair in the ground today. Not by a long shot.

22: Gerrard, who barely gets out of loping mode all game, gives the ball away softly twice in as many minutes. Then he stops. And does nothing. He's a player capable of doing great things. Only a fool would deny that. But I reckon if he'd been schooled at Old Trafford he'd be a great player, full stop. Liverpool have spoiled him by letting him fanny around in a free role.

RONALDO! POST! (23): Mascherano fouls Giggs on the right and snipes at the linesman… again. Giggs picks himself up and curls over a free-kick that Vidic flicks on and Ronaldo, who only sees the ball at the last moment, nudges against the far post.

26: Liverpool's first mildly dangerous attack ends with Gerrard's shot deflecting behind off Vidic. As Gerrard goes over to take the corner he's serenaded with 'Chelsea rent boy' by the Stretford End. I wonder what would have happened if he'd gone. Would United have won the League last year? Would so much of his stuff have been robbed?

31: As Reina fluffs another goal-kick the Diego song rings around the ground. "He comes from Uruguay, he made the Scousers cry". It just goes to show. Win a game at Anfield and you'll be remembered forever – no matter how crap you are.

In fairness, though, Diego isn't crap any more. His record in Spain is exceptional – 56 goals in three years with Villareal and now 16 in his first first year with Atletico Madrid. In fact the three ex-Red forwards in La Liga – Diego, Ruud and Rossi – are all doing much better than Fergie must have hoped when he sold them. The trio would end the season with a combined tally of 47 goals from just 95 games.

31: Giggsy gives it away. He and Gerrard seem to be having a contest on who can concede possession more lazily.

32: What am I talking about? Ferdinand drills a ball to Giggs's patch on the left, he takes it down brilliantly and curls in a cross that the flustered Reina almost flaps into his own goal.

33: The Anfield theme continues as the crowd bursts into a rendition of 'When Jonny comes running down the wing'. It's a reminder that Liverpool under Benitez have conceded goals to some unlikely figures. Mickey Silvestre scored both goals in the first Benitez game. O'Shea's scored a winner. So has Rio. I wonder why I've brought that up now. Oh that's right...

ROONEY! BROWN! GOAL! (33):10: Another terrible Reina moment gifts United the lead. Rooney crosses right-footed from the left, Brown attacks the ball brilliantly, Reina hardly jumps and as Wes's momentum spins him around, the ball cannons off his back and into the net. "Campeones, campeones" fills Old Trafford as Tyler scratches around for some Wes stats. Finally he gets hold of a couple. Wes has played for United for 10 years now. But this was only his third United goal. The other two, if you're interested, came in 2–1 wins against Juve in 2003 and Newcastle in 2005.

35: As Crouch warms up on the touchline, Tyler informs us that it's now more than 10 hours since Liverpool scored against us in the League. Crouch, of course, did score the winner in the Smudge FA Cup game in 2006.

36: Torres collapses for the umpteenth time under pressure from Vidic and whines at Bennett. Maybe that's the reason why Fergie gave up on trying to sign him. Torres has looked like a world beater all season. But is he a mummy's boy when defenders get tight to him? Mind you, he'd look a hell of a better player here if he had some support. Liverpool are committing absolutely no one forward. It looks like their Plan A is to keep a clean sheet and try and pinch something late on… and Plan B is to keep United to one and try and pinch something.

37: As 'We've got Wesley Brown' rings round the stadium, Kuyt boots the ball over. Ordinary isn't he?

CHANCE! ROONEY! (39): Ronaldo's free-kick – given for another foul by the chuntering Mascherano – clips the top of the wall and balloons into the area. Giggs wins the flick on, Rooney anticipates where the ball is going to drop but can't get enough power to seriously trouble Reina. Reina, who keeps on switching from the sublime to the ridiculous to the plain appalling, then sends a quick throw straight at Anderson. Luckily for him, Viv's shooting is nowhere near as good as his passing and the ball balloons miles over the bar.

40: The cameras show Benitez in the dugout smiling and cracking jokes with his coaching team. Yeah right. As always, he looks like a waiter whose customers have all done a runner. And that goatee? Awful.

TORRES! YELLOW! MASCHERANO! RED! (43): The inevitable finally happens. Ferdinand bundles over Torres, and Torres whines himself into Bennett's notebook. Mascherano's not having that, and he races 20 yards to moan at Bennett. Bennett's not having that either, and he sends him off. In a sense Mascherano is unlucky. He's done no more mouthing off than Terry and Ballack do every week. Or that Keano did in his D'Urso days. But to launch into 30 minutes of sarcastic sniping on the very weekend that the referees were most likely to flex their muscles against dissent was madness. 'Fair play to the ref' – Alan Smith says. Fair enough.

45+: There's still time for Torres to collapse to the floor again before Bennett brings the half to an end. As the Liverpool players chip away at the officials on the way to the tunnel, Tyler hands back to the studio with, "We have an Easter Bennett here. But Steve Bennett will surely have the sympathy of the majority for his handling of two cases of dissent, first from Torres and then Mascherano."

No, I don't know what Tyler was on about either.

RONALDO! SITTER! NO! (46): It should have been all over in the first attack of the second half. The little genius, Scholes, takes the Liverpool defence out of the game with a beautifully scooped pass. Ronaldo beats Reina to the ball but doesn't get enough height on his flick and Reina beats it down with his arms. Ronaldo, who sinks to his knees and cups his hands over his face, can't believe he isn't celebrating his first Liverpool goal.

52: Anderson was brilliant at Anfield. He's just as good here. His latest charge forward is halted by Arbeloa on the left corner of the area. As Arbeloa gets booked, and Carragher whines phlegmily at the Easter Bennett (why? it had to be a yellow), Giggs and Rooney come over to chat with Ronaldo about the free-kick. I'm not sure why they bothered. They've both get as much chance of taking it as Liverpool have of winning the League. Ronaldo shoos them away, measures out his run up and dips one just wide of the far post.

ROONEY! CHANCE! SAVE! ANDERSON! NO! (56): Benitez is fond of making lists during games. If he'd made a list of everything Liverpool should have done better here, then dealing with long balls would have been right at the top. This time Van der Sar pumps the ball forward, Rooney gets free of the ball-watching Skrtel, pulls down the ball brilliantly with his right toe and in the same motion lashes a low left-footer at Reina. Reina, whose afternoon is having a turn for the better (don't worry, it won't last), makes a decent save with his legs and Anderson batters the rebound into the Stretford End.

59: Torres collapses again under pressure from Rio and this time buys the free-kick. Rio then gets booked for kicking the ball away.

TORRES! RED! NO! (63): Torres, who might be braver than I though, chops down Vidic from behind. It's a routine yellow card, but Bennett lets him off. Lucky boy. Funnily enough, Benitez seems to forget his star man's let-off when he launches into a predictable tirade about the referee later. It's not the only thing that slips his mind either. Carragher should have walked after five minutes. United should have had a penalty at the same time. And Arbeloa was a lucky man for getting away with two poor challenges on Giggs after his yellow. Forget the idea that Easter gifted United the match, Liverpool could conceivably have spent the last 20 minutes with eight men.

65: Benayoun comes on for Babel. Why are Liverpool so obsessed with buying average wingers?

67: So far it's all been too easy for United. They were too good for Liverpool with 11 men. And they're much too good for Liverpool with 10 men. But they still haven't killed them off. And for the first time Liverpool are showing signs that they might make us live to regret it. First Gerrard's free-kick from the right bounces dangerously across the six-yard box. Then Torres spins in from the left and is only stopped by excellent work from the excellent Ferdinand…

70: …and then Gerrard slams a shot just wide from 25 yards. It's getting really tense now. We should be watching a ritual humiliation. Instead we'd all settle for a dour last 20 minutes and a scruffy 1–0.

72: That's better. Rooney charges down the left, makes a clown out of Carragher and then shows superb awareness to square the ball to Anderson. Once again, the crowd rises in anticipation of Anderson's first goal. Once again he finds the Stretford End. He's class with his foot. But he shoots like Nicky Butt… (sorry)

72: Fergie's had enough of United's wastefulness. Off comes Anderson, who's played well, and Giggs who hasn't (you have to say he doesn't influence these big matches from the wing any more). On comes Tévez and Nani. And the double-change almost pays off straightaway…

TEVEZ! SHOT! GREAT SAVE! (72): Rooney's attempted through ball to Nani is deflected into Tévez's path eight yards out, and his instinctive left-footer is superbly saved low to his left by Reina.

RONALDO! SITTER! NO! (78): I don't believe it. Ronaldo's done it again. This time Tévez's neat chest pass sends him clear, he hesitates and then, when he finally realises that Arbeloa's played him onside, he casually pokes the ball against Reina and behind off the bar. What do we have to do to score against Reina in the second half…?

RONALDO! GOAL!: 78: That's right. We do the same as we did in the first half – we expose his weakness against crosses. Nani curls in the corner from in front of the tunnel, Ronaldo loses Alonso, Reina comes and gets nowhere and Ronaldo nods into the empty net. It's his firs-ever goal against Liverpool, but as it should have been his third today he's not in the mood to celebrate. Instead, as his teammates pile on his back, he does one of those haughty celebrations that he obviously thinks looks cool. He can't pull if off like Eric though. Remember that celebration after his Sunderland chip in '96? What a star.

ROONEY! NANI! GOAL! (80): Old Trafford is still rocking to Ronaldo's second when Rooney and Nani concoct a brilliant third. Rooney takes out three Liverpool defenders with a reverse ball through the hapless Carragher's legs. Nani runs across the slow-turning Skrtel and lashes the ball into the left corner. Reina, who'll need a dark room to get over this one, just waves it by. As Nani somersaults into the arms of Brown and the excited Fergie almost loses his glasses, Tyler screams 'HOW ABOUT THAT?'. Not bad Martin. Not bad at all.

82: Liverpool officially hoist the white flag by bringing on Riise for Torres. And that's about it as far as the action goes here. Now for the next big question of the day. Who to support during the second half of 'Set Up Sunday'. Arsenal, Chelsea or neither? I went for Chelsea to finish off Arsenal's season. It seemed like a smart idea at the time.

It didn't seem quite so clever just a few weeks later...

Scouse-busting quotes of the day

- 'The 3–0 scoreline wasn't flattering. Not at all. Rooney could have had a hat-trick, Ronaldo could have had a hat-trick...we certainly had the better chances and the better penetration. I was disappointed we didn't finish them off earlier. When we did get the second goal there was relief right around the ground.' – Fergie.

- 'I could see two games out there. There was one game before the sending-off and another one after it.' – Benitez can see a lot. But he can't see that United were easily better than Liverpool when Mascherano was on the pitch.

- 'I don't know why the boy got involved. He had been booked, so he put himself on a knife-edge with what he did. This last week the focus has been on dissent – people have been talking about it – and in that context it was clear it was going to be an issue at the weekend.' – Fergie again.

Line of the day

'The pity for United is that Javier Mascherano's buffoonery, and the debate it conjures up about the behaviour of modern-day footballers, will inevitably divert attention away from what was, in essence, a performance of authentic brilliance. Liverpool were dismantled from A to Z' – *The Guardian*

Bitter line of the day

'Stretching right back to the 1977 FA Cup final they [United] have a knack of finding the back of the net in ways which defy science and gravity. They say fortune favours the brave, but in these clashes it sometimes seems as if fortune just favours United.' – It could only be the *Liverpool Echo*.

Match facts

United: Van der Sar, Brown, Ferdinand*, Vidic, Evra, Ronaldo, Scholes, Carrick, Anderson (Tévez 73), Giggs (Nani 73), Rooney
Liverpool: Reina, Arbeloa*, Carragher, Skrtel, Aurelio, Mascherano† 44, Alonso, Kuyt, Gerrard, Babel (Benayoun 66), Torres* (Riise 82) [Benitez]
FAPL 12.45, Old Trafford. Att: 76,000. Ref: S. Bennett. Half-time: 1–0
*Yellow card † Red card

Other scores
Chelsea 2 (Drogba 2) Arsenal 1 (Sagna)

League table
1. United 73 (31) 2. Chelsea 68 (31) 3. Arsenal 67 (31) 4. Liverpool 59 (31)

Liverpool to Villa

'Then you have Cristiano Ronaldo. I have never seen such a creation.'

The return of the Bell Enders
You'll never believe who was voted in first and second place for Man of the Match at Old Trafford on the Liverpool Official Website. Yep that's right – Pepe Reina and Javier Mascherano.

Looks like Red scamps have been busy on t'internet again...

The 3rd Knight
Egil Vindorum, head of the Oslo palace chancellery, announces that the world's most famous Norwegian Ole Gunnar Solskjaer is going to be knighted. Remarkably it appears that his 261 career goals have nothing to do with it:

'What is being honoured are his attitudes, his way of being,' Vindorum said. 'He is a role model for children and young people. What he did on the soccer field has nothing to do with it.'

International friendly Reds
Ferdinand captains England to a 1–0 defeat in a dull and pointless friendly in Paris. Rooney, Hargreaves and Brown also play. More significantly, Becks becomes only the fourth Englishman to win 100 caps. Anderson comes on as a second-half sub as Brazil beat Sweden 1–0 at the Emirates. Arsenal no-marks boo his every touch. Fletcher is ruled out for six weeks with knee ligament damage sustained during Scotland's pointless draw with Croatia. Vidic's Serbia lose 2–0 to Ukraine. Park's South Korea draw their World Cup qualifier against Korea DPR 0–0. Manucho scores Angola's goal in their 1–1 draw against Japan, er, Under-23s.

'Youngsters these days' moment of the week
From *football365*:

'Rio Ferdinand takes a lengthy swig of water and gobs a jet of it on to the floor of the tunnel in the Stade de France right in front of the watching TV cameras. A role model' – *The Guardian*. Honestly, kids with their hair, and their clothes, and their music with no proper words…

Overblown debate of the week
'Is Beckham worth 100 caps?'

It's the question that launched a thousand dull conversations this week. Many people seem to believe that the 100-cap club should only be reserved for the very best England players. Others can't stand Beckham purely because of the circus that surrounds him. Or believe he was only first choice in Euro 2004 and Germany 2006 because of his name. But, frankly, who cares. Becks isn't the best player ever to play for England (was Billy Wright?) but he has been our best right-sided midfielder for the best part of a decade. And if he'd been fortunate enough to captain a better England team he would never have been begrudged his 100 caps. In fact he'd probably already have been knighted.*

Quote of the week
'I have been privileged to work with some of the best players in the world on a daily basis. Zidane, Figo, Ronaldo, Raul, Roberto Carlos, David Beckham. And I think Cristiano is the finest and most complete football player. You think about Figo the winger, Ronaldo the forward, Zidane the playmaker – and you add the strength of Fernando Morientes in the air! Then you have Cristiano Ronaldo. I have never seen such a creation.' – Carlos Queiroz.

* Just wait for the furore when he is…

United 4 Aston Villa 0   29/03/2008

Ronaldo 17, Tévez 33, Rooney 53, 70

Rooney emerges from United's 11th four-goal demolition job of the season – and 14th straight win against poor Villa – and tells the waiting press that playing for this United team is like playing for Brazil. I'm not sure about that Wayne. The Brazilians have never had centre-backs as good as ours…

Goal action

1–0 (17): What a player! Villa fail to clear a corner, the ball falls at the feet of Ronaldo near the penalty spot, and before the four surrounding Villa defenders can say 'Holy mother of…' he flicks it between Laursen's leg and past Carson. Ronaldo's grinning celebration says it all. He'd even managed to impress himself.

2–0 (33): Ronaldo doesn't make as many goals now he's reinvented himself as a goal-happy inside-forward rather than a stepover-happy winger. But this assist was well worth the wait. Scholes feeds Ronaldo on the right, and his floated cross to the back post practically begs the onrushing Tévez to nod it into the net.

3–0 (53): In Paris in midweek it had been obvious to every man and his poodle that Rooney enjoys playing for his country just as much as Scholesy used to. Back in Red he looked 100 per cent in love with the game again. And he looked even happier when he finally broke his Old Trafford drought that stretched back to October. Ronaldo's fortunate flick-on from Giggs's pass takes Laursen out of the game, and Rooney walks the ball past Carson and into the Stretford End net.

4–0 (70): Ronaldo plays in Rooney on the left side of the area. Carson expects him to curl the ball across him, Rooney reads him and rolls the ball in at the near post.

Cocky question of the week

How many Brazilians would get into United's team?

Brazil Copa America-winning XI 2007:
Doni, Maicon, Juan, Alex, Mineiro, Gilberto, Josue, Baptista, Elano, Robinho, Vagner Love

Brazil World Cup-losing XI 2006:
Dida, Cafu, Lucio, Juan, Carlos, Silva, Ze Roberto, Juninho, Kaka, Ronaldinho, Ronaldo
I reckon we'd only take Kaka and a right-back off them at the moment.

Worst headline of the day
'Just Like Watching Backheel' – *The Mirror*. Brazil, backheel. Get it? Thought not.

Villa – the verbals
☻ 'That's what you have to aspire to. I thought United were really brilliant. Many teams would have struggled like we did. We lost at home to Sunderland last week, and I was very down. We've lost 4–0 at Old Trafford, but I'm actually OK.' – Martin O'Neill's been here so often he can't even get disappointed.

☻ 'To be at this club, with the football we play at times, is brilliant. It's something every player would want to be a part of. It's brilliant. Growing up, I used to love watching Brazil. The football we play in this team is similar to the way Brazil play. It's an honour to be in this team.' – The white Pelé.

View from the broadsheets
☻ 'On this evidence, Manchester United are a club on the brink of implosion. Age, finally and inevitably, has caught up with Ryan Giggs and Paul Scholes.

'The fundamental lack of understanding between Rio Ferdinand and Nemanja Vidic leaves them lethally vulnerable to counter-attacks, while Wayne Rooney is overweight and out of touch. Cristiano Ronaldo is the single most overrated player of this new century.

'That is how the scouts sent to Old Trafford by the Roma manager, Luciano Spalletti, before tomorrow's Champions League quarter-final ought to report back. On no account should Spalletti be shown a video of this display by a side at the height of their already considerable powers. The man who saw United score seven times in last year's quarter-final will despair.' – *The Telegraph* gets its tongue stuck in its cheek.

Match facts
United: Kuszczak, Brown, Ferdinand (Hargreaves 62), Vidic*, Evra (O'Shea 62), Ronaldo, Carrick (Anderson 61), Scholes, Giggs, Tévez, Rooney
Aston Villa: Carson, Reo-Coker, Mellberg, Laursen, Bouma* (Osbourne 80), Agbonlahor, Petrov, Barry, Young, Harewood (Salifou 69), Carew (Maloney 41) [O'Neill]
FAPL 17.15 (Set). Att: 75,932. Ref: M.Halsey. Half-time: 2–0
*Yellow card

Other scores
Bolton 2 (Taylor 2) Arsenal 3 (Gallas, Van Persie pen, og); Chelsea 1 (Carvalho) Boro 0;
Liverpool 1 (Torres) Everton 0

League table
1. United 76 (32) 2. Chelsea 71 (32) 3. Arsenal 70 (32) 4. Liverpool 62 (32)… 8. Villa 49 (32)

Villa to Roma

'Ronaldo is better than George Best and Denis Law.'

Look at your shoes and try not to giggle
'Yes, I have contributed to putting them under pressure – but that's for the protection of
my players. I don't think there is a manager who would question the integrity of officials.'
– Fergie talking about how much he respects referees.

I predict a riot
From *The Guardian*:
'As Manchester United fans started to arrive for tonight's Champions League quarter-
final with Roma, UEFA warned that the city might be stripped of the right to host next
season's Final if there are any more stabbings.' – UEFA reveal their criteria for choosing
which stadium hosts the Champions League Final. If you only stab English fans on four
visits out of every five, it's all yours. Michel Platini really can't stand the rosbifs can he?

Mixed messages
- 'When I heard we would face Manchester I put my arms in the air and shouted "Hell,
yes, at last!" Finally we have the chance to put things right. This is the perfect
opportunity for us to wipe out the memory of last year.' – Roma coach Luciano
Spalletti, on the eve of the Roma game.
- 'There were many bad words spoken in our dressing room as soon as the draw was
made. We have to play them again and once again we have to play at home first and then
go to Old Trafford. We all know what happened there last time. This is a disaster for
us, a nightmare. For us, it is the same old story.' – Roma defender Marco Cassetti,
when the draw was made.

Quotes of the week
- 'For me, Ronaldo is above the rest, and if he keeps scoring in this rhythm and stays in
this sort of form then he will prove that he is the best. Ronaldo is better than George
Best and Denis Law.' – Praise indeed from Johan Cruyff.

⚽ 'United are the best team in the world, but it's a long time since they got a very important win abroad. They're fantastic at Old Trafford, but they never dominate a match away. They are very good on the counter-attack, but they aren't good at controlling games.' – Spalletti plays a dangerous game.

⚽ 'Everybody here, including myself, will never forget last season. The memory is so bad that everybody still talks about a 7–0 defeat. It was 7–1! I scored a goal!' – The Old Trafford wounds run deep for Roma midfielder Daniele de Rossi (and they're not about to get any better).

Changing his tune

'I don't think his Diaby's tackle was malicious – it was more protective' – Arsene Wenger backs up Abou Diaby after he was sent off at Bolton for a shin-high challenge that was just as bad as Martin Taylor's lunge on Eduardo. The real difference? The victim of Diaby's lunge, Gretar Steinsson, got up.

Benitez used to be a girl

…well it's more believable than this piece of wisdom from *The People*:

'Sir Alex Ferguson is considering an offer to MK Dons boss Paul Ince to join his coaching team at Manchester United'.

Yes, that's the same Paul Ince who Fergie famously labelled a bully and 'a f***ing big-time Charlie'. I can't see it, can you?

Roma 0 United 2   01/04/2008

Ronaldo 39, Rooney 66

In 2004 Ronaldo was Man of the Match in the FA Cup Final and starred for Portugal as they made it to the Final of Euro 2004. He was 19. In 2005 he was sensational in the Cup Final travesty against Arsenal. He was 20. In 2006 he was the Man of the Match in the World Cup semi-final. He was 21. In 2007 he had quiet games against Milan and Chelsea. Ignoring his CV, the football know-alls jumped at the chance to label him a big-game bottler, someone who's a world beater against Charlton and a cameo merchant against Chelsea. It was a ridiculous notion, really. And it looked even more ridiculous by the time Ronaldo had finished with Roma here. A Cristiano beating up Romans. I'm amazed the tabloid boys missed out on that…

Goal action

1–0 (39): Gay icon wingers aren't supposed to score goals like this. When Rooney marginally overhits his pass to Scholes on the right of the box, Ronaldo is still dusting himself down after being clattered by Mexes. He's not even in the frame. By the time Scholes stands up a crafty ball to the far post he's racing in with a demonic ferocity. Normally athletes who take off after running this far, this quickly, know that a sand pit is waiting for them. Ronaldo only has a stray head, elbow, boot or shoulder to look forward to. It doesn't put him off. He launches himself, like Frank Stapleton with a rocket up his arse, into the smoky Roman air, and meets the ball perfectly just above his over-pampered eyebrows. Pizarro gets there in time to make Ronaldo's landing a painful one but can't do anything about the header. Neither can Doni. What a goal. What a player.

2–0 (66): Before Ronaldo's opener, Totti-lite Roma had struggled to get at United. After the break they looked far more dangerous, especially down the left-sided channel patrolled by Tonetto and Mancini. Still, they only make three or four half-chances before their 'keeper shoots them in the foot. Brown launches a deep ball from the right, Park nods it back across goal, Doni makes a hash of a simple catch and Rooney prods in. 2–0. And tie over (almost).

View from the broadsheets

⚽ 'Never does it in the big matches, does he? Never does it when the pressure is on against the best teams. Never scores the ones that matter.

'So, how to explain this and satisfy those who still doubt? Noted small-game player Cristiano Ronaldo set Manchester United on the way to an entirely meaningless Champions League semi-final with a not-at-all brave header against the completely useless second-best team in Italy in the benign atmosphere of the dilapidated cowshed that is the Olympic Stadium. There, that should please them.' – *The Times* quashes the Ronaldo bottle rumours.

Roma – the verbals

- ☻ 'To be honest, I don't remember much about the goal. I went down and I felt pain. I didn't enjoy it. But I will have to watch it on television. Others say it's a good goal. To win 2–0 away is a great result for us.' – Ronaldo.

- ☻ 'His header was absolutely fantastic, his spring and courage to go in front of the defender. I think the defender thought he was going to get it. It was the spring [that did it]. It was a centre-forward's header. It reminds me of myself.' – Fergie's reached that age…

- ☻ 'Manchester United have proved what a great team they are. It's clear that for us it now becomes an almost impossible task. The second goal hit us hard. It came at the worst possible time, just when we were playing at our best and we looked closer to finding the equaliser. But we have made mistakes, both in attack and on defence – and against a team like Manchester, you pay a high price for them.' – Daniele De Rossi would have sounded even more depressed if he'd known what was in store for him at Old Trafford.

- ☻ 'I said in the Press Conference yesterday that people always maintain Italian clubs play defensive and on the counter, so in that case Manchester United are the most Italian team I know!' – Spalletti compliments United – I think.

What was good?

No Reds tear-gassed in France. And now no Reds stabbed – or beaten up – in Rome. I don't know, you can't rely on anything these days…

What was bad?

The sight of Vidic limping off with a badly twisted knee revives bad memories of the defensive injury crisis that crippled United's Euro bid last year.

No-mark of the night

'There is no doubt that he has quality, but it is also true that he has a big head. Some of his little tricks in the middle of the pitch were unnecessary, and he needs to show some respect to his opposition. You can bet that we will have something to say about it in the return leg.' – David Pizarro gets his knickers in a twist about some Ronaldo 'showboating' that no one else saw.

Match facts

Roma: Doni, Cassetti, Mexes, Panucci, Tonetto (Cicinho 69), De Rossi, Aquilani (Esposito 76), Taddei (Giuly 59), Pizarro, Mancini, Vucinic [Spalletti]

United: Van der Sar, Brown, Ferdinand, Vidic (O'Shea 34), Evra, Park, Carrick, Scholes, Anderson (Hargreaves 55), Rooney (Tévez 84), Ronaldo

CLQF 19.45 (ITV) Stadio Olympico. Att: 80,023. Ref: F. De Bleeckere (Bel). Half-time: 1–0

Champions League quarter-finals:

Schalke 0 Barcelona 1; Arsenal 1 Liverpool 1; Fenerbahce 2 Chelsea 1

Roma to Boro

'I watched the game with Roma and, for me, Manchester now have eight of the best players in the world.'

More details needed

According to *The Daily Star*, Danny Simpson has 'diplomatically moved off to join Ipswich on loan' after being linked with Emmerdale 'sex kitten' Roxanne Pallett. Intriguing.

Scandal of the week

The Independent alleges that a player with 'a Premiership club on his CV' got himself sent off on purpose. Didn't Denis Law use to do that every Christmas?

'A footballer with a serious gambling problem has admitted accepting a £50,000 bribe to help throw a game in Britain, *The Independent* can reveal. According to a source familiar with the circumstances, the player – who has a Premiership club on his CV – racked up a £50,000 debt with a bookmaker. The bookmaker said he would write off the debt if the player got himself sent off and also persuaded three teammates to get booked in a specific game. The player agreed, and the incidents were fixed as requested. His team lost the match, which was played in the past two years, the source said.'

Thanks but no thanks

The Ferguson boys – Alex and Darren – land a unique family double in the latest LMA Managers Performance Awards (no, I hadn't either), finishing first and second. And what does Fergie Snr get for his troubles? A holiday for four in, er, Newfoundland, that's what. Bizarre.

Quotes of the week

⚽ 'Before the game with Switzerland, I was eating with the England players, and I got a roll with my soup. I said to Ray Clemence: "where's the butter?" Clem said there wasn't any. Fabio doesn't like butter.' – Trevor Brooking reveals that the changes under Capello are more sweeping than any of us could have possibly imagined.

⚽ 'I am unable to recognise the Ronaldo who left Sporting. Sporting is good at development, but he has responded to playing for Manchester United. I watched the game with Roma and, for me, Manchester now have eight of the best players in the world. Ronaldo has become number one by being at Manchester United, playing in the best League in the world and by playing every year in the Champions League.' – Sporting president Filipe Soares Franco raves about Ronaldo and United. Who do you reckon the three players he didn't fancy so much were? Brown, Park and…?

⚽ 'I was delighted to see the generally excellent behaviour of the travelling Manchester United fans. They were a credit to themselves and the club.' – The British Embassy praises the Red Army after a trip to Rome finally passes without trouble.

Middlesbrough 2 United 2   06/04/2008

Ronaldo 10, Alves 35, 56, Rooney 74

When a title-chaser draws a game towards the end of the season, the press normally asks the same question. Is it a point won or a point lost? They didn't bother this time, it was a no brainer. For 35 minutes United looked like flicking Boro aside. Carrick set up Ronaldo for a simple first, a careless flag stopped Rooney adding a second, and Scholes and Carrick were like kids in the playground who don't want anyone else using their ball. But then Alves profited from the Vidic-free zone in United's defence to score the first, Boro started sweating self-belief and United began to get a bad case of the wobbles…

When Alves scored his second and the wind started driving the smoggy snow into United eyes, it looked like the Boro bogey was going to strike again. When Boro kept on making chances, and Ferdinand hobbled off with a foot injury, even Avram Grant must have come close to breaking into a smile. But then came the season's next big turning point. Park, once again showing that he's much better than the press pack will ever give him credit for, took young left-back Andrew Taylor back to school, Rooney flicked his cross past Schwarzer and the contours of Grant's face returned to normal (think bullfrog with PMT). United's lead might have been reduced to three points, but, crucially, Rooney's finish meant we could lose half of their upcoming summit meetings against Arsenal and Chelsea and still win the League.

Goal action

1–0 (10): Deceptively simple. Giggs's corner runs deep to Carrick on the left of the area. He returns the ball back into the six-yard box and Ronaldo stabs in.

1–1 (35): Eight hours and 16 football minutes since they last lost a goal (Newcastle's consolation on 23 February) United concede again, and it's a shocker. O'Neill's aimless ball somehow bypasses the entire United defence, Alves escapes Carrick (why was he the last man back?) and the £12 million Brazilian shoots low and hard for his first Boro goal.

1–2 (56): Alves's second is almost as poor from United's point of view, but the finish is a good one. Brown and Aliadiere compete for a hopeless up-'n'-under, the ball drops into the path of Alves and he opens up his body to curl his second.

2–2 (74): Thank god. Park cuts inside Taylor on the right, and Rooney does the rest with the help of a deflection off Wheater.

What was bad?
- United's defending highlighted just how important Vidic is to the team. It also showed why O'Shea should never be trusted in central-defence. Why didn't Pique start?
- Ferdinand left the ground with his left foot encased in a surgical boot. Had the curse of the late-season metatarsal struck United again?

What was good?
- Alves. Annoyingly terrible the previous week at Stamford Bridge, where he missed two open goals. Annoyingly good here.
- The injury bulletin the next day. Rio was OK.

View from the broadsheets
'The road to the Premier League title is frequently booby-trapped and Manchester United were forced to negotiate a particularly hazardous stretch as they passed through Teesside yesterday. As if playing in a swirling snowstorm was not sufficiently off-putting, Sir Alex Ferguson's side had to cope with an additional attacking blizzard from an exhilaratingly high-tempo Middlesbrough whose Brazilian striker Afonso Alves scored his first two goals in English football.

'Throw in some technical area needle featuring a palpably tense Ferguson and Gareth Southgate indulging in a bout of mutual finger jabbing and shouting at the end and it is easy to imagine that United will not care to dwell on the weekend their lead over Chelsea at the top of the Premier League was trimmed to three points.' – *The Guardian.*

The Riverside – the verbals
- 'The nature of this club is that we never give in, and that's a great quality to have. That sends out a signal to other players and fans that we won't give in. It could prove to be a vital point.' – Fergie.
- 'I'm really proud. We had them rattled.' – Southgate.

Match facts
Boro: Schwarzer, Young*, Wheater, Pogatetz, Taylor, Aliadière (Johnson 90), Boateng*, Arca, Downing, O'Neil*, Alves (Tuncay, 78) [Southgate]
United: Van der Sar, Brown, Ferdinand (Pique 70), O'Shea (Hargreaves 67), Evra, Carrick, Scholes, Giggs, Ronaldo, Tévez (Park 63), Rooney*
FAPL 13.30 (Set). Riverside Stadium. Att: 33,952. Ref: M. Riley. Half-time: 1–1

Other scores

FA Cup semis: Cardiff 1 Barnsley 0; Portsmouth 1 West Brom 0

Arsenal 1 (Bendtner) Liverpool 1 (Crouch); City 0 Chelsea 2 (og, Kalou)

League table

1. United 77 (33) 2. Chelsea 74 (33) 3. Arsenal 71 (33) 4. Liverpool 63 (33)...14. Boro 35 (33)

Boro to Roma

'I don't know if Ronaldinho wants to play in the InterToto Cup next season.'

News

Liverpool beat Arsenal 4–2 in the second leg of their Champions League quarter to progress 5–3 on aggregate. For most Reds, disgusted by the idea of the Scousers sneaking another European Cup on pens (retrospective giggles all round), it was a disappointing result. But there were at least a couple of reasons to be cheerful. There was a good chance that Arsenal would arrive for the weekend's Old Trafford showdown with a nasty psychological hangover. And we got to watch and listen as Arsene Wenger drank from the bitter cup of defeat again. Like reruns of Ole's and Giggsy's goals in '99, it's one of those things you just never get tired of...

J'accuse

'We have a feeling of disappointment and injustice tonight...It is difficult to take, the players in the dressing-room are very down because they believe week after week the decisions are going against them.' – Wenger takes the Anfield defeat, which effectively condemned Arsenal to a third straight season without a trophy, with typical grace.

Transfer link of the week

'Manchester City have launched an audacious bid to sign Ronaldinho, the former world footballer of the year.' – *The Guardian*

Seriously, I haven't laughed so much since Eddie Large was in his pomp.

They're all out to get us

It's another bad moment for Arsenal. *The Guardian* reckons they'll lose points in the future if they can't kick their favourite habit of hissing at Tottenham fans:

'English football clubs could be docked points from their League campaigns as part of a new zero-tolerance policy against fans who engage in antisemitic or Islamophobic abuse, the FA said yesterday. The announcement came as the FA, the Metropolitan police, the Board of Deputies of British Jews and the National Association of Muslim Police attended football's first faith summit aimed at tackling such incidents on the terraces and near grounds.'

Clock watching

The Times comes up with a leftfield explanation for Owen Hargreaves's limited appearances in his debut season.

'Hargreaves's strangely peripheral role at Manchester United is not down to poor form but disciplinary issues. In particular, Sir Alex Ferguson is known to have been angered by the player's poor timekeeping, with Hargreaves turning up late for several team meetings.'

Quote of the week

'I hope it's true. But I don't know if Ronaldinho wants to play in the InterToto Cup next season.' – Sven Goran Eriksson is nothing if not perceptive.

Runner-up

'Ronaldo is an excellent player. He is a very exuberant player and a very fair player.' – Luciano Spalletti perhaps overdoes it as he covers for David Pizarro's 'showboating' whining in Rome.

United 1 Roma 0 09/04/2008

Tévez 70

When Roma won the Scudetto in 2001, Italian sex siren – and diehard Roma fan – Sabrina Ferilli showed her gratitude by stripping down to a flesh-coloured bikini in front of a million people in the city centre. This year she upped the ante, vowing to do the Full Monty if Roma won the Champions League in Moscow. Every hot-blooded man in Italy was left salivating over the prospect. Judging by his first-half penalty gaffe here, I reckon Norwegian referee Tom Ovrebo quite fancied seeing more of her too*...

Fortunately, the penalty – awarded for a perfect slide tackle on Mancini by Brown – didn't influence the course of the tie. De Rossi duffed his spot-kick into the Stretford End and, though Roma had a good spell just before the break, United's rejigged defence effectively cruised through the rest of the match. Tévez's winner merely confirmed what we'd all suspected since Doni dropped Park's header in Rome the previous week. Signora Ferilli would have to wait another year at least before dropping her knickers in the Circo Maximo.

Goal!
1-0 (70): Hargreaves whips in his umpteenth superb cross and Tévez stoops at the near post to flick a header past Doni. For once he leaves the dummy in his pants but he does lift up his shirt to reveal a birthday message to his brother. 'Feliz cumpleanos Ariel', as they say in Fuerte Apache.

What was good?
Hargreaves's performance in an unusual advanced position on the right...It almost sounds sacrilegious considering what Beckham did for us, but it could be the best display of crossing I've ever seen.

Question of the day
When will a United-following actress follow Sabrina Ferilli's lead and promise to strip off in Albert Square? (Put your hand down Lisa Riley.)

What was predictable?
We're playing Roma. Simone Perotta plays for Rome. Which means that Tyler or Tyldesley will feel obliged to tell us all about his roots in Ashton-under-Lyne. Every time he touches the ball. Geoff Hurst grew up there as well, did you know? Grrrrrgh.

*I'm joking of course. I would never actually suggest that Tom Ovrebo would ever give a bad decision on purpose or that he would get turned on by naked Italians, etc.

What was not?

I wasn't prepared for a bearded Eric turning up for the match looking like – I hate to say it – the sort of guy who would have seagulls following his boat...

Or for the sight of Gary Neville making his comeback as a sub, certainly not as a centre midfielder anyway. His facial hair wasn't anywhere near as impressive as Eric's, but after all the rumours that Gary would never play again it was just good to see him back.

View from the broadsheets

☼ 'For Sir Alex Ferguson it is back to the Nou Camp for the first time since the miracle of 1999: Barcelona, how could we forget? Nine years on since his greatest moment as manager of Manchester United, Ferguson must look at his latest generation of players and think that if this team cannot win the club's third European Cup then perhaps he will never lay his hands on it again.

'Carlos Tévez's goal 20 minutes from time was the difference last night but it was not the second half that will concern Frank Rijkaard and the boys from Catalonia. It was in the first 20 minutes that United showed the devastating style which has earnt them the title of bookmakers' favourites for the Champions League title. In that time their passing and their running demolished the Roma defence and they did it with a team that did not even include Wayne Rooney or Cristiano Ronaldo.'
– *The Independent*

Worst Headline Of The Day

'Threesy Does It – *The Daily Mirror* combines 'easy' with the number of times United have beaten Roma this season. Genius.

Match facts

United: Van der Sar, Brown, Pique, Ferdinand, Silvestre, Hargreaves, Park, Carrick (O'Shea 74), Anderson (Neville 81), Giggs (Rooney 74), Tévez
Roma: Doni, Panucci, Mexes, Juan, Cassetti (Tonetto 56), De Rossi, Pizarro (Giuly 69), Taddei (Esposito 81), Perrotta*, Mancini, Vucinic [Spalletti]
CLQF 19.45 (ITV). Att: 74,423. Ref: T. Ovrebo (Nor). Half-time: 0–0
*Yellow card

Champions League quarter-final results:

Barcelona 1 Schalke 0 (2-0), Chelsea 2 Fenerbahce 0 (3-2), Liverpool 4 Arsenal 2 (5-3)

Roma to Arsenal
'This is what I do for a living: I f**k companies.'

Sensible move of the week

'Sir Alex Ferguson has made Manchester United's Player of the Year bash a black tie affair with WAGS.' – *The Daily Star*

Crazy in love

- 'To be sitting on the bench behind somebody who only started to play when he was 30 is not funny. I am very angry' – The brilliantly nutty Jens Lehmann can't believe he's second choice to Manuel Almunia.
- 'To have someone here who hates me is just amazing. I know he hates me. Every morning I wake up I know it is going to be the same. I've had to put up with it every day since he was out of the team and even before then. I wake up, and I know what it is going to be like' – Almunia can't believe Jens Lehmann full stop. Neither can we.

Changing Times

After Fergie blasts their Hargreaves 'time-keeping' exclusive as 'utter rubbish', *The Times* does a swift U-turn:

'Two starts in Europe this season tell one story, but as Hargreaves reflected on a frustrating eight months at the club after arguably his best performance for United in the 1–0 quarter-final, second-leg victory over Roma, another tale emerged, one that may alarm supporters but also helps to explain his limited impact so far.'

So what was this second tale *The Times*'s top sleuths uncovered? It's that Hargreaves hasn't been fully fit all season. Which would have been sort of 'alarming'…if we hadn't all known about it for months.

In the frame

'Did anyone actually believe that? I've got a good watch, a Swiss watch, and it's perfectly on time, thank you.' – Is it just me? Or has Owen Hargreaves got that trademark Bayern arrogance about him?

As a snake

A businessman bidding to own Mansfield is planning to rename the club Harchester United after the former Sky series *The Dream Team*.

John Batchelor said: 'Football supporters in general have to understand that if they want professional football in their town, they have to accept it has to be done on a commercial basis. Harchester is more promotable than Mansfield. That's not any form of insult to Mansfield at all because it's a club with a long tradition, but it's just a fact of life. One club has been on the television for 10 years and the other one hasn't.' Inspired.

The April fools

City get all giddy as the European Cup-Winners' Cup, the European Cup and the UEFA Cup are all displayed. According to the *Red Issue*, one internal memo carried the frothy-mouthed line, 'We have now made history by becoming the first English football club or museum to display all 3 European trophies at the same time.'

'F***ing brilliant', as the *RI* put it.

Stupid girl

After Darren Ferguson was fined £2,000 for assaulting his estranged wife, Nadine, on his dad's driveway in October the press reveals his defence. Apparently he didn't kick his wife in the stomach, she had 'run into his raised leg'. For god's sake son, you'd have been better off if you'd used your dad's line about needing a poo.

Quote of the week

'This is what I do for a living: I f**k companies' – Potential owner John Batchelor sends out a message of hope for Mansfield/Harchester fans. Will someone in the FA sort out a 'Fit and proper person' test soon, please?

Still laughing

'Ronaldinho has fallen from grace to such an extent that Manchester City recently thought about buying him' – *The Daily Mail* won't let it go.

United 2 Arsenal 1 13/04/2008

Adebayor 48, Ronaldo 54 (pen), Hargreaves 72

Fergie was right, this was torture. But it was the sort of torture that gets middle-aged accountants to pay women to dress up in leather and whip their backsides. When the final whistle blew, Arsenal's season lay in ruins and United were two wins from the title. Who could have asked for a better ending than that?

How the match unfolded

ADEBAYOR. MISS! (12): Arsenal had been devastated by their Champions League defeat at Anfield. In fact, one of their players, Senderos, had cried so hard in the dressing room afterwards that Wenger gave him two days off. United, meanwhile, had enjoyed a cruise against Roma. But if you'd asked an uninformed observer at half-time to choose which team had just been through an emotional wringer they'd have said United. There's no getting around it, Arsenal were better than us in midfield, where Scholesy's legs looked like they were struggling to keep up with his brain. And they created more decent chances than any other visitors to Old Trafford this season. Fortunately, the best of them fell to Adebayor, and after recently swapping his dreadlocks for a mini-Afro he seemed to be suffering from a bad case of Samson syndrome.

This was perhaps the best of his misses. Eboue's cutback from the right catches both Pique and Ferdinand off balance, Adebayor just about gets his telescopic legs sorted in time but Ferdinand recovers well to block his lunging shot.

PARK. MISS! (14): The press box were rightly impressed by Arsenal's first-half performance. But the hacks who claimed they should have been three or four up at half-time mustn't have been paying attention. Arsenal created three great chances. But United created three even better ones. Moments after Adebayor's chance, they should have taken the lead. Hargreaves, picking up where he left off against Roma, digs out a cross from the left which seems destined for Ronaldo's forehead and then the net. Unfortunately, Park gets in Ronaldo's way and he heads it wide on the stretch.

ROONEY. SAVE! (22): What a pass! With a nonchalant swoosh with the outside of his left foot, Evra releases Ronaldo down the channel between the centre-backs and Toure.

Ronaldo dinks the ball cutely over the lunging Song and squares the ball to Rooney just a couple of yards out. He should score, but his uncertain side-foot hits Lehmann's leg and deflects behind.

ADEBAYOR. BALLOON! (27): Adebayor balloons his shot miles over the bar after being teed up by Fabregas. If he'd missed that badly 20 years ago he would have taken out the Wonderfuel Gas sign.

ADEBAYOR. MISS! (34): Hleb dances past the leaden-footed Pique and sends Adebayor clear on the left side of the box. A Solskjaer or Henry would have opened up their body and curled the ball into the far corner. Adebayor opens up his body and rolls the ball apologetically into the midriff of Van der Sar.

ROONEY. SAVE! (35): A misplaced pass from Carrick is allowed to run all the way to Rooney. He runs away from three covering defenders and seems to have done everything right when he flicks a shot towards the far corner, but Lehmann reacts brilliantly with his left foot and the ball skids just wide.

ADEBAYOR. HANDBALL! NO, GOAL! (47): Adebayor finally gets lucky…very lucky. After a training-ground free-kick routine goes wrong, Arsenal recycle the ball to Van Persie on the left. His cross dissects Ferdinand and Van der Sar, who both seem to leave the ball for each other*, and Adebayor bundles it in with his elbow.

VAN DER SAR! SAVE! (50): Ferdinand was probably United's Man of the Match, along with Evra, but he had a nightmare couple of minutes here. Adebayor crosses from the right, Ferdinand inadvertently diverts the ball goalwards, and it takes a smart reaction save from Van der Sar to stop Arsenal going two up.

GALLAS! RONALDO! PENALTY! (51): Van der Sar's save looked crucial at the time. It looks even more crucial a minute later. Carrick knocks a hopeful ball into the area and Gallas, under slight pressure from Park, clearly handles. 'Would you believe it?' Andy Gray barks on Sky, for probably the 73,000th time.

RONALDO! GOAL! NO (52): Lehmann's got a 50:50 record with penalties at Old Trafford. Make that 33:67. Hold on, Howard Webb's making Ronaldo take it again, and you can see why. Ronaldo stutters for so long in his run up that Park almost beats him to the ball.

---

* Ferdinand later reveals that he left the ball after hearing someone shout ''keeper's'. Van der Sar denies it, which suggests that an Arsenal scamp was playing dirty tricks.

RONALDO! GOAL! (54): Lehmann, who gets more yellow cards than any other 'keeper I've ever seen, gets himself booked for trying to convince Webb to change the rules and award Arsenal a free-kick for Park's encroachment. The mind games don't put off Ronaldo who shows off his cojones by sweeping the ball low past Lehmann's right hand.

OFF! ADEBAYOR! NO! (62): The frustration of watching a season's work get ruined finally gets to Adebayor, who chops down Anderson with a leaping, two-footed, scissors-style scythe from behind. It could easily have been a red card. In fact it should have been a red card, but Webb – no doubt remembering that Arsenal never kick anyone – only gets out his yellow.

VAN DER SAR! SAVE! (66): What is it with United's defenders today? First Ferdinand forces a great save from Van der Sar. Now it's Brown's turn, though in fairness he doesn't have much chance with this one. Clichy crosses low from the left, the ball flicks off Brown and Van der Sar does brilliantly to get across and touch the ball onto his near post.

ROONEY! CHANCE! (70): Clichy was voted into the PFA team at left-back this season. It wasn't a terrible decision, just the wrong one. Clichy is a very good player and might just have the edge over Evra defensively, but he just doesn't offer the threat going forward that his countryman does. This time Evra surges through the middle, gets the ball back from Tévez and threads a terrific ball through to Rooney, who slams his shot straight at Lehmann's legs.

HARGREAVES! GOAL! (72): Arsenal's reprieve doesn't last long. The ball ricochets back to Evra, he is brought down by Gilberto near the 'D' and Hargreaves whips a superb dipping free-kick over the wall and into the bottom left corner. As Old Trafford goes berserk, Lehmann screams something at his wall. I don't know what he thought they could do though. That was about as perfect a free-kick as you could get.

GIGGS! ON! (89): Fergie brings on Giggs for Hargreaves. Is it to waste time? Or is it to make sure Giggsy gets the chance to beat Sir Bobby's record this season?

BENDTNER! CHANCE. (90): Arsenal need two goals and a miracle to stay in the title race, but an equaliser here would at least have given them the consolation of damaging United's own title bid. Fortunately, when Arsenal's chance does come, Bendtner heads it straight at Van der Sar. I'm surprised Adebayor didn't chin him.

GAME OVER! SEASON OVER! (93): Ronaldo launches into an outrageous display of all-kicking, all-dancing showboating near the tunnel which ends with him getting a (deserved?)

kicking from Hoyte. By the time the referee has written down Hoyte's name, time is up. On the match, and on Arsenal's season. Just a couple of months after the media crowned Wenger's team the 'new Invincibles', the three-horse race for the title was down to two.

Views from the broadsheets

☺ 'It takes a certain kind of confidence to tell Cristiano Ronaldo to stand aside when there is a potentially crucial free-kick to be hit, but then there has been a certain kind of confidence about Manchester United all season. Enter Owen Hargreaves stage right: an unlikely match-winner in a title race that is starting to look entirely predictable.' – *The Independent*

☺ 'When the title race is run, when forensics set to work analysing the scene, the moment that defined the season is likely to have come in the 73rd minute here. Patrice Evra's nimble surges have been one of the many joys of United's season and when he was cut down by Gilberto Silva, Ronaldo and Owen Hargreaves took command of the dead-ball situation.

'It was about 25 yards out, perfectly placed for one of Hargreaves' little up-and-over-the-wall attempts. Watched by Fabio Capello, Hargreaves took three steps before his right foot came down, lifting the ball in. Looks of horror invaded the face of every Arsenal player in the wall, stirring heartache in Adebayor, Gilberto and Robin van Persie as they turned to see where the ball had ended up.

'There it lay in the back of Lehmann's net, mocking Arsenal and mortifying Chelsea, whose title dream surely rolled to a standstill with Hargreaves' dead-ball. For United, this was one of those precious "name on the trophy" moments.' – *The Telegraph*

Quote of the day

'We have to accept we will not win the title.' – Arsene Wenger.

Runner-up

'I think Arsenal have been unlucky not to get something from the game. You couldn't ask for more from a team than Arsenal produced today, and we've still managed to win.' – Fergie really sticks the knife in by being nice about Arsenal.

Match facts

United: Van der Sar, Brown*, Ferdinand, Pique, Evra, Ronaldo, Carrick*, Hargreaves (Giggs 89), Scholes (Anderson 55), Park (Tévez 55), Rooney
Arsenal: Lehmann*, Toure (Hoyte* 85), Gallas*, Song Billong, Clichy, Eboue (Walcott 61), Fabregas, Silva, Hleb, Van Persie* (Bendtner 76), Adebayor* [Wenger]
FAPL 16.00 (Sky). Att: 75,985. Ref: H. Webb. Half-time 0–0
*Yellow card

Other scores
Liverpool 3 (Gerrard, Torres, Voronin) Blackburn 1 (Santa Cruz)

League table
1. United 80 (34) 2. Chelsea 74 (33) 3. Arsenal 71 (34) 4. Liverpool 66 (34)

Arsenal to Blackburn
'To be part of a team I have supported all my life is a great honour.'

News

Yes. Wes Brown finally agrees a new four-year contract, saving him from wasting his career away at Newcastle or Villa. Ferdinand and Carrick both agree contract extensions too. Brucie makes himself even more popular among Reds by masterminding Wigan's 1–1 draw at Chelsea. Unfortunately, Everton don't do us any favours at Goodison, which means that the lead is down to two points going into the weekend's game at bogey ground Ewood. Just as at Anfield, Wenger takes the defeat at Old Trafford on the chin. Yeah right.

Everyone thinks they have the best excuse at home

☻ 'This team has been punished in the past seven weeks more so than any team I have seen since I arrived in England 11 years ago. Every single decision has gone against this team in every single game recently.' – Wenger isn't paranoid. Everyone really is out to get him. Just think about that handball goal at Old Trafford that was allowed to stand. Hang on, that was Adebayor's handball…

☻ 'It is very difficult to swallow because we feel there is not a great difference in technical quality between ourselves, Chelsea and Manchester United. The confidence, however, has dropped in the last two months.' – Wenger still refuses to accept that United are better than Arsenal. Which is great. If he never comes to terms with the fact that Arsenal's style is far more suited to winning plaudits than titles, they'll keep on drawing blanks when the trophies are handed out.

Sing it Edith

Wenger reckons that 'this team has been punished in the past seven weeks more so than any team I have seen since I arrived in England 11 years ago'. Let's see…

☻ Birmingham (a) 2–2: Eduardo suffers his horrific break and Clichy concedes a very soft penalty. Verdict: Arsenal unlucky… but they should still have done better against a team that only had 10 men for 87 minutes.

- ❂ Aston Villa (h) 1–1: Aston Villa are denied a deserved win in the 34th minute of injury time. Verdict: Arsenal lucky to get a point.
- ❂ Milan (a) 2–0: Everything goes right as Arsenal become the first English side to turn over Milan in the San Siro.
- ❂ Wigan (a) 0–0: Laboured performance. Hardly any chances. Verdict: No complaints.
- ❂ Boro (h) 1–1: Adebayor has a goal wrongly ruled out for offside before Boro score on the break. Arsenal have all the play but make few chances until Toure heads in a corner near the end. Mido is then harshly sent off for Boro. Verdict: Adebayor's goal could have made all the difference.
- ❂ Chelsea (a) 1–2: Arsenal can't cope with Drogba and Anelka and lose a game they were leading. Sagna picks up an injury that keeps him out all season. Verdict: No complaints about the result. Losing Sagna is unfortunate, but another top team has been deprived of their first choice right-back for far longer.
- ❂ Bolton (a) 3–2: Diaby is rightly sent off for a horror tackle in the first half. Bolton go two up and should have scored a third. Arsenal's late comeback is sealed with a shot from Fabregas that pinballs off five Bolton defenders and Lenny the Lion. Verdict: Got away with it.
- ❂ Liverpool CL (h) 1–1: Kuyt gets away with a tug on Hleb in the area. Bendtner blocks a certain goal on the Liverpool goalline. Verdict: Unlucky with the penalty, but Hleb did go down very easy. Definitely seen them not given.
- ❂ Liverpool (h) 1–1: Wenger sends out a weakened team and can have no complaints with the 1–1 result.
- ❂ Liverpool CL (a) 2–4: Gerrard scores the decisive penalty after Toure pulls back Babel. Wenger goes mad, but it's a definite penalty. Verdict: Ref was spot on.
- ❂ United (a) 1–2: Arsenal outclassed United for an hour and should have been 12–0 up, blah blah blah. In fairness they played well, but Adebayor's goal shouldn't have stood and the penalty Gallas conceded was a stonewaller. Verdict: Arsenal might not have deserved to lose but can't complain about the decisions.

In other words, Arsenal's seven-week punishment amounted to one bad injury, one dubious offside call and one 70:30 penalty claim. Savage eh?

Talking sense

Five real reasons why Arsenal didn't win the League:

- ❂ Not enough goal threat from midfield.
- ❂ Running Fabregas into the ground (again).
- ❂ No proper captain (see below).
- ❂ Phillipe Senderos.
- ❂ They're not as good as United. Or Chelsea.

How times change

From *football365*:

- ❂ 'When Arsène Wenger made William Gallas Arsenal's captain, responses varied only from "oh" to "really?" On Saturday, Gallas underlined why Wenger made the right choice' – *The Times* after Gallas scored Arsenal's winner against Wigan, 23 November.
- ❂ 'For all his qualities and achievements, Arsène Wenger, the Arsenal manager, has often appeared to possess certain blind spots – identifying goalkeepers, centre-backs and recognising any wrongdoing among his own players, for example – but his failure to find a suitable leader for his outstanding young team could be the most damaging oversight of all…Gallas has lacked the maturity to cast aside his frustrations and focus on the good of the team' – *The Times* after Arsenal failed to win the title, 14 April.

We've got Wesley Brown

'Manchester United is a fantastic club, and I am delighted to have signed a new deal. To be part of a team I have supported all my life is a great honour. I can see this team winning many trophies in the coming seasons, and it will be great to share in that success. – Wes is overjoyed to be staying. So am I. It's not just that Wes is the sort of versatile player that wins you Championships. His new contract means we'll still have a local lad at Old Trafford when the last of the class of '92 retires. By the way, I reckon that's another reason why Arsenal keep falling short. It makes a huge difference when managers can call on home-grown players with a real feeling for the club. Chelsea have Terry. Liverpool have Carragher and Gerrard. United have Brown, Scholes, Giggs and the honorary Mancs, Sheasy and Fletch. Arsenal haven't had anyone like that since Keown hung up his monkey suit.'

Blackburn 1 United 1   19/04/2008

Santa Cruz 21, Tévez 88

This could have been the story of how a bald American cost United the title. It could have been the story of how an Old Trafford legend cost United the title. It could even have been the story of how Rob bloody Stiles (no penalties again!) cost United the title. Instead, it was the story of how a man bull from Fuerte Apache put United a Chelsea draw away from the title. Ronaldo scores great goals and is a great goalscorer, Rooney scores great goals and is a good goalscorer, but if you need a guy to score the goals that really matter, look no further than Carlos Tévez. Since 2 February, United had stolen late, late equalisers in three crucial games – at Spurs, Lyon and now Blackburn. Tévez, the goal-hanger supreme, bagged all three.

Goal action

0–1 (21): Sloppy. Ferdinand and Vidic both get attracted to Pederson's hopeful long throw and, as the ball gets stuck between them, Rio accidentally backheels it towards the unmarked Santa Cruz. Fittingly for a player sponsored by 'Blackburn's Holly Tree Fish & Chip Shop – Quality Assured', the Paraguayan scores with ease.

1–1 (88): After half-time United keep knocking at the door. And knocking. And knocking. But Friedel won't let them in. With two minutes to go it looks like the title is back in Chelsea's hands for the first time in months, but then Scholes flicks on Nani's corner at the near post and Tévez twists his neck to score at the far post. As Florencia's dummy comes out again, so does a version of the classic United quote, this time from Mark Hughes: 'United never say they lost. They say they ran out of time.'

What was good?

⚽ Brad Friedel – The former Scouse flop has been tagged the 'bald fraud' by some Reds on account of his routine brilliance against United and his routine inability to do anything useful at Anfield. He's never been better than he was here. The saves from Ronaldo (point-blank header from a corner), Rooney (one-on-one), Rooney again (low bullet) and O'Shea (point-blank left-footer) were all excellent. The one from Tévez (surprise shot that nutmegged a defender) might just have been the best from an opposing 'keeper all year.

What was bad?

☻ Rob Stiles – He'd already missed three stonewall United penalties this season. At Ewood he doubled his tally, missing Reid's first-half trip on Rooney, Vogel's mistimed second-half slide tackle on Ronaldo and, worst of all, the handball by Emerson that blocked Carrick's goalbound header. What was that story about Abramovich's drive again?

Views from the broadsheets

☻ 'Cristiano Ronaldo's reaction to Carlos Tévez's late equaliser showed exactly why Manchester United make such formidable opponents. As Tévez sprinted away to milk the jubilant reaction of fans who turned the Darwen End into the Stretford End, Ronaldo collected the ball from the net and raced to the centre-spot.

'Tévez, newly arrived this season, still learns the United way, that equalisers are not enough, that a team moulded in the hungry image of Sir Alex Ferguson always hunts victory, however satisfying a draw may feel. Ronaldo, far more cognisant of United's tradition for late triumphs, just wanted to get the game re-started. The champions ran out of time, but Ronaldo never ran out of determination, and that is what makes United so special.

'This confluence of technical expertise, seen in the dazzling footwork of Ronaldo, Tévez and Wayne Rooney, and passion for victory elevates United to the foremost team in the land for goals, drama, style and silverware. Chelsea make mighty roundheads, Arsenal gloriously flawed cavaliers, but no one quite captures the imagination like Manchester United.' – Excellent stuff from *The Telegraph*...

☻ 'Prayers, presumably, were being offered in the mock Tudor mansions of Cobham and Esher, the multimillionaire players of Chelsea reduced to nervous, desperate wrecks as they pleaded for divine intervention. The heroics of Brad Friedel had offered them hope, but, as Manchester United set up camp in the Blackburn Rovers penalty area in the final 15 minutes, it needed something more. Would United score? As their rivals would grudgingly concede, they always bloody score.' – And *The Times*.

Match facts

Blackburn: Friedel, Emerton, Samba, Nelsen, Warnock, Bentley, Reid*, Vogel (Mokoena 85), Pedersen, Santa Cruz, Roberts [Sparky]

United: Kuszczak, Brown (O'Shea 81), Ferdinand, Vidic, Evra, Ronaldo, Carrick, Scholes, Giggs (Nani 46), Tévez, Rooney* (Park 90)

FAPL 17.15 (Set) Ewood Park. Att: 30,316. Ref: R.Styles. Half-time: 0–1

*Yellow card

Other scores
Fulham 0 Liverpool 2 (Pennant, Crouch); Arsenal 2 (Adebayor, Gilberto) Reading 0

League table
1. United 81 (35) 2. Chelsea 78(35) 3. Arsenal 74 (35) 4. Liverpool 69 (35)...9.
Blackburn 52 (35)

Blackburn to FC Barcelona
'I've got an arch in my back and my bum sticks out.'

News
Rob Styles's latest penalty cock-up earns him a demotion to Division Two for the
weekend's thriller between Shrewsbury and Chester. Styles at Shrewsbury? It's an
amusing image. But it doesn't really make up for the loss of those two points at Ewood
does it? The police reveal that more than 50 supporters were arrested before and after
the Blackburn game. Strangely, the papers make nothing of it. Isn't it in their interests
to mention any trouble these days? Chelsea get lucky in the first leg of their Champions
League semi at Anfield as John Arne Riise scores an hilarious injury-time equaliser in
front of a gobsmacked Kop. Luckily for Riise, Craig Bellamy and his golf clubs aren't
around any more...

Come again
'I watch Ronaldo every weekend and he is massively impressive. He carries United
on his back in some matches. Barca have no idea how spectacular Ronaldo is or how
far ahead of every other player in the world he is right now. But if they keep the ball
away from him Barca will get to the Champions League Final.' – Fernando Torres
accuses United of being a one-man team. He's not been watching Liverpool much
has he?

King of the stone age
'A homosexual cannot do the job of a footballer. The football world is not designed for
them. It's a special atmosphere, in which you stand naked under the showers. There are
no gays in football, I don't know if players are against having them in their team but I
definitely am. I'm old school, but I know the ambience of football, and a gay wouldn't be
able to survive within it.' – The ever-charming Luciano Moggi, Juve's shady former general
manager.

Gossip

United are linked with moves for Palacios and Valencia from Wigan, Sporting's Moutinho and Veloso, Klaas-Jan Huntelaar (again), Heerenveen's Miralem Sulejmani, Rennes's Stephane Mbia and Cruzeiro's Bolivian striker Marcelo Moreno.

Quotes of the week

- 'The Newcastle fans aren't as good as everybody says. They think they should be winning things – but why? They've not won a trophy for 50 years.' – Clearly, Titus Bramble speaks better than he plays.
- 'The sly joker is Fletch. People don't suspect him, but when something's going on he is normally involved. Pique and Fletch are always at the centre of pranks with players' clothes.' Rio lifts the lid on the United dressing room for *manutd.com*
- 'I've got an arch in my back and my bum sticks out.' – Wolves striker – and former Red reserve – Sylvain Ebanks-Blake responds to suggestions that he might be a touch, er, chunky.
- 'Romantic, funny, hard working.' – How Wayne Rooney describes himself on his official website.
- 'What can I say? I decided to stoop and head the ball in the direction it came from. But it was a swerving cross, the ball was wet, and it slid right off my forehead. It was a shock to see it lying in the goal.' – It wasn't shocking John Arne. It was hilarious.

'Lucky Escape' stat of the week

'Harry Kewell will have cost Liverpool a massive £157,554 a GAME when his Anfield career comes to an end this month.' – *The Sun*

FC Barcelona 0 United 0   23/04/2008

First, the good news…United didn't lose, they defended well – far better than in Fergie's previous Euro semis – and they showed that Barcelona, for all their talent, have the same ingrained flaw we all hoped they had. They play nine out of 10 football outside the box but can't help disappearing up their famous backsides once they're inside it.

Now the bad news…A 0–0 away draw isn't the result it used to be. If Ronaldo had got it right from the spot, Reds would have effectively had one foot in the Luzhniki. As it was, we had to face a week of newspaper reminders of what happened the last time we got scoreless draws away – at Monaco in '98 and Real Madrid in 2000. God, we even went out when we drew 0–0 at Rotor Volgograd.

And the worst part of the night? The ultra-negative tactics which saw Rooney play as an auxiliary right-back, Tévez stalk Toure and basically left Ronaldo to do all the attacking on his own. Teams like Liverpool need to hide behind tactics at places like Barcelona because they know they'd get murdered in a pure football contest. Manchester United don't have to, particularly against teams with as soft a centre as Barca. Before the game, the Culers must have been choking on their chorizo worrying what a lightning counter-attack led by Rooney, Ronaldo and Tévez would do to Marquez, Puyol and co. They needn't have worried. Barcelona might be a team in transition but, as the world watched, they did at least stay true to their magical history. United, unfortunately, never even tried.

The moments that mattered

PENALTY! RONALDO! NO! (2): Ronaldo's madly ambitious free-kick from the best part of 40 yards cannons off the Barcelona blockers and bounces behind. When the corner comes in, Ronaldo's header is smothered by Milito. The referee points to the spot, Ronaldo stares out Valdes and then, for some reason, decides to abandon his normal stuttering penalty technique. Instead he opens his body up and shanks the ball wide of the right-hand post.

PENALTY! RONALDO! NO! (29): The penalty shock knocks United out of their stride and also acts as a giant pick-me-up to Barcelona. But even though Xavi, Toure, Iniesta and the brilliant Messi boss the game, it's United who threaten next. Iniesta gifts the ball to Ronaldo, and he is taken out in the box by the pony-tailed Marquez. It was as much a penalty as the first one (and that was a no brainer) but, perhaps wondering how he was going to beat 94,000 people to the airport, the Swiss ref lets the Mexican off.

ETO'O and ETO'O (51): Barcelona continue to dominate possession and decorate the night with the angles and cleverness of their passing. But they only give United two genuine scares, both of which come in the space of a minute early in the second half. First Eto'o shows good sportsmanship by refusing to go down under Ferdinand's sliding challenge. Then thrilling one-touch play ends with Iniesta flicking on to Eto'o and Eto'o lashing his shot into the side netting.

CARRICK! MISS! (53): United's only chance away from the penalty spot falls to Carrick but, after bamboozling Marquez, he lashes his shot into the side netting too. Amazingly, as far as major moments go, that was that. For the first time in the history of United–Barcelona, we'd been served up a dud.

Views from the broadsheets

- ✪ 'To summarise Barcelona on last night's evidence, think Arsenal in their moments of most brilliant and most wasteful excess. They seduced with their intricate passing and they failed to fashion much that was incisive or dangerous inside the United area. The touch and the fluency had their support in raptures until it slowly dawned that minutes, a half and eventually a whole game had passed and they had not fashioned the killer chance for a winning goal.' – *The Independent*
- ✪ 'There was plenty of Barcelona-style football, but it looked like it had been put on at 33rpm rather than 45. By half-time United seemed to sense the team pressing towards their goal – and having the odd shot too – were attacking them with the footballing equivalent of a plastic dagger.' – *The Guardian*
- ✪ 'This season United have travelled England and Europe breaking down obstinate defences and five-man midfields. Last night it was their turn to spoil and thwart, and they did it beautifully. Yes, they rode their luck at times but there was no good fortune in the defiance of Edwin van der Sar and Rio Ferdinand, in particular, who held together a patched-up back four missing Nemanja Vidic.' – *The Independent*
- ✪ 'The best you could say about United's performance was that they worked hard and concentrated hard, with the feisty Patrice Evra probably their stand-out player.' – *The Guardian*

Bitchy line of the night
'True Real players don't miss penalties at Camp Nou.' – Marca sticks it to Ronaldo (just weeks before launching a full-blown campaign to sign him up).

Quote of the night
'Barcelona had a lot of the ball but they didn't create chances. We are going to win.' – Ronaldo's bullish, despite that miss.

Match facts

Barcelona: Valdes, Zambrotta, Marquez*, Milito, Abidal, Xavi, Toure Yaya, Deco (Henry 77), Messi (Bojan 62), Eto'o, Iniesta [Rikjaard]

United: Van der Sar, Hargreaves*, Ferdinand, Brown, Evra, Ronaldo, Carrick, Scholes, Park, Rooney (Nani 76), Tévez (Giggs 85)

CLS/F 19.45 (Sky). Camp Nou. Att: 98,000. Ref: M. Busacca (Switz). Half-time: 0–0
*Yellow card

Champions League semi-final:

Liverpool 1 Chelsea 1

FC Barcelona to Chelsea
'It'll be great to go back to Old Trafford on Tuesday, and that'll be a proper atmosphere.'

Story of the week

'Smitten soccer star CARLOS TÉVEZ has penned a love song – for his Manchester United teammates. The Argentinian striker, who fronts a band in Buenos Aires, is also singing the praises of his adopted home city. Tévez, 24, has called his ditty Mi Amorosa Aventura, which means My Love Affair. He will record it this summer with his group Piola Vago, which translates as Sly Idol.' – The Sun

ABU ** of the week Part I**

Step forward The Sunday Times's Rod Liddle:

'I've tried to remember if there was some occurrence over the past two or three years that gave me more intense pleasure than Ronaldo missing that penalty against Barcelona on Wednesday night.

'The birth of my daughter? The look of pleasure on the faces of my children when they awake to their presents on Christmas Day? Nope – nowhere near. This, you might argue, is the statement of a bitter and pathetic little man – but then "we are what we are", as the Labour MP Ron Davies announced shortly after he'd been espied interfering with badgers in a wood near the M4 a few years back.'

News

Nothing much to report from Old Trafford, but it's a busy week in Medialand: Ian Wright quits the Match of the Day team after getting the huff for being used as a comedy jester. He then takes his first step towards serious journalism by signing up for, er, Gladiators. Steve McClaren signs up for the Five Live's commentary team for Euro 2008.

So the man who wasn't good enough to get to the competition will be there to criticise the managers who did. YCNMIU. And ex-Red flop, and Talksport presenter, Alan Brazil is banned from driving for 20 months after being found twice over the legal drink-driving limit.

ABU **** of the week Part II
Liddle's still spouting...

'Ronaldo's faux-nonchalant, side-footed slice of a spot-kick provoked me to open a bottle of champagne I'd bought when Ashley Cole was caught out with some slapper a month or so ago, but in my euphoria had entirely forgotten about and left at the back of the fridge.

'I was so happy I even thought about buying some Pringles and asking the neighbours round. And there was still plenty in the bottle to toast Cristiano's fall-down-like-a-great-big-girlie-in-the-penalty-area routine half an hour later. If you were a referee, would you ever give Ronaldo a penalty, unless you actually saw the gun taken out of the holster and pointed at his head? As Sir Alex Ferguson has frequently pointed out, his little Portuguese moppet is often denied decisions which should rightly have gone his way; such was the case, I would reckon, against Barcelona (although in the good old days it would have been an indirect free-kick at best).'

Quote of the week
'It was a lovely atmosphere, a great stadium. It was a bit quieter than I expected really. It'll be great to go back to Old Trafford on Tuesday and that'll be a proper atmosphere. We're going to attack Barcelona, get at them and let's see if they can deal with that.' – More straight-talking from Owen Hargreaves, the season's second most quotable Red (after the brilliantly bonkers Paddy Evra).

Must try harder
'I think this case has shown that the law is a grey area. It is rather like the offside law. I am disappointed with the verdict. I work long hours – I'm entitled to drive at 50mph. I'm the first guy to be done for driving too slowly' – Alan Brazil pleads his innocence over his drink driving conviction, though his argument loses some of its credibility when it emerges that he told police he'd earlier drunk a bottle of wine. Not such a grey area then is it Alan?

A strange kind of story
'Ronaldo is a disgrace to football, he cheated the referee and his own teammates. The people on the BBC and SKY call him a genius, the best player in the world...it's an

insult to Rooney, Scholes. You can throw me off this panel, but I am going to speak my mind.' – RTE's Eamon Dunphy, Rod Liddle's favourite pundit, during the Barcelona game.

Understatement of the week
'I'm a bit disappointed in the transition between defence and attack.' – After the Nou Camp 0–0, Fergie opts for a technical term to say what we could do with a mix of the words 'we', 'were' and 'crap'.

Chelsea 2 United 1   26/04/2008

Ballack 45, 86 (pen) Rooney 57

Ever since the win in Rome I'd had a dream. On Wednesday night we'd go to the Nou Camp and give an exhibition of attacking football that would leave the Barcelona fans crying in their white hankies, and elevate this United team to the same attacking pantheon as the '60s one. Then on Saturday lunchtime we'd go to Stamford Bridge, destroy their proud – and let's face it, pretty stunning – unbeaten home record and in the process all but clinch the title. Right in front of Peter Kenyon.

Instead we got this. A dour betrayal of our roots in the Nou Camp. And an ultra-defensive reserve team at the Bridge. United did OK after Carvalho gifted Rooney his equaliser. They had two shots cleared off the line at the death. And I personally thought we were unlucky with the penalty. But we were embarrassingly timid, disjointed and off the pace in the first hour. And we really should have lost by a lot more...

United's superior goal difference always meant we'd still be odds-on for the title regardless of what happened here. So you can sort of see why Fergie took the risk of resting players for the Barca rematch. But why end the season worrying about a trip to Wigan when we could all have spent the last fortnight smoking a big fat figurative cigar?

The moments that mattered

8: Bad news. Vidic, who's only just back from his Roma knee injury, is concussed after Drogba accidentally catches him with his knee. That's the last we'd see of him till Wigan on the final day.

0–1 (45): Drogba is allowed to pivot and cross on the edge of the box and Ballack, arriving unchecked from the far post, heads the ball decisively across Van der Sar.

1–1 (57): United equalise with a goal out of nothing. Carvalho rolls a back pass straight at Rooney, he accelerates towards goal and finishes off the inside of the upright.

63: It's ironic. On the day that Fergie opts to rest half his team, two of the stars he does pick up bad injuries. After limping through most of the second half, Rooney finally goes off after aggravating his Blackburn hip injury. We wouldn't see him again until Wigan either.

72: Ballack and Drogba become involved in a furious – and hilarious – row over who should take a free-kick. Drogba even races to the sideline to argue with the Chelsea coaches before returning to force Van der Sar into a fine save.

1–2 (86): It looks like United have got away with it. Then Carrick blocks Essien's cross with his hand. It's a definite handball. But intentional? I'm not sure how he could have got his arm out of the way. Ballack never looks like missing.

90: Ashley Cole clears Ronaldo's shot off the line. Then Shevchenko races back to do the same to Fletcher's volley. I don't know how Darren Campbell can look at himself in the mirror...

120: And now the fun really starts. Ferdinand kicks a wall – and an unfortunate female steward – on his way down the tunnel. Then United's players come out for a warm down on the pitch, Evra gets involved with a groundsman, punches are thrown and a mini war breaks out featuring more than 30 players, ground staff and stewards.

Views from the broadsheets
- 'Manchester United were like a tipsy tightrope walker as they balanced title ambitions against Champions League aspirations. They kept their poise out of sheer habit for a while but it was no surprise when they fell. It is that weakness as much as the outcome that stimulates hope of the Premier League trophy for Chelsea, who had an intensity and quality the visitors never matched.' – *The Guardian*
- 'For Ferguson this was a selection gamble gone horribly wrong.' – *The Observer*
- 'Let's face it, if Sir Alex Ferguson had to choose between a result against Chelsea on Saturday or one against Barcelona tomorrow it would be the latter every time.' – *The Independent*

Quote of the day
'It was absolutely diabolical. It is a major decision. Granted, it hit his hand. But he has not lifted his hand above his shoulders, above his head, anything like that. It is going straight to Rio Ferdinand. The referee should have seen that rather than the linesman. If we're not going to get those decisions then we are under pressure' – Fergie goes mental about the penalty (he doesn't mention it's the first we've had against us in the League all season).

Reaction of the week
'It shouldn't have to be like this. Here we are, stood on the verge of greatness with a European Cup/Premiership double within our grasp, and I'm reduced to watching us

player with my f***in fingers over my f***in eyes. This is just barmy. A season in which we've played some sublime attacking football is ending with a total betrayal of our roots that could easily leave us with f*** all...

'At Stamford Bridge we were on the back foot from the start, only got back into it because of a defensive mistake, and never looked like winning it in a million years. Our new winger, some chap called Rooney, spent his afternoon chasing stupid aimless balls into the corners while ace centre forward Ryan Giggs gave Terry and Carvalho such a torrid time that they spent much of the first half doing a Sudoku puzzle for money. Meanwhile a 38-goal winger languished on the bench alongside an Argentine goal poacher. And when the changes did come, amazingly it was the impressive Anderson who was hauled off to accommodate the considerable bulk of John O'Pie...

'I'm just baffled, and very, very angry. We have a deserved double without our grasp after a season of spectacular football and suddenly Ferguson decides that we're f***ing Liverpool. Well bollocks to that. This is not the United way.' – Mr Spleen, G-Stand Grumbler, *Red Issue*.

Overreaction of the week
'Over a matter of days, Manchester United have gone from the fearless, swashbuckling people's choice for the League title and European crown to a strangely rattled, snarling pack beset by self-doubt, paranoia and tactical indecision.' – *The Mail*

Match facts
Chelsea: Cech, Ferreira (Anelka 66), Carvalho, Terry, A. Cole, Ballack*, Mikel*, Essien, Kalou (Shevchenko 81), Drogba*, J. Cole (Makelele 87) [Grant]
United: Van der Sar*, Brown*, Ferdinand*, Vidic (Hargreaves* 14), Silvestre, Fletcher, Carrick, Anderson (O'Shea 65), Nani, Rooney (Ronaldo 63), Giggs
12.45 (Sky) Stamford Bridge. Att: 41,828. Ref: A. Wiley. Half-time: 0–1
*Yellow card

Other scores
Birmingham 2 (Forsell, Larsson) Liverpool 2 (Crouch, Benayoun)

League table
1. United 81 (36) 2. Chelsea 81 (36) 3. Arsenal 74 (35) 4. Liverpool 70 (36)

Chelsea to FC Barcelona
'I'll stick my pitchfork up your a**e.'

News I

Ronaldo is named PFA Player of the Year again but loses the Young Player of the Year prize to Fabregas (go figure). Ferdinand and Vidic are also picked in the PFA Team of the Year. Giggsy can now claim the United appearance record this season after it emerges that Sir Bob's tally included an FA Cup game against Bolton in 1962, which he actually missed because of a last-minute illness. The press tries, and fails, to sort out what happened at Stamford Bridge. It's clear that Evra was punched and abused by Chelsea staff, but did he start the aggro? And was he racially abused? Will the Chelsea spin doctors kill this one dead? Will the FA ever get to the bottom of it? Don't hold your breath…

Immigrant song

- ☉ 'It was handbags really. It was not as bad as it appeared. I've been told not to say anything about what actually happened.' – Sam Bethell, the groundsman who took a swing at Evra, reckons nothing much happened.
- ☉ 'Patrice received a grave insult from a member of Chelsea's staff. He demanded an explanation and from that moment these men just wanted to attack Patrice. I have never seen anything like this in my career.' – Tévez begs to differ…
- ☉ 'Basically this came about because of the provocation of somebody who works for Chelsea. Patrice wanted an explanation, but these men were very aggressive. Even now I just do not understand the reaction of these people. If the images are stored in the CCTV cameras, then it will be impossible for them to say that the players were not provoked.' – As does Gerard Pique.

The Crying Game

Ronaldo – the tubby one – swerves away from the textbook recovery programme as he battles against his latest career-threatening knee injury. From *The Mail*:

'International football star Ronaldo had a fight with three prostitutes he brought back to his Brazil motel room after he discovered they were actually men, it emerged today. Police became involved when an "altercation" happened as the 31-year-old AC Milan striker came to the shocking realisation that the call girls he had paid to have group sex with after his night out were in fact transvestites.'

I haven't got the pictures to show you here. But I can tell you the only thing shocking about them was that Ronaldo ever thought they were women. Next time he's feeling randy in Rio, he should give Viv a call.

News II

Leeds lose their long drawn-out appeal against their 15-point penalty for going into administration. Amusingly, it turns out that the appeal was rejected because – stop laughing – Leeds accepted the points deduction last August and promised not to appeal against it. City make themselves look stupid too, as it emerges that Thaksin Shinawatra wants rid of Sven. Has he forgotten what a mess the club was in when Psycho left?

Quotes of the week

- ☺ 'I sit on a mower watching some of the world's greatest players play football. It's a hard job, but someone's got to do it.' – Sam Bethell's *Facebook* page makes an unlikely appearance in the nationals.
- ☺ 'I'll stick my pitchfork up your a**e.' – What an unnamed Chelsea employee allegedly told a United player.
- ☺ 'We are filing a report and it will be sent to the FA, and we are very happy with that. We're hoping that the FA investigates it. But one question I want to ask – why were the lawnmowers on the pitch after the game to cut the grass? Aren't they supposed to cut it before the match?' – Fergie makes a decent point. Had Chelsea deliberately kept the grass long to stop United's counter-attacking game? And here's another question no one was answering. Was there any real need for the Chelsea lawnmowers to be out for the few minutes United needed for their warm down? Looking at the Sky pictures it was like a game of Frogger out there.

PFA Team of the Year

James, Sagna, Ferdinand, Vidic, Clichy, Ronaldo, Gerrard, Fabregas, Young, Adebayor, Torres

United 1 FC Barcelona 0   29/04/2008

Scholes 14

When I was 18 I spent a summer travelling round Europe with mates. In truth, I can't remember much about it. Just the odd blurred images of good girls, bad girls, ouzo fountains and naked nuns (don't ask). But there is one thing I know for sure about that holiday. It was the best one I've ever had.

This match was just like that summer. Even writing now, just a couple of days later, I've got almost no memory of what actually happened on the pitch. Just the odd blurred image of Messi's mesmeric feet, the demonic energy of Tévez, Puyol's floppy hair and the magical moment when you just knew Valdes wasn't going to get near Scholesy's shot. But there is one thing I know for sure, the feelings I got as the deafening, scarf-twirling Red Army brought United home were some of the best feelings I've ever had.

How the match unfolded
MESSI (1): The evening starts badly for United with the news that Rooney hasn't beaten his hip injury and Vidic hasn't beaten his concussion. The game almost follows suit. Messi darts past Brown on the right and Scholes takes him down inches outside the box. Messi picks himself up to take the free-kick but hits it straight at the wall. The 'Ginger Motty' in the seat behind me screams abuse at Brown and, bizarrely, Carrick, in the process smashing his own record for the time it takes to turn on your team.

GOAL! SCHOLES! (14): Old Trafford is sweating passion, but neither team is doing a great job of getting at the other's defence (though, in fairness, Barcelona are getting nowhere with a lot more poise and style than United). Then something very special happens. Zambrotta takes the ball off Ronaldo and kindly donates it back to Scholes. He flicks the ball up slightly and thumps his right foot through it from 25 yards. Valdes never looks like he's going to get there, and he doesn't.

MESSI (19): United are ahead in the big fight. But the Messi versus Ronaldo fight on the undercard is going very much the way of the Argentine. How can someone so squat, small and, let's face it, unathletic looking, be so damn quick? Here he surges past Scholes and Brown, eats up 40 yards in next to no seconds and curls in a left-footer that brings a good diving stop from Van der Sar,

PARK (21): Ronaldo makes his own point, working a crossing position on the left and then picking out Park on the edge of the area. Park adapts his body position brilliantly to send a low side-foot fractionally wide of the far post.

PANIC (28): Barcelona's defence have clearly been shaken by Scholes's goal and the incessant badgering they're getting from Tévez and Park. And their loss of cool nearly costs them a second goal. Valdes – how does he get a game for a club like Barca? – flaps at a cross, Ronaldo just fails to get the right contact on his header and Puyol has to knock his own man, Milito, out of the way to clear from underneath the bar.

ETO'O and DECO (37 and 39): The first 15 minutes were Barcelona's. The second 15 were definitely United's. Now Barcelona get their game back together and come close twice in as many minutes. First Eto'o drives just past the left post. Then Deco curls just past the right one. It's a nervy time for Reds, but it's worth remembering that the United defence has still not given Barca a chance inside the area. In fact, in two evenings of pretty constant Barcelona possession, Van der Sar has hardly had to make a save worthy of the name.

NANI (41): The chance of the night. Park cuts the ball back onto his right foot and whips in a centre from the left that Nani flicks inches wide of the far post. If only he'd gone for full-length Kool and the Gang hair rather than the short version…(I've always wondered if a big Afro can help a player's heading – if so, imagine how dangerous Dion would have been if he hadn't shaved).

PENALTY! NO! (50): Milito was a lucky boy at the Nou Camp. And he gets lucky again here as the German referee, Fandel, ignores his blatant barge on Ronaldo.

UNITED PRESSURE (52–55): United's only sustained spell of second-half pressure brings three half-chances in quick succession. First, Abidal prevents Nani sliding in Ronaldo's low cross. Then Valdes saves smartly from Tévez's fierce near post shot. And finally Nani ends a weaving run by blasting the ball into the corporates in the Stretford End.

HENRY! (61): Henry comes on to warm applause all round. Yeah right. The booing and whistling is deafening.

HENRY (77): I think my heart actually stopped here. Henry takes himself out of Hargreaves's pocket for a moment, gets on the end of Xavi's corner but ends up heading the ball feebly straight at Van der Sar.

PLEAT (84): Pleat talks a lot of nonsense on ITV. But he has a good moment here, observing: 'They're still weaving patterns and they're pretty patterns, but they're not getting near Edwin van der Sar in the Manchester United goal.' He's right. And that's partly down to Barcelona's tendency to overplay – and over-rely on Messi – and mainly down to the brilliant performances across the United back line. Amazingly, Vidic isn't being missed.

BARCA PRESSURE (60–90): In the last half hour Barcelona crank up the pace of their attacks, while United all but give up on attacking. But, with Tévez defending like a rabid lion from the front and Ferdinand and Brown too strong for any combination of Eto'o, Henry, Bojan, Messi and Gudjohnsen, Barca only create quarter-chances at best.

(90+6, yes 6!): Ronaldo concedes a free-kick on the right to give Barca one last chance. Valdes comes up but doesn't get anywhere near the ball, and as Tévez boots his clearance into the Manchester air, the referee finally blows his whistle. So that's it. Sell your daughters, lie to your boss, book a yak trip from Katmandu, do whatever you have to. We're going to Moscow, and what makes the feeling even better is that this time Scholesy's going to be there too. The football fates have got a sense of fair play after all…

Views from the broadsheets

- ✪ 'Scrub the blinis and caviar from the Moscow menus and prepare for the full English. Replace the ice-cold vodka shots with warm beer. It's Cossack hats for goalposts in Red Square. Russia's capital will belong to the English on May 21, after Salford's finest, Paul Scholes, set up an all-Premier League European Cup Final.' – *The Telegraph*
- ✪ 'Sir Alex Ferguson may one day remember it as the prelude to his finest hour; the rest of us will consider it the siege of Old Trafford or the night when Manchester United took on Lionel Messi for a place in the European Cup Final. The little Argentine might just have done it on his own were it not for the extraordinary contribution of Paul Scholes, whose goal pitched a match, a night, the whole history of his famous club into a thrilling new chapter.' – *The Independent*
- ✪ 'This was not the type of spectacle associated with Old Trafford. United's great virtue here and at Camp Nou has been the capacity to thwart Barcelona and secure clean sheets. The outstanding players in this win were the left-back Patrice Evra, carried off in stoppage time, and the centre-half Wes Brown. The captain, Rio Ferdinand, was nearly as unyielding.' – *The Guardian*
- ✪ 'Official statistics revealed that United enjoyed the ball's company for 42 per cent of the game, but UEFA's number-crunchers must have included the kick-in. Barcelona

dominated possession, moving the ball effortlessly between Lionel Messi, Deco and Xavi but they lacked a predator.' – *The Telegraph*

☉ 'Admiration for Barcelona's purist football has to be qualified by the recognition that they were largely innocuous over the three hours of the tie. Evra was outstanding in the key task of containing Lionel Messi, the single Barcelona player untouched by the decline at the club as the Frank Rijkaard era comes to its end.' – *The Guardian*

Barca – the verbals

☉ 'Fate is fate, but I think the important thing is that we're in the Final. We have a fantastic chance, whoever we play.' – Fergie looks forward to marking the 50th anniversary in the ultimate style.

☉ 'It was a marvelous night. This club deserves to be in the Final, for the history and the support. It was the fans who got us over the line.' – Fergie again.

☉ 'We can leave with our heads held high. We did everything but score. We possibly had the better of the play, but they got the goal.' – Frank Rijkaard's typically cool reaction to the result that cost him his job.

☉ 'What got us through was our discipline and one moment of quality from a fantastic player. I can't really put it into words, but what a goal.' – Rio.

☉ 'I thought there would be goals, I must admit, but when we concentrate we have great defenders.' – Fergie.

☉ 'United never dominated the two games, and we deserved to reach the Final. This was a big disappointment as we had it in our grasp. We were better, and it's difficult to accept losing. People talked up a battle between Messi and Ronaldo. But I played better than the Portuguese player in the two games. It just came down to a solo goal.' – You can sort of see why Xavi is so bitter – then again, if you don't create any chances…

☉ 'I can't believe how good I am.' – Paul Scholes. Only kidding. True to form, he marked the most important goal of his career by grabbing a quick shower and heading off home.

Worst headline of the day

'Paul Of Fame' – *The Sun* stinks the place out.

Runner-up

'Goalsey!' – *The Daily Mirror* rhymes Scholesy with, er, a made up word. Terrible.

Match facts

United: Van der Sar, Hargreaves, Ferdinand, Brown, Evra (Silvestre 90), Park, Scholes (Fletcher 76), Carrick*, Nani (Giggs 76), Ronaldo*, Tévez.

Barcelona: Valdes, Zambrotta*, Puyol, Milito, Abidal, Toure Yaya* (Gudjohnsen 88), Messi, Xavi, Deco*, Iniesta (Henry 60), Eto'o (Bojan 72) [Rikjaard]

CLS/F 19.45 (ITV). Att: 75,061. Ref: H. Fandel (Ger). Half-time: 1–0

*Yellow card

Champions League semi-final:

Chelsea 3 Liverpool 2 (4–3)

FC Barcelona to West Ham

'The fans were legends. They were absolutely brilliant. If anything, they were the ones that got us going and we never looked back.'

King Ronaldo II

Ronaldo is voted Footballer of the Year by the Football Writers' Association for the second season running. Fernando Torres finishes second and David James, strangely, comes third. OK, James had a decent season and he enjoys talking to the press, which has always counted more than it should. But he's not fit to drop the ball at the boots of Rio Ferdinand, the only Englishman who would walk into this season's world XI.

Good news

⚽ Chelsea beat Liverpool 3–2 in the second leg of their Champions League semi-final to book their ticket to Moscow. The result means that United will be spared the ball-crushing possibility of losing to the Scousers in the biggest game in English history.

Bad news

⚽ Chelsea beat Liverpool 3–2 in the second leg of the Champions League semi-final to book their ticket to Moscow. The result means that United can no longer earn us a lifetime of bragging rights by giving Benitez's team another stuffing in the Final. It also means we're going to have to share Moscow with Chelsea's ragbag collection of hooray Henrys, Johnny-come-lately city boys and white-van-man drivers. One thing seems certain. It's not going to be anything like Barcelona '99, for all sorts of reasons...

P***ing on our parade I

The hangovers from the Barcelona win hadn't even worn off when the press boys began their scare stories about what awaits us in Russia. The Telegraph starts the ball rolling...

'There are genuine fears that extremist groups and Russia's own brand of hooligans – who fly the Union Flag as their emblem in supposed recognition of their English role models – could create ugly clashes with Manchester United and Chelsea fans coming for the Final. Each leading Russian club have their own firm of hardened "Ultras", who carry knives and metal staves and regularly meet away from the main stadiums for formal fights that leave participants bloodied and sometimes dead.'

...*The Sun* picks up the baton...

'The OMON [Putin's fearsome riot police] are just one of several minefields English fans will have to tiptoe around in Moscow. Equally frightening are the drink police, who round up drunks at night in mobile cells. They take them to secure "sobering houses", where they are stripped naked and chained to bare metal beds until they have sobered up.

'Security sources told *The Sun*: "Sobering houses are not a good way round the cost of hotels. They are an exercise in Soviet-style humiliation, very, very uncomfortable."'

...And keeps running with it...

'Russia is awash with fake vodka made with methanol, a byproduct of the oil industry. Each year 40,000 people die there from alcoholic poisoning, so buying cheap vodka at stalls or from touts is a no-no.'

...And running...

'Beware offers of free booze from new Russian friends made in Moscow's pubs and bars. The Russian Mafia and bar girls are known to spike Westerners' drinks with date-rape drug Rohypnol, leaving tourists waking up to hangovers and missing wallets.'

...Until they just get silly...

'In addition, Moscow is in the grip of a plague of wild dogs which have been killing old or drunken street sleepers.'

P***ing on our parade II

Red Football Ltd – the company the Glazers use to own United – choose the day after Barcelona to confirm what every Red who's stopped believing in Santa (or believing David Gill) already knows. The world's richest club is almost certainly also the poorest. According to the results in the year to 30 June 2007, borrowings were up to £666 million, by far the highest of any English club ever. The total owed to all creditors was up to £746 million. And the total interest payable was £81 million per annum. Or, to put it another way, the profits that Gill bragged about in January won't even cover the interest payments.

P***ing on our parade III

United also use the post-Barcelona euphoria as a smokescreen for their latest ticket hikes (it's an old trick – they did it after last year's Milan semi win too). Next year's season tickets will cost an average 6.5 per cent more than this year's, although we will at least be able to opt out of buying League Cup tickets. Next year, a season ticket will cost from £494 in the East/West Lower to a bargain £912 in the North/South Upper Centre. Throw in the extra Cup games (nine this year), and you're looking at up to £1,350 of your net salary going straight to the Glazers' hedge funds.

Pub quiz question of the week

Ronaldo is the eighth player to have won the Football Writers' Award more than once (though only he and Henry have won it in successive seasons). Who are the others?*

Quotes of the week

- 'Cristiano was an overwhelming winner and, given his age, he has the potential and ability to dominate this award for years in an unprecedented way.' – Chairman of the FWA, Paul Hetherington, hasn't heard about Ronaldo's Real dream.
- 'Fans are entitled to ask, "At what long-term price is our current success being bought?"' – Nick Towle, chairman of the Manchester United Supporters' Trust worries about the debt.
- 'What should we be doing now? Congratulating ourselves for having 42,000 Brits coming to town, or start regretting it?' – *Sport Express*, Moscow's leading sports paper, has mixed feelings about the all-English Final.

Curb your enthusiasm

- 'It would be a great injustice if Manchester United were to lose the Premier League title. I would raise a glass if United win the title. It would be, of course, a toast to Alex Ferguson, the best there is and may ever be.' – Alan Curbishley forgets that West Ham have still got to visit Old Trafford, 21 April.
- 'I don't know about wanting to favour either Chelsea or Man United. I will raise a glass to whoever wins the title because they will have deserved it.' – Alan Curbishley backtracks furiously after Chelsea get all conspiratorial, 2 May.

Thought of the week

United owe £81 million in interest this year. Leeds were brought to their knees by a debt of 'just' £78 million.

Quote of the week

'The fans were legends. They were absolutely brilliant. If anything, they were the ones that got us going, and we never looked back.' – Wes Brown raves about the Barca atmosphere.

*Answer: Danny Blanchflower, Finney, Matthews, Dalglish, Barnes, Lineker, Henry

United 4 West Ham 1   03/05/2008

Ronaldo 3, 24, Tévez 26, Ashton 28, Carrick 59

When United all but lost the League at West Ham in 1992, Fergie blasted the Hammers players for their 'obscene' effort. Avram Grant would have been entitled to say the same thing about the shift the West Ham players put in here, particularly in the 50-plus minutes that remained once Nani had butted them back into the game. For months I was convinced that Dinamo Kiev would run away with the award for the most yellow-bellied visitors seen at Old Trafford this year. After watching West Ham in action here I'm not so sure...

Having said all that, any West London talk of a Curbishley–United conspiracy was way off the mark. West Ham had clocked off for the summer weeks before this game – since March they'd won only twice in 10 League games, and one of those was against Derby. They were missing five or six defenders, which meant they had to play a 17-year-old kid (Tomkins) alongside an average full-back (Neill) in central-defence. Most relevant of all was the fact that, before this game, Curbishley had handed United three defeats on the spin. Not even Chelsea could say that they'd helped Chelsea out as much as that.

Match action

1–0 (3): Ronaldo makes a mug of Neill on the right touchline, the back-pedalling McCartney all but ushers him into the area and then deflects Ronaldo's low shot past Green.

2–0 (24): More terrible defending from West Ham as Hargreaves's left-footed cross from the right is allowed to reach Ronaldo at the far post. He reacts well to deflect the ball in with his thigh to become the first Red to score 30 League goals in a season since the Lawman in 1964. Amazing.

3–0 (26): Tévez jinks in off the left flank and smashes a stunning 30-yarder over Green. Even the West Ham fans can't help but laugh and applaud.

3–1 (28): Tévez's goal would have been the stand-out moment in 99 per cent of matches. It wasn't even the stand-out moment of the half as Dean Ashton – bizarrely linked with United recently – capitalises on a bad header from Brown to thump an overhead kick into the top corner.

RED CARD (36): Ashton's goal didn't affect the party mood. Nani's stupid retaliatory headbutt on the serial irritant Neill did...

4–1 (59): After Nani's dismissal, United had no choice but to switch from their normal cavalier stuff and conserve their energy in the sunshine. The second half was a festival of back passing that would have left Liverpool fans from the 1970s and 80s purring. But West Ham were so feeble even with an extra man that United still managed to add to their lead, Carrick strolling forward unchallenged to fire a fourth with the aid of a deflection off the hapless Neill.

West Ham – the verbals

- ✪ 'I recognise that my action was a thoughtless one...I want to publicly ask for forgiveness, firstly of my teammates, who were forced into a greater effort during more than 60 minutes, secondly of my manager and coaches, and thirdly of the United fans who have given me so much affection.' – Nani begs for mercy after becoming the second Portuguese Red to be sent off for butting this season.
- ✪ 'The game was marred by immaturity from Nani, real immaturity. He retaliated when he didn't need to and the referee didn't have any option but to send him off.' – Fergie doesn't mention that he's been sent off as many times as anyone this year.
- ✪ 'The fans were fantastic again. It's strange to do a lap of honour when you've not won anything, but the fans deserve it. We wanted to honour them because they've been superb this season. On Tuesday against Barcelona they were out of this world. Hopefully we can all celebrate in a big way next Sunday at Wigan.' – The Birmingham furore is forgiven and forgotten.
- ✪ 'How many players could score that many? He is improving all the time. Plus he has spent 90 per cent of the season on the wing.' – Fergie on you know who.

Views from the broadsheets

- ✪ 'What a difference three years makes. In May 2005, after their final home game of a profoundly forgettable campaign, the traditional end-of-season lap of honour was an excruciating affair for Manchester United's players. They had been forced to applaud Chelsea, the newly crowned champions, on to the pitch and, after a 3–1 defeat, they had trudged around Old Trafford to a backdrop of discontent and empty seats, not to mention anger and anguish at the imminent takeover by the Glazer family. A weary Sir Alex Ferguson went to pick up the microphone and, like a sober man in a karaoke bar, decided against it. There was nothing to say.

    'Fast-forward three years and the scene could hardly have been more different. As his smiling players congregated in the centre circle after strolling past the meek challenge of West Ham United, Ferguson, looking remarkably fit and healthy for a 66-year-old, bounded over, took the microphone and urged a packed stadium to congratulate the "absolutely fantastic" efforts of the players, of his staff and of the fans themselves.' – *The Times*

☻ 'Ferguson paid tribute, in order, to his players, the club's medical staff, his assistant, Carlos Queiroz, the rest of his backroom team, the supporters and, with a lump in his throat, his good mate Alan Curbishley, who, he said, would always be a friend of Manchester United. OK, OK, the bit about Curbishley is an exaggeration, but the West Ham manager has only himself to blame if he is prime meat for a cheap shot or two. On Saturday, the lack of wisdom he had shown before the game – when he used his newspaper column to express his hope that United, rather than Chelsea, would win the title – was surpassed only by the mystifying, strangely naïve, way he set up his team to play.' – *The Guardian* takes the mick as Fergie takes the mic.

☻ '[United are] in the luxurious position of knowing the only club who can stop them now is not, in fact, Chelsea but Wigan Athletic. It is a Wigan side, admittedly, that is playing better than at any other stage this season but, all the same, it is unlikely Ferguson will lose too much sleep about the prospect of throwing it all away at a ground where there are advertising hoardings for Poolies Pies and Uncle Joe's Mint Balls.' – *The Guardian's* confident we won't regret the lap of honour.

Line of the day

'Tuesday night, to me, was one of the greatest pieces of impact for you to make on our team, well done. As the lads make their lap of honour, a tribute to you, the fans, enjoy yourself in Moscow, and hopefully next week at Wigan! Well done!' – Fergie pays tribute to the Red Army in his end-of-season speech.

Match facts

United: Van der Sar, Hargreaves, Brown, Ferdinand, Evra, Nani† 37, Carrick, Scholes (O'Shea 72), Park (Giggs 61), Ronaldo* (Fletcher 64), Tévez
West Ham: Green, Pantsil, Tomkins, Neill*, McCartney*, Noble, Parker, Mullins (Sears 75), Boa Morte (Solano 52), Ashton (Cole 56), Zamora* [Curbishley]
FAPL 12.45 (Sky) Att: 76,013 Ref: M.Riley. Half-time 3–1
*Yellow card † Red card

Other scores

Newcastle 0 Chelsea 2 (Ballack, Malouda); Arsenal 1 (Bendtner) Everton 0; Liverpool 1 (Torres) City 0

League table

1. United 84 (37) 2. Chelsea 81 (36) 3. Arsenal 80 (37) 4. Liverpool 73 (37)…10 West Ham 48 (37)

West Ham to Wigan
'I'm not a Manchester United fan, but I want them to beat the southerners any time.'

Moscow news

The Russians end the visa debacle by announcing that travelling fans will be allowed to use their match tickets to gain entry to the country for 72 hours. Typically, there are no plans to refund the fans who had already shelled out £65-plus for their visas. United invite the surviving members of the Babes, the 1968 European Cup-winning team and the 1948 FA Cup winners to watch the Final. They've learnt from the Wigan Carling Cup Final at least.

Lovely place for a trip away

Moscow scare stories number 29:

The Mirror reports on the horror Butyrka jail, which – if you believe the scaremongering – Reds could end up in if they fight, need the loo, meet a policeman, drink or smile.

'The rat-infested, disease-ridden, gang-run fortress is where any Chelsea or Manchester United fan arrested during the Champions League Final on Wednesday will be taken. Here prisoners sleep in shifts because cells designed for 20 inmates often house 80. Aids and TB are rife – 37,000 prisoners in Russia are HIV positive. Twenty per cent of inmates are intravenous drug users and more than 60 per cent of them share needles. Inmates survive on porridge for breakfast, then soup, salt and water for lunch and more porridge for dinner plus a hunk of bread and one sugar lump. There are regular beatings and last month prisoners rioted in protest.'

Sounds like Joey would love it…

Chairman of the week

Before the West Ham match Chelsea played mind games with Alan Curbishley. Before the Wigan decider they tried to put pressure on Brucie because of his connections with United. But they picked the wrong manager to mess with, and they certainly picked wrong chairman. Here's what Dave Whelan had to say:

'I'm not a Manchester United fan, but I want them to beat the southerners any time. I've met Abramovich once, the first time he came here. He flew into the JJB area in his helicopter. I said I'd send a car to pick him up, but he said "no". He had a bullet-proof car pick him up. He had two people examine the security at The JJB Stadium and check out whether there was any risk involved. He wouldn't eat or drink anything here. Did he have a pie? Nothing. I might be unkind, but I can't see Bolton getting anything at Chelsea because they've nothing to lose there. But we'll have the champagne for United, no question.'

Rumour of the week

'Soccer stars from outside the EU are to be banned from playing for British clubs unless they can speak English. Players like Manchester United's Argentinian Carlos Tévez and Arsenal's Brazilian Denilson will have to get their English up to scratch to play in the Premier League. They will be among groups restricted under rules being introduced from October in a bid to reduce the number of migrants each year by around 30,000' – *The Sun*. Poor old Peter Beardsley would never have got a game.

News

FC United win their third successive promotion with a 4–1 Play-off win against Skelmersdale United. Next season 'that mob' will play in the Northern Premier League, just three Leagues below the Football League. Fergie will be pleased. Avram Grant suggests that United and Chelsea should meet in a title Play-off if they both finish on the same points. You know, I think he was being serious! Wigan persuade the rugby league team to delay their game at the JJB from the Friday to the Monday so that the awful pitch would at least have some grass on it for United's visit. The move leads to another rash of media hand-wringing about Wigan's stomach for the battle. Funnily enough, the press boys aren't too fussed when it emerges that Chelsea's final-day opponents, Bolton, warmed up for the weekend with a jolly at Chester races...

Lovely place for a trip away

Moscow scare story number 218:

'Manchester United and Chelsea fans travelling to Moscow for the Champions League Final will be sent to special "gulags" to prevent them from fighting with each other. Fans will be ferried from the airport to the special holding pens near the stadium, which will have just one entrance, be guarded by armed Moscow police and will not sell alcohol. They could remain there for up to eight hours.' – *The Daily Mail*

Quotes of the week

- 'It's a normal practice. We use them in our country, and the fans call them "settling tanks". It doesn't matter who comes here – even a bunch of penguins – if our laws are violated we'll take full measures allowed by our law to clamp down. We will not differentiate.' – Police chief Major Igor Konovalov on the gulags awaiting Reds in Moscow. Sounds like fun...
- 'Let's go to Moscow and it can be winner takes all. Sometimes you can score more goals against weaker teams. But if you have the same points, you are at the same level.' – Avram Grant talks utter nonsense. The reason United's goal difference is so superior, Avram, is that we attack.

⚽ 'The Russians' general stereotype of the English is almost something from Jeeves and Wooster, not the lager louts and football hooligans. It could be a real culture clash.' – Marc Bennetts, from *Russian News* agency Ria Novosti, gets the gong for understatement of the week.

Competition of the week

Football365 spots the flaw in *The Daily Star's* prize of a 'Luxury coach trip to see the Champions League Final from Top Balcony coaches':

'A once-in-a-lifetime chance to travel through Finland and Russia to see the match of the century in Moscow,' brags the 'paper'. Hmmmm. A quick glance at Top Balcony's website reveals that the package does not include a match ticket, and the coach journey sets off from the maverick location of Birmingham at midnight on Sunday 18 May and arrives in Moscow at 5pm on Tuesday 20 May. This makes it a piffling 65 hours on the road, at the end of which you won't get to watch the 'match of the century'.

PS: They were also charging £590 for the pleasure!

Fib of the week

'I want to thank you all for your brilliant journalism this season. You've enthralled me with your honesty, your integrity, and your nonsense.' – Fergie to the press before the Wigan game.

Wigan 0 United 2   11/05/2008

Ronaldo 33 (pen), Giggs 80

Whoever wrote the script for the 2007–08 title race did a damn good job. Excitement, quality, surprises, roller coaster fortunes, three genuine contenders and a neck and neck finish…it really did have it all. As the nation switched on Sky for the final time this season, they must have been hoping for one last twist. Thankfully, it never came. This was a nervy afternoon for United fans, particularly in the first half when Steve Bennett emerged as the most unexpected hero of the season. But for neutrals and Chelsea fans it must have had a feeling of inevitability about it. And when the history man, Ryan Giggs, provided the classic Hollywood moment with the decisive second, you sort of knew it was always meant to be.

So how does the latest set of United champions compare with the ones that went before? And how does Fergie's 10th title compare with the other nine? As Fergie himself said, as he celebrated in the Wigan rain, they're right up there. And in terms of the competition they had to beat, this title might just have been the biggest achievement yet. Just think about it. To win the title this year United had to see off two teams that reached the semi-finals of the Champions League, and one team good enough to outclass Milan in Milan. When United won the league in 1993, they had to see off Aston Villa and Norwich.

And one more thing. United's season didn't get going until September this year. Imagine how good we'll be when we play 38 games like everyone else…

The final 90 minutes – how the title race was won…and lost

(Chelsea v Bolton action in italics)

15.00: Good news for United. Forget the scare stories about Rooney being out for Moscow, he's in his kit and he's starting. Actually make that double good news. Vidic is back from his concussion too.

15.10: What a miss! Drogba shins the ball wide from a yard out.

15.12: Bad news for Chelsea. Terry collides with Cech and is carried off with a dislocated elbow. Amazingly, he announces afterwards that he'll still be fit for Moscow. It's not the first time that Terry has recovered ridiculously quickly from injury either. Has Abramovich got a stockpile of spare body parts or something?

YELLOW! SCHOLES! 15.13: Scholesy is booked for a trademark bad tackle on Palacios.

FERDINAND! HANDBALL? NO! 15.22: Wigan look in the mood to be awkward and United are having some uncomfortable moments. First Boyce hooks over after a game of scrappy head tennis in the United box. Then Koumas bends in a hopeful curler which Ferdinand leans into and blocks with either his shoulder, or the top of his arm, or a mix of the two (it's hard to tell, even in slow motion). Steve Bennett, rightly taking the view that you can't give a penalty if you're not sure, awards a corner. That doesn't stop him getting a verbal beating from the media afterwards, mind.

15.22: A roar goes around Stamford Bridge. It's a false alarm. Someone must have thought Bennett pointed to the spot.

15.25: United keep looking like they're on the verge of something good. But somehow it's just not happing. It takes them 25 minutes to create a half-decent chance. Ronaldo's low free-kick wobbles in the air and dips awkwardly in front of Kirkland who dives to his left and pushes it away.

ROONEY! PENALTY! RONALDO! 15.33 (1–0, 0–0): Then comes the breakthrough. Boyce takes out Rooney in the box, and Ronaldo sends Kirkland the wrong way for his 31st League goal of the season – just one short of Dennis Viollet's 48-year-old record. Brucie raged about the penalty decision afterwards, and there was a lot of guff written about it in the press. But Boyce never got near the ball, and he clearly took Rooney down. Forget United being lucky, even Rob Stiles would have given us that one.

15.37: United weren't lucky with their penalty. But they enjoyed a huge break here. Palacios bursts past Scholes on halfway, and Scholes can't resist barging him over. As Andy Gray, who normally can't stand the idea of players being sent off for anything less than decapitation, screams for a second yellow (it was obvious all afternoon that Sky were desperate for a twist in the title race), Bennett gives Scholes a lecture. And then nothing. Absolutely nothing.

Paddy Crerand sums it up best on MUTV, 'Oh Paul, you're a lucky, lucky man, son. Oh Paul, Paul, Paul!'

Half-time: Wigan 0 United 1, Chelsea 0 Bolton 0

GOAL! SHEVCHENKO! 16.26 (1–0, 1–0): United look far more like themselves after half-time. But as the rain thumps down at the JJB, they can't kill the game off. First Bennett fails to spot Bramble's obvious penalty box foul on Scholes, then Kirkland makes a series of excellent stops from Rooney, Ronaldo and Tévez. To add to the tension, United lose their get-out-of-jail card when Shevchenko finally puts Chelsea ahead at the Bridge. A Wigan goal now and the title's Chelsea's.

16.29: Three minutes later they come bum-squeakingly close to doing it. Koumas sends over a free-kick, and Heskey thumps in a header that beats Van der Sar and just clears the bar. This is horrible.

16.31: History is made. Giggsy comes on for Park to equal Sir Bobby's record of 758 United appearances.

CHAMPIONS! 16.44 (2–0, *1–0*): And 13 minutes later fate provides him with the perfect memento. Rooney cuts in from the left and plays in Giggs who's sneaked into a gap between Bramble and Scharner. Giggs kills the ball with his first touch and then coolly slips the ball past Kirkland with his next. For a moment the magnitude of the moment seems to paralyse him. But then, just as he had at the Riverside all those years ago, he drops his shoulder and sets off running, leaving Rooney trailing behind him before sliding to a halt on his backside.

GOAL! BOLTON! 16.57 (2–0, *1–1*): Giggsy's goal guarantees that United will be champions on goal difference. Matt Taylor's sloppy late goal at the Bridge guarantees that when Giggs is presented with the Premier League Trophy by Roger Byrne jnr – a nice touch – United would be champions on points too.

Views from the broadsheets I

- ⚽ 'When the moment arrived it was poetic that it should fall to a man that spans the generations and the Ferguson years. There have been three, arguably four, great teams produced at Manchester United by Sir Alex Ferguson, but only one player has been constant through them all. Ryan Giggs, 758 games old, if one considers his legs, or young, if one studies the spirit in which he plays each game, slipped between two Wigan Athletic defenders and ensured that the league trophy will remain at Old Trafford for another season' – *The Times*
- ⚽ 'By virtue of leading Manchester United to their 10th League title under his managership, Sir Alex Ferguson yesterday cemented his reputation as the greatest club boss in the history of the English game. Even given the huge commercial power that United wield as a worldwide brand, it is still an astonishing record in an era when those charged with bringing success on the football field have never had to work under such unremitting pressure.' – *The Independent*

✪ '"This has been the best Premier League season ever," enthused Richard Scudamore yesterday and it was impossible to disagree with the elite division's chief executive. For excitement, switchback fortunes and sheer technical brilliance, the 2007–08 season has been pure Hollywood with United's swaggering Cristiano Ronaldo rightly cast as the leading man.' – *The Telegraph*

JJB – the verbals

✪ 'Paul Scholes will go down as one of United's greats. Everything about him is top, top drawer. But he knows he got away with it today. Had it been any other day it was another yellow card and he should have been off. You should ask the referee about his integrity, not about my team.' – Brucie does a great job of making out he's upset. But deep down…

✪ 'We are bouncing into that Final now. If we'd lost the title it would have been different. If this team goes on now and wins the European Cup, it will be my best ever.' – Fergie's eyes turn to Moscow.

✪ 'First I want to congratulate Manchester United. They had a great season and I have sent a message to Alex Ferguson congratulating him. He is a great manager and a great person. I like him personally. I wished him all the best. It is amazing what he has done. I remember at the start when he had problems so it is an amazing achievement.' – Anyone else think that Avram Grant seems a decent bloke?

Views from the broadsheets II

✪ 'Sir Alex Ferguson would doubtless laugh at the notion that United owed their seventeenth league title to any referee, let alone Steve Bennett. The simple truth is that United are champions because they have been the outstanding team in England this season and it would have been an injustice had it been Chelsea celebrating at 5pm yesterday' – *The Times*

✪ 'Admit it: he's been brilliant. If last season was about Cristiano Ronaldo and Wayne Rooney, then this season has really mainly been about Ronaldo. His goal tally piling up game after game, the posturing around free-kicks and then the dispatching of those free-kicks, cannonball-style, into the top corner. The expectation that something will happen every time he gets the ball; the anticipation of having a real superstar on the pitch.

'Manchester United's 10th Premier League title, the class of 2008, will be remembered as one man's season above all' – *The Independent*

Worst headline of the day

'Ryan King' – *The Sun*

Giggsy – the verbals

- 'It was like slow motion really. I put it in the net and did not know what to do. I couldn't remember how to celebrate because I had not scored for so long. But with the rain, it was the perfect weather for doing a slide, so that is what I went for.' – Giggsy on his celebration…

- 'I am not going to play it down, I can't really. To equal someone like Sir Bobby Charlton is special. He is the embodiment of everything that Manchester United stands for.'…and the record.

Quote of the day

'If I could choose someone to break it, it would be him. The day he came to Manchester United, I knew he was special. He is a great athlete, a great person and a great footballer. His record with United is unbelievable, and I'm really proud of him.' – Sir Bobby on the 784 man.

Match facts

Wigan: Kirkland, Boyce, Bramble, Scharner, Figueroa, Valencia*, Palacios*, Brown (King 81), Koumas, Bent (Sibierski 70), Heskey* [Brucie]
United: Van der Sar, Brown, Ferdinand, Vidic, Evra, Ronaldo, Carrick, Scholes* (Hargreaves 67), Park (Giggs 67), Tévez, Rooney*
JJB Stadium 15.00 (Sky). Att: 25,133. Ref: S. Bennett. Half-time: 1–0
*Yellow card

Other scores

Chelsea 1 (Shevchenko) Bolton 1 (Taylor); Sunderland 0 Arsenal 1 (Walcott); Spurs 0 Liverpool 2 (Voronin, Torres); Boro 8 (Alves 3, Downing pen, Aliadiere, Rochemback, Johnson) City 1 (Elano)

League table

1. United 87 (38) 2. Chelsea 85 (38) 3. Arsenal 83 (38) 4. Liverpool 76 (38)…14. Wigan 40 (38)

Wigan to Chelsea
'I'm carrying on, I still have a bit of damage to do yet.'

Quotes of the week

- 'The club should be prepared to fight because it is really important that we continue to be regarded as the most successful club in the country. That record has been built up over decades of hard work and doing things the right way, and it has to be preserved.' – Ian Rush is getting worried now that Liverpool are just one ahead. Brilliant!

⚽ 'My last Final holds bad memories for me. But I joke that I went to the Final with Monaco in a Fiat now I am going with the Ferrari. But now I need to drive the Ferrari very well. This is the biggest game in my life now and I do not want to lose again.' – It could only be Pat Evra.

⚽ 'I'm carrying on, I still have a bit of damage to do yet.' – Fergie stresses he's not bowing out in Moscow. Rushie will be pleased.

Wrong one lads

The Daily Star gets all excited after the Wigan decider, writing, under the headline, 'Hookers Won It For Us':

'Goal ace Cristiano Ronaldo lifted the Premier League trophy yesterday, and admitted Manchester United's success was all thanks to his raunchy romp with hookers.'

Cor blimey, we all thought. That's quite an admission. Oh no, hang on a minute, Ronaldo's actual quotes were: 'The fans sing your song when you've done something good, which is nice.' I think they were trying to make a link with the 'class with the brass' song. It's not even Ronaldo's...

Retrospective quote of the week

'He possesses, neither by experience nor talent, any managerial ability at all.' – A Glasgow industrial tribunal's ruling on St Mirren's sacking of Alex Ferguson in 1978 (27 trophies ago).

News I

Ronaldo picks up the Barclays Player of the Season and Golden Boot awards. Fergie is named the LMA Manager of the Season. Ronaldo also wins the Treble – Player of the Year, Players' Player and Goal of the Year (for the Portsmouth free-kick) – at the club's awards ceremony. Richard Eckersley wins the Reserve Team Player of the Year and Danny Welbeck wins the Young Player of the Year.

Chelsea continue their habit of signing players we're linked with by splashing out a hefty £16 million on Porto right-back Jose Boswinga. Rangers fans shame themselves by fighting with the GMP following their UEFA Cup Final defeat to Zenit St Petersburg. One policeman was hit so hard that his earpiece ended up embedded in his head and had to be removed by doctors...

It's a mystery

'Could Anything Have Stopped It?' asked *The Daily Mirror* headline. Erm, let's see, maybe stopping Rangers fans drinking Manchester dry by 4pm?

Bolt from the blue

Manchester's police and council can't say they weren't warned. Remember the open letter Barcelona's Elmundo Deportivo wrote to Rangers fans last year?

'Stay at home and vomit in your own living-room, urinate in your sitting-room corners, fight with your neighbours, the Celtic supporters (who deserve a prize just for putting up with you) and foul the streets of Glasgow instead. Don't come back here again, because it is not a laughing matter. And, by extension, don't play in the Champions League either. You are not at that level neither in a sporting nor human sense.'

(see p82 for their rant in full)

The oldest tunes

'Those scenes obviously are dreadful and I've seen them myself and we have been informed…that those scenes were caused by supporters that don't normally attach themselves to our support' – Rangers chief executive Martin Bain reckons it was Chelsea.

P***ing on our parade (literally)

Manchester city council reacts to the UEFA Cup Final violence – a one-off incident caused by idiots from a city 200 miles away – by cancelling the party for the Champions League Final. There would be no big screens showing the game in the city centre. On top of that, there would be no triumphant parade if United won in Moscow.

In fairness, you can see why they made the decision they did. After all, those victory parades, with all those kids and families and happiness, are notorious for kicking-off.

Prediction of the week

May 4: *The Sunday People* exclusively reveals the identity of QPR's new manager:

'WORLD Cup legend Zinedine Zidane is the sensational name in the frame to take over as boss of QPR. Rangers owner Flavio Briatore has promised a major announcement before today's final match of the season at home to West Brom – and informed whispers insist he'll name Zidane as Loftus Road boss.'

May 14: Ian Dowie is unveiled as the new QPR boss.

News II

City sneak into the UEFA Cup via the Fair Play League (again!). It also emerges that every United European Cup Final ticket includes a hidden £11 charge to pay for the buses we might, or might not, be using to get to and from the airport. Charming, that. UEFA drag us all the way to Moscow, the Russkis fleece us for every penny they can and we have to pay for the 'complimentary' coaches that many of us will never sit on. Typically, United refuse to follow Chelsea's lead by footing the bill.

Fair play

'Manchester City face the prospect of having to start their UEFA Cup campaign next season at another stadium because of a Bon Jovi concert at their ground. The club are looking at alternative venues – with Huddersfield Town's Galpharm Stadium under consideration – amid concerns that the pitch at Eastlands will not be ready in time.' – *The Guardian* reckons City have done it again.

News III

Portsmouth scrape past Cardiff at Wembley to win the trophy that should have been the second part of another Treble. The loveable – but increasingly terrible – Motty marks his last Cup Final by failing to realise that Kanu's winning goal had been given. Joey Barton is sentenced to six months with the family for his Christmas McAttack in Liverpool city centre. The court hears that he assaulted two men, one of whom he hit 20 times while he was on the floor. United announced that Ole will take charge of the reserves next season. The Ronaldo to Real rumours resurface again, and this time they just won't go away.

Keeping it real

Sir Bob throws a wobbly after Marca winds up for another go at Ronaldo:

'Ronaldo's on a long-term contract with us. I don't have to say we expect him to honour it because he will honour it unless something tragic happens. Do I think Ronaldo will be at United next season? Absolutely. It really irritates me how people can set rumours going and undermine people through the media. It's unethical. They have not got the right to undermine the way we have helped this lad.

'Everybody seems to think that Real Madrid or Barcelona are the two greatest clubs in the world. I don't think I have to tell Cristiano that Manchester United is the biggest club in the world.'

Underwhelming thought of the week

We're going to have to play Portsmouth in the Community Shield. Bizarrely, we're also going to play them in a friendly in Nigeria in the summer.

Staying up

After Fulham complete their great escape at Portsmouth, news emerges of the incentive Mohamed Al Fayed had used to motivate his players – a £5,000 Harrods hamper packed with caviar, champagne, smoked salmon and…Viagra.

Gossip

United are strongly linked with Cardiff wonderkid – and future Arsenal man – Aaron Ramsey, as well as Micah Richards and Sevilla's Brazilians, Luis Fabiano and Dani Alves. Seb Coe calls for Fergie to manage the Great Britain football team at the 2012 Olympics.

Footballer of the week

From *The Telegraph*:

'Birmingham City midfielder Olivier Kapo has stunned one of the club's youth players by giving him a car [a £30,000 Mercedes] as a thank you for polishing his boots. James McPike, an apprentice at St Andrews, had asked Kapo for his boots as a souvenir after Birmingham's final game of the season. However, the French playmaker had already taken them home and so, in an incredible act of generosity, he threw the 20-year-old his car keys instead as an end-of-season present.

'When McPike told Kapo that he could not afford the insurance on such a powerful vehicle, Kapo even said he would pay for a year's worth of cover so that the youngster could drive it.'

Fan of the week

'We like Wayne Rooney a lot in Russia. He's very popular. He looks like Shrek' – Russian fan Ruslan Matveev in *The Guardian*.

Quote of the week

'Everybody seems to think that Real Madrid or Barcelona are the two greatest clubs in the world. I don't think I have to tell Cristiano that Manchester United is the biggest club in the world.' – It's so good it just demands a repeat.

United 1(6) Chelsea 1 (5)   21/05/2008

Ronaldo 25

For raw emotion and pathos, Wembley 1968 will never be beaten. For sheer 'oh my god' heart-stopping drama, 1999 will always stand on its own. But if you're after drama, emotion, euphoria and blood-draining tension you'll have to wait a long time to get a better night than this one. In front of the Munich survivors, United paid the ultimate tribute to the Babes by winning the trophy the fates had snatched from them. And they did it in a way that only United can. By scaring us all senseless.

It was an amazing night. It was a surreal one too. And it will live in the mind of English football – and possibly scar the psyche of every Chelsea fan – forever. But I'm not sure I'd want to go through it again. At least not the part after Lampard scored anyway.

Here's how the torture – the beautiful torture – unfolded:

Pre-match preamble:
There's no fat lady singing on the pitch this time. Instead there's an army of local kids in red-and-gold masks and capes dancing around and releasing balloons. Didn't they see what happened at Bramall Lane?

As the teams emerge hand in hand with their opponents' mascots, and 'Believe' is spelled out in white plastic sheets in the United end, Tyldesley and Tyler have a 'stat-off' in the commentary booths. Tyldesley tells us there are three previous Champions League finalists playing for United and four playing for Chelsea while United's average age is 28. Tyler easily trumps him by giving us the number of times the Chelsea and United teams have lined up together before tonight. The answer? Remarkably, none.

Then, as the captains, Ferdinand and Terry, meet for the toss, it's time for the speeches. Tyldesley launches into one of his trademark Churchillian epics, finishing with 'Only the engraver's knife will decide for which team it is forever memorable.' Tyler counters with the corny, 'Alex Ferguson, like a footballing Indiana Jones, has seen this trophy as his Holy Grail'. And then the quite brilliant, and quite awful, 'Lubos Michel, like the turf he's going to patrol, comes from Slovakia.' Crikey, Martin. Didn't you have time to think about this on the plane? It's no contest. Tyldesley wins on points.

As for the teams, there are no real surprises. Fergie goes for Hargreaves in midfield and Tévez in attack. Chelsea go for Drogba on his own up front. The biggest news for United is that Parky's in a suit not a tracksuit. He can count himself really unlucky, especially after his performance in the semi. Asia will have to wait another year for its first Champions League finalist...

Match facts

United: Van der Sar, Brown, Ferdinand, Vidic, Evra, Hargreaves, Scholes, Carrick, Ronaldo, Tévez, Rooney

Subs: Kuszczak, O'Shea, Fletcher, Silvestre, Nani, Anderson, Giggs

Chelsea: Cech, Essien, Carvalho, Terry, A. Cole, Ballack, Makelele, Lampard, Joe Cole, Drogba, Malouda

Subs: Cudicini, Shevchenko, Obi, Alex, Belletti, Anelka, Kalou

CLF, Luzhniki Stadium 22.45. Att: 67,310. Ref: Lubos Michel. Half-time: 1–1

The match:

0: As the match starts, Tyler, probably sensibly, goes quiet. Nothing's stopping Tyldesley though. 'Manchester United won the war on the home front,' he tub-thumps. 'Now for the historic battle for overall supremacy. May the best team win.' I'm not sure about that Clive. I haven't emptied my Nan's Christmas club tin to come and watch United do defeat with honour. I'd settle for another Nou Camp grab and run right now.

2: Malouda digs in the first dangerous cross which Vidic, playing on his old home ground, clears well. Ferdinand then rolls a pass to Scholes in centre field. It's the touch he's been waiting nine long years for. I wonder what Keano's thinking watching it on TV. Maybe he's not bothering. If I was him, I'd be out walking Triggs right now.

4: Anderson's not in the starting line up. But it's his song that rings around the Luzhniki first. Anderson...son...son. *Agadoo* being sung in Moscow...I bet that didn't happen much in the '80s. The Iron Curtain wasn't all bad news you know.

5: Sticking with Black Lace for a moment, did you ever hear what happened to them? One member had a bit of a Kleberson moment in his sex life and ended up changing his name. The other one died after the tour bus crashed in a hailstorm in Germany. Very Spinal Tap.

6: Nothing much is happening here. Vidic dominates Drogba in the air and Drogba collapses to the ground. 'Such a big player at his best, such a big Jessie at his worst', tuts Clive.

7: The first dangerous cross, swung over by Hargreaves, is well defended by Terry. Interestingly, Hargreaves is playing wide on the right of midfield rather than in a tight midfield three. Andy Gray poses the question whether United's unexpected 4–4–2 formation has thrown Chelsea. Not just yet. But as the half wears on it's clear that Fergie has won the first battle of the tactical war. Hargreaves pins Ashley Cole back on the right, Ronaldo pins Essien back on the left and Chelsea can't get going on either flank.

8: Essien looks bemused by Ronaldo's quick feet. This time he buys a stepover, Ronaldo bursts to the line and clips in a left-footed cross that just clears Hargreaves's mop at the back stick. The first *Viva Ronaldo* of the game sweeps round the stands behind Van der Sar's goal.

12: Tyler makes a telling remark. Chelsea should have been the first English team in Europe, not United. But they didn't have the balls to stick it to the FA like Sir Matt did. 13: 'I told my mate the other day...that I had found the white Pelé'. From behind the goal it feels like all the noise is coming from United. The TV gives the same impression.

15: The first shot of the bench. Fergie's in a nice shiny grey suit (just as he was in Barcelona), Carlos is in his black trackie and Mickey P's in his shorts. It's not a good look. But at least he doesn't look like Hitler any more.

17: 'Nothing much in it at the start. You just get the feeling that Manchester United have settled the better. They've used the ball better, worked it a little bit better, probably shaded possession.' Quite right Mr Gray. Quite right.

19: Ronaldo is pushed over on the left by Drogba who whines that he went down to easy. Ronaldo grins at the irony. Pot. Kettle. Anyone?

SCHOLESY! YELLOW! (20): Hargreaves's free-kick doesn't clear the first man, the ball breaks for Makelele, Scholes challenges him clumsily from behind and takes him down. As Makelele hits the turf, his studs catch the Ginger Prince flush on the nose. As the blood drips into his cupped hands, the unsympathetic Lubos Michel shows Scholesy a yellow. Makelele also gets himself into the book for trying to start a minor scuffle. When he realises he's in trouble the Frenchman puts on his best 'Why me?' face. I'll tell you why, Claude. Because you could start a fight in an empty room. What is it about Chelsea midfielders?

22: Tévez is caught in possession on the left, and Lampard drives in a cross that Vidic heads almost out of Van der Sar's hands. It looks messy, but there's no real danger and the corner comes to nothing.

22: Scholesy's still not back on. Don't say the Final jinx has struck again. Hold on. He's back – though his nose doesn't look good. A bit like Fergie's on New Year's morning. Hold on, I shouldn't say that. Oh, what the hell.

SCHOLES! BROWN! RONALDO! GOAL! (25): Scholesy repositions whatever's soaking up the blood in his nose and shows himself for a throw-in on the right. Brown throws it to his feet. A snappy, flicked one–two gives Wes the time and space to float a left-footed cross to the back stick. Essien gets drawn beneath the ball, Ronaldo jumps, hangs in the air and deflects the perfect header into the corner. 'Manchester United strike,' Clive screams, 'and guess who? Essien can't deal with him.'

Amazing. It's Ronaldo's 42nd goal of the season in just his 49th game – and his first ever against Chelsea. Surely that small game player nonsense has to stop now. As Clive says, Ronaldo doesn't play many small games these days.

27: Tyldesley's way ahead of Tyler on points now: 'The only time in a Champions League Final a team has come from behind in the game itself is United in Barcelona and Barcelona against Arsenal.' Barcelona isn't involved in any way tonight so things are looking good.

29: Ronaldo destroys Essien in the air again, but United haven't got anyone in the six-yard box and Terry clears his header back across goal. 'It's a mismatch,' Clive screams.

30: Drogba's needing the physio's attention again after jumping for a high ball with Ferdinand. I wonder if his hair band's too tight. 'Wouldn't it be ironic if he had something genuine,' Pleaty says, dryly.

31: Amazing. Drogba's fine.

31: The possession stats show that it's 65 per cent v 35 per cent to United. Chelsea haven't got to grips with United's 4–4–2, they can't get people forward in support of Drogba, and when they do have the ball in United's half they can't do anything with it. Scholes and Carrick are outnumbered three to two but they're having the time of their lives.

31: Ned Boulting, ITV's version of Geoff Shreeves, reveals that Avram Grant hasn't spoken to anyone – players or coaches – since the goal. Instead he stands alone in the technical area looking like he's just downed some of his wife's home brew.

32: As *We shall not be moved* starts up, Rooney gives the ball away twice in 10 seconds. He doesn't look quite right. I wonder how fit he really is.

FERDINAND! VAN DER SAR! SAVE! (33): Drogba heads Lampard's cross back across the six-yard box, Ferdinand, under massive pressure from Ballack, gets his header all wrong and Van der Sar has to make a fine, one-handed save.

TEVEZ! CHANCE! CARRICK! CHANCE! (34): It's not Rooney's night. But you can't keep a good man down. Here he pickpockets Carvalho near United's right corner flag and sprints down the touchline before lashing a 60-yard diagonal ball into the stride of Ronaldo. Ronaldo sucks in Cole and Essien before firing a left-footed cross into the six-yard box. Tévez gets there before the lumbering Terry but his diving header is too close to Cech's feet. The ball falls beautifully for Carrick but he gets just too much height on his shot and that allows Cech to make a stunning tip-over save.

Clive takes the positive line: 'Wonderful Manchester United counter attack.' Martin comes over all negative: 'They might live to regret this.' Yes and no, Martin. Yes and no.

40: Brown brushes Ashley Cole off the ball. Clive calls Wes a quiet superstar and then suggests he 'might be the only member of the United team you could bump into in Waitrose without recognising'. Not sure about that Clive. He's orange.

ROONEY! TEVEZ! CHANCE! (41): United almost score again. Hargreaves slides in Rooney down the right. His low cross takes out the Chelsea defence, but Tévez can't sort out his feet in time and the ball squirms wide. 'There's absolutely no doubt Chelsea are fortunate to still be in this game,' Andy Gray growls.

RIO! YELLOW! (43): Ferdinand takes down Lampard as he charges towards the box and is booked. Drogba and Ballack keep their toys in the pram this time and Ballack curls the ball tamely over.

43: They're doing their half-time round-ups in the commentary booths. Andy Gray says, 'It's been as good a first half of a Champions League Final as I can remember. Maybe not from Chelsea's point of view. But an entertainment point of view'. Clive, who's hardly let Pleaty get a word in this half, says 'So far, so good, Manchester United'.

I think they call that the commentator's curse...

ESSIEN! VIDIC! RIO! LAMPARD! GOAL! (44): I don't believe it. Essien thumps in a hopeful long shot that takes a double deflection off Vidic and Ferdinand. Van der Sar slips and Lampard has an easy task from no distance at all. As Lampard, who'd just lost his mum, looks to the heavens, Gray rolls his 'r's and growls 'Verrrry, verrrry lucky'. Is it destiny that Lampard will win the Cup for his mum? It certainly feels like that right now.

YELLOW! CARVALHO. (45+): Cavalho's terrible studs-up challenge lands halfway up Ronaldo's shin. He gets a yellow, but the more the challenge is replayed the more it looks like it could have been red.

45: Chelsea saunter out for the second half a full two minutes after United. Fergie's not best pleased and is right in Lubos Michel's ear when he emerges from the tunnel. Drogba makes it his business to get involved too. Nothing new there then.

49: Joe Cole takes Carrick out late, then Ballack has a cheap shot at Ronaldo. As Ronaldo picks himself up, Ballack and Drogba are straight at the referee. Why? Michel must feel like a hen-pecked bigamist – or should that be polygynist? – out there tonight.

51: Cole doesn't get a corner and charges at Michel a la David Pleat at Maine Road in '83. Ballack's already in his face. 'They've done a lot of complaining tonight Chelsea. A lot,' Clive mutters. You can certainly say that again CT. United have had their fair share of referee botherers in their time, but Chelsea are taking moaning to a whole new level.

53: The first decent move of the half. Ronaldo sends a cute pass to the overlapping Evra, and his chipped ball to the far post is just too high for Hargreaves. It's frustrating. If Hargreaves had been Frank Stapleton he'd have scored three headers already tonight.

54: Essien, who's obviously decided that attack is the best form of defence against Ronaldo, charges through the inside-right channel, cuts inside Evra but duffs his left-footed curler onto the running track. The same running track that Wells, Ovett and Coe won Olympic medals on in 1980.

55: 'It's midnight Clive,' Pleaty points out. It's true. It's United's first two-day game. More meaningfully, it's now 22 May, the day that George Best was born.

55: The cameras pick out the Charltons in the executive seats. Norma is biting her lip but Bobby is perfectly still. So still, in fact, he looks like one of those other Russian premiers from the early '80s – you know, the ones that the West claimed were dead.

55: One more thing about Bobby. He's got nothing on his head. I was sure he'd wear his Russian hat tonight. Half the Reds in the stadium haven't been able to resist getting one.

56: Chelsea's first decent attack. Ashley Cole gets clear down the left, but his cross is taken off Drogba's toes by the superb Vidic.

56: The camera pans to the United bench where Giggsy is sat cross-legged with his white socks pushed down to his ankles. Kenneth Williams couldn't have looked camper.

56: Ballack is allowed to travel 20 yards before thumping a shot well wide. Chelsea are definitely finding more room in midfield now – and Hargreaves and Ronaldo are being pushed further and further back. It looks a different game now, even though Chelsea still haven't made a genuine chance.

65: Three more Chelsea shots are blocked in the space of a minute. 'Its just not happened for United since half-time,' Clive notes. 'Does he [Fergie] bring Anderson on?' queries Pleaty. He might well have done in another game David. But Fergie's got the Giggsy factor to think of here. There's absolutely no way he won't be making history tonight, which means we'll have to save the other subs for later.

67: Rio collapses with cramp. Is it the pitch? The nerves? The time of the night? Fortunately, after hobbling around for a few minutes, he's OK.

70: United finally get in their first shot of the half, but Carrick's drive is blocked.

75: The 'ground covered' stats appear at the bottom of the screen. Joe Cole and Ballack have done the most running with 9,310m and 9,219m respectively. It would have been a lot less if Michel hadn't moved around so much.

76: Evra does what every Red has dreamt about. He dumps Joe Cole on the floor. It's getting spicier now.

DROGBA! GOAL! NO! (77): The sound of bums squeaking echoes around Manchester. Drogba spins and hits a 20-yard curler that cannons wide off the post.

78: Ballack collapses to the floor after a minor clash with Tévez. Pathetic.

79: More brilliant defending from Vidic. Rooney gives the ball away to Ashley Cole, Ferdinand slips and Malouda is away down the left. His low cross is a good one, but Vidic wants it more than Drogba, and the ball is back on the running track.

80: Tyldesley has spent the last nine years sprinkling his commentaries – and annoying the hell out of ABUs – with references to 'that' night in Barcelona. With the clock ticking towards injury time, he can't resist doing it again. This time he's talking about potential subs and reminiscing about what happened last time a United player came on in a European Cup Final. If United win here I've got a bet with myself that Clive will tell us to 'party like it's 1999'.

81: Tévez hammers in a shot from the left angle of the box, but the ball starts wide and finishes even wider. Amazingly, Cech hasn't had a single thing to do all half. Mind you, Van der Sar hasn't exactly been busy either. It's undoubtedly been Chelsea's half but United are still ahead in terms of clear chances.

81: Clive's back on the 1999 theme, reminding the viewers of Fergie's half-time speech at the Nou Camp. I'm not sure that his words have been quite as inspiring this time. United desperately need to get the Holy Trinity (Version II) in the game again. Ronaldo's been good, Tévez looks strong and Rooney's almost set up two goals but they can't do anything without the ball.

GIGGS! 784! (86): History is made. Giggsy comes on for Scholesy to break Sir Bob's appearance record. It's an incredible achievement. As Giggsy waits to come on, ITV show a clip of him jogging on for his debut against Everton in 1991. It's a nice touch. How skinny was he then?

89: Clive can't stop himself. 'Nine years ago, United were still 1–0 down at this stage.' You can imagine Chelsea fans throwing their beer cans at the TV.

90+: The Red Army – no, not that one – lets out an almighty roar as United win a series of throw-ins deep in Chelsea territory. The last of them finds Ronaldo who clips in a dangerous cross that just escapes Tévez's reach. We could really have done with someone with some height up front tonight. If only Saha was made of something more reliable.

90+: Michel blows for time. United still haven't won a European Cup final in the first 90 minutes. That's the bad news. The good news is that we still haven't lost one either.

90 minutes: United 1 (Ronaldo) Chelsea 1 (Lampard)

Extra-time:
90: 'The big night out in Moscow will go on and on,' Clive booms as *U-N-I-T-E-D (United are the team for me)* fills the United end.

91: United's best move since Lampard's equaliser. The ball fizzes between Carrick, Giggs, Tévez and Rooney, but Tévez just fails to beat Cech to Rooney's flicked through ball.

91: Kalou comes on for Malouda.

LAMPARD! BAR! LET OFF! (93): The night's Carsten Jancker moment. Or was it Mehmet Scholl who hit it the second time? Chelsea put together an intricate, incisive move of their own which ends with Lampard spinning and digging out a shot from just inside the box. Van der Sar is beaten but the ball bounces off the bar and on to safety via Joe Cole's snatched volley.

96: Good stuff in the crowd as a couple of United fans swap their United shirts for some army boys' caps. The army caps and beer bellies make them look like that fat bloke from Full Monty. The army boys are cracking up (they're probably in some Siberian salt mine by now).

96: Joe Cole throws himself onto the floor looking for a free-kick and gets cramp as a reward. United sportingly kick the ball out of play, but instead of giving it them straight back Chelsea kick it out deep in United territory. The significance of that would become clear in 20 minutes or so.

98: Anelka comes on for Joe Cole. The significance of that would become clear in 30 minutes or so.

99: It's taken him a while, but Clive doesn't let us down: 'You know Bayern hit the woodwork twice in that game.' Which game's that Clive? Oh yeah, I remember. Look what minute it is too. Nice work CT.

GIGGSY! DESTINY! NO! (99): Giggsy sealed the League title on the day he equalled Sir Bobby's record. He could have won us the European Cup on the night he went one better. In fact, scrub that. He should have done. Evra – my man of the season along with Ferdinand – surges past three Chelsea men, draws Cech out of goal and cuts the ball back to Giggs. If he'd turned his body he could have passed the ball into the net with his left foot. Instead, the weight of history seems to get to him and his awkward prod flicks off Terry's head and over the open goal.

100: Nani comes on for Rooney who throws his shirt onto the ground as he trudges to the bench. I reckon it's a sign of his frustration and disappointment rather than petulance. It's just not been his night.

102: Tévez, who's getting stronger and stronger as the night goes on, cuts in from the left and thumps a drive straight into Cech's midriff.

109: The bright start to extra-time doesn't last. Chelsea in particular aren't doing anything to win the game now. Perhaps it's tiredness. Clive's getting tired too. After noting how many Glazers are in Moscow he makes a 'Double Glazers' gag. Terrible.

110: Vidic gets a yellow for taking down Anelka near the area. Drogba bends the free-kick tamely wide.

TÉVEZ! BALLACK! DROGBA! RED! 113: A minor flurry of blocked United shots ends with the ball in Cech's grasp and Carvalho collapsing onto the turf with cramp. Cech volleys the ball out of play. And then things get interesting...

Tévez, still smarting from Chelsea's behaviour earlier on, knocks the ball out for a throw-in and beckons his teammates forward. Chelsea completely overreact. Terry gets himself right in Tévez's face. Ballack barges into him. Tévez doesn't flinch. Then, as United players arrive to back their man up, another melee forms and Drogba slaps Vidic across the chin. Michel sees everything and makes up his mind straightaway. Ballack gets a yellow. So – harshly – does Tévez. And Drogba sees red.

114: Drogba is only the second player to be sent off in a European Cup Final (Lehmann was the first in 2005). As he trudges from the field you can see him thinking about confronting Vidic. And then you can see him thinking again. Considering his pain threshold it's a very sound decision. At the other end of the field Terry shows yet another unsavoury side to the Chelsea team, nustling up to Tévez and firing a Choccy-style snot torpedo into his hair. What a charming man. What a charming team.

117: Essien gets booked for his umpteenth foul on Ronaldo.

120+: As Reds belt out 'We'll never die', Tévez almost gets his head on one Ronaldo cross while Nani smashes heads with Ashley Cole trying to get on the end of another. But in truth neither side look like scoring. It's going to be penalties, and both managers prepare for the shootout with late changes. Belletti comes on for Makelele while Anderson replaces Brown. I love Wes, but I wouldn't want him anywhere near an important penalty either. Funnily enough, I wouldn't have fancied Rooney or Scholesy much either. Both have had their penalty problems, particular Scholesy. Remember, it was his miss that allowed Arsenal to steal the Cup in 2005.

Full-time: United 1 (Ronaldo) Chelsea 1 (Lampard)

That's it. 'A season which started back in August with a shootout between these two will end exactly the same way' says Clive. Hopefully the result will be the same, but no one's putting their house on it. United are brilliant at penalty shoot-outs in the Community Shield. But they're terrible in the ones that actually count for something. Videoton in '85, Torpedo Moscow and Southampton in '92 and Arsenal in 2005…We haven't won a single one. And Van der Sar is Dutch, so his record is terrible too. I'm not looking forward to this…

Penalties

1–0: As Steve Ryder, whose hair hasn't moved since 1978, talks more bland nonsense in the ITV studio, and Hughesie advises every penalty taker to just get their foot through it, United get a double break. They win the toss to take the penalties at the United end. And they also get to take the first one. Tévez gets them off to the perfect start, passing the ball firmly into the right corner.

1–1: Ballack never looks like he's going to miss, and he doesn't.

2–1: Carrick scored in the Community Shield shootout. And he scores again with a confident slot to Cech's right.

2–2: Belletti, the only player on the pitch with previous experience of scoring in a Champions League Final, steps forward with the driving Moscow rain dripping off his nose. He hasn't touched the ball yet, but you'd never know it. Van der Sar goes to the left. Belletti's penalty goes to the right.

2–2: 'Maybe the best player in the world against maybe the best goalkeeper in the world,' Clive stammers. Yes, it's Ronaldo versus Cech. And it's a disaster for United. Ronaldo reverts back to his trusted stuttering technique, but he stutters for too long, loses all momentum and can only sidefoot the ball tamely to the left. Cech guesses the right way and that's it. Is Ronaldo's epic goalscoring season going to be remembered for the one he missed…?

2–3: It certainly looks like it as Lampard beats Van der Sar low to his left.

3–3: As Hargreaves steps up, Clive reminds us he was the only player to score for England in their penalty shoot-out defeat to Portugal in the last World Cup. He's also spent most of his professional life in Germany. So he should score. And he does, rifling the ball into the top left-hand corner.

3–4: Is that United's last chance gone? Van der Sar gets a big left hand on Cole's side-footer but pushes it into the net rather than wide. The dream looks over for United now.

Up in the stands, I've decided that penalties only count for Scousers anyway. The cameras focus on the drenched United players in their halfway line embrace. Ferdinand, Brown, Ronaldo… all of them look the same pallid white.

4–4: Nani, with Vaseline smeared over his banged-up head, just squeezes the ball past Cech's right hand. And that means it's all going to come down to one kick…

4–4: Would Drogba have taken this penalty if he'd still be on the pitch? If so, how different would this night have ended up? It hurts just thinking about it. Fortunately, we'll never know. Instead John Terry emerges from the pack and marches towards the area. As he places the ball on the spot, and Van der Sar seems to shrink, I'm wondering how I'll possibly cope with the media love-in that's going to follow. 'Mr Chelsea', 'Captain Courageous', that sort of thing. But then something extraordinary happens. Terry runs in, opens up his body and slips. He still makes a decent contact but gets his aim wrong and the ball brushes the post and goes wide. United are still alive. Maybe the Babes are controlling what happens here after all…

5–4: Terry looks like he's just been in a car crash as he takes the walk of shame back to halfway. Anderson passes him the other way and lashes the ball down the centre. What a time to score your first United goal. What a first touch. What a boy.

5–5: The momentum is all with United now. But Kalou's penalty is calmness personified. Now it's the history man's turn…

6–5: Giggsy scored the first of his 25 Champions League goals against Gothenburg in 1994. Until this season he'd scored in a record 11 consecutive Champions League seasons. On the way he's scored some great goals (the slalom in Turin in 2003), some lucky goals (Porto in '97) and some vital goals (the late semi equaliser at Old Trafford in '99). But nothing he's ever done before is as important as this. Come on son, don't let this opportunity go. There's no chance of that. Giggsy sends Cech to the left and calmly sweeps the ball into the right. Match point again…

Penalty 14
Anelka has scored against us for City and Arsenal, he's played for Liverpool and he scored the winner against us for Bolton in November. But can he handle the pressure now? Van der Sar thumps his gloves together, jumps up and down on his line and points to his left. Fatally, Anelka ignores his advice and sidefoots the ball the same direction that Ronaldo did. The ball arrives at Van der Sar at that perfect height commentators always talk about and the big Dutchman almost breaks into a grin as his gloves close in on it.

As Van der Sar hits the turf there's a moment of quiet as 70,000 people in the Luzhniki, and millions more people worldwide, digest what's just happened. Then Tyldesley screams 'VAN DER SAR'S SAVED IT!' and bedlam breaks out…

Van der Sar gets buried underneath a mountain of players. There's red shirts, tracksuits and grey suits everywhere. The red end bounces likes it's 1999 (I lost my bet – Clive never said it). Ronaldo, the drama queen, sobs on the Moscow turf. Terry is blubbing like no hard man should. Anelka is walking round on his own like someone deafened by a bomb blast. Carvalho has got a prayer sign stuck to his lips. Carrick and Saha are screaming. Parky's doing a Maysie. Giggsy is hugging anything that moves. Red-nosed Scholesy quietly commiserates with Terry. Terry blubs some more. *Always look on the bright side of life* fills the Moscow night…

And then ITV's pitchside man Gabriel Clarke invades the celebrations and asks Van der Sar, the hero of Moscow, to sum up the moment. Van der Sar gulps back the emotion and then utters two simple words:

"F***ing hell"

You could stay up all night. You could bring Hemingway, Dickens, Shakespeare and Kafka back from the dead. But nothing any of them could come up with could do a better job of summing up the night – nay, this whole incredible season – than that…

The End

Statistics

League tables

Final League Table

Pos		Pld	W	D	L	F	A	GD	Pts
1.	**Manchester United**	38	27	6	5	80	22	58	87
2.	Chelsea	38	25	10	3	65	26	39	85
3.	Arsenal	38	24	11	3	74	31	43	83
4.	Liverpool	38	21	13	4	67	28	39	76
5.	Everton	38	19	8	11	55	33	22	65
6.	Aston Villa	38	16	12	10	71	51	20	60
7.	Blackburn Rovers	38	15	13	10	50	48	2	58
8.	Portsmouth	38	16	9	13	48	40	8	57
9.	Manchester City	38	15	10	13	45	53	-8	55
10.	West Ham United	38	13	10	15	42	50	-8	49
11.	Tottenham Hotspur	38	11	13	14	66	61	5	46
12.	Newcastle United	38	11	10	17	45	65	-20	43
13.	Middlesbrough	38	10	12	16	43	53	-10	42
14.	Wigan Athletic	38	10	10	18	34	51	-17	40
15.	Sunderland	38	11	6	21	36	59	-23	39
16.	Bolton Wanderers	38	9	10	19	36	54	-18	37
17.	Fulham	38	8	12	18	38	60	-22	36
18.	Reading	38	10	6	22	41	66	-25	36
19.	Birmingham City	38	8	11	19	46	62	-16	35
20.	Derby County	38	1	8	29	20	89	-69	11

All-time Premier League table

	P	W	D	L	F	A	Pts
United	**620**	**394**	**137**	**89**	**1220**	**538**	**1319**
Arsenal	620	332	168	120	1048	547	1164
Chelsea	620	310	168	142	977	606	1098
Liverpool	620	306	157	157	992	607	1075
Aston Villa	620	230	187	203	783	724	877
City (14th)	430	129	120	181	487	579	507

Top scorers

Premier League top scorers 2007–08

Ronaldo	**United**	**31**
Adebayor	Arsenal	24
Torres	Liverpool	
Santa Cruz	Blackburn	19
Benjani	City/Portsmouth	15
Berbatov	Spurs	
Keane	Spurs	
Yakubu	Everton	
Tévez	**United**	**14**
Carew	Aston Villa	13

Champions League top scorers 2007–08

Ronaldo	**United**	**8**
Messi	Barcelona	6
Torres	Liverpool	
Drogba	Chelsea	
Gerrard	Liverpool	
Babel	Liverpool	5
Ibrahimovic	Inter	
Kanoute	Sevilla	
Raul	Real Madrid	
Deivid	Fenerbahce	
Kuyt	Liverpool	

United top scorers 2007–08

	FAPL	CL	FAC	Other	Total
Ronaldo	31	8	3	0	42
Tévez	14	4	1	0	19
Rooney	12	4	2	0	18
Saha	5	0	0	0	5
Nani	3	0	1	0	4
Giggs	3	0	0	1	4

United top 10 goalscorers (in one season)

	Season	League	FA Cup	League Cup	Europe	Others	Total
Law	1963–64	30	10		6		46
Van Nistelrooy	2002–03	25	4	1	14		44
Ronaldo	2007–08	31	3		8		42
Law	1964–65	28	3		8		39
Van Nistelrooy	2001–02	23	4		10	1	36
Taylor	1956–57	22	4		8		34
Herd	1965–66	24	3		5	1	33
Whelan	1956–57	26	4		3		33
Viollet	1959–60	32					32
Best	1967–68	28	1		3		32

Premier League top scorers ever

Cole	Newcastle	1993–94	34
Shearer	Blackburn	1994–95	34
Ronaldo	**United**	**2007–08**	**31**
Shearer	Blackburn	1995–96	31
Shearer	Blackburn	1993–94	31
Philllips	Sunderland	1999–2000	30
Henry	Arsenal	2003–04	30